Higher Education
for a better tomorrow

Higher Education
for a better tomorrow

Dr. M. Rajaram

STERLING PUBLISHERS PRIVATE LIMITED
Regd. Office: A-59, Okhla Industrial Area, Phase-II,
New Delhi-110020. CIN: U22110PB1964PTC002569
Tel: 26387070, 26386209; Fax: 91-11-26383788
E-mail: mail@sterlingpublishers.com
www.sterlingpublishers.com

Higher Education for a better tomorrow
© 2015, Dr. M. Rajaram
ISBN 978 81 207 9841 0
Reprint 2016

All rights are reserved. No part of this publication may be reproduced, stored in a retrieval system or transmitted, in any form or by any means, mechanical, photocopying, recording or otherwise, without prior written permission of the original publisher.

PRINTED IN INDIA

Printed and Published by Sterling Publishers Pvt. Ltd., New Delhi-110 020.

"Education is a powerful tool for human progress and empowerment. It is also a strong driver of social thinking and transformation."

"Universities are 'engines' of innovations that churn out new ideas for national growth."

– Selvi J Jayalalithaa
Hon'ble Chief Minister of Tamil Nadu

Contents

Foreword — ix
Preface — xi

1. **Higher Education: A Panoramic View** — 1
   - Structure — 1
   - Religion and Higher Education — 8
   - Higher Education and Indian Constitution — 10
   - Challenges in Higher Education — 14
   - Environment of Higher Education — 25
   - Regulatory Authority — 27
   - University Grants Commission — 36
   - University–Government Relationship — 38
   - Autonomy for Central Educational Institutions — 42
   - Constraints in Higher Education — 46
   - Institution–Industry Interaction — 48
   - Orientation Programme — Objectives — 51
   - Research — 64
   - Universities — 67
   - Vice-Chancellor — 95

2. **Conceptualising Higher Education** — 99
   - Vision For Education In India — 99
   - Mobilisation of Resources — 108
   - Future View of Higher Education in India — 110
   - Higher Education Stakeholders — 122
   - Opportunities in Higher Education — 124
   - Globalisation and Massification — 143
   - Internationalisation of Indian Higher Education — 150
   - Higher Education in Rural Areas — 158

Contents

3.	**Higher Education: Privatisation Way**	**161**
	• Management and Administration of Private Colleges	161
	• Higher Education: Private Players Demonstrating Excellence	166
	• Myths and Facts of Privatisation of Higher Education	168
	• Important Private Universities in India	173
4.	**Relevance of Foreign Education**	**186**
	• Foreign Education	186
	• Higher Education in the United States of America	190
	• Higher Education Under WTO Regime	196
	• Top Ten Universities in the World	204
5.	**The Need to Revamp Curricular Pattern**	**208**
	• Curriculum Reconstruction	208
	• Choosing the Right Career	209
	• Designing of New Courses	213
	• Some Key Emerging Career Fields	216
	• Teacher Training For Higher Education	222
	• Remodeling Classroom Instruction	232
	• Quality Improvement in Teaching	233
	• Improving University Teaching	242
	• New Integrated B.Ed. Course (NIB.Ed.)	248
	• Open Universities and Study Centres	251
	• Continuing Education for Engineers	255
	• Quality Enhancement	257
	• Total Quality in Higher Education	261
	• Overview of Total Quality	269
	• Prohibition of Unfair Practices in Technical Education, Medical Education and University Bill 2010	273
	• Revamping of Medical Courses	275

6. **Higher Education for the Future**   **279**
   - Higher Education for the 21st Century   279
   - Educational Priorities in the 21st Century   283
   - Humanistic Education   287
   - Physical Education   290
   - Women's Education   291
   - Architecture and Education   299
   - Technical Education in the 21st Century   301
   - Education Technology   311
   - Public Relations   313
   - Information and Communication Technology (ICT) in Education   314
   - M-learning (Mobile learning) and E-learning   317
   - Life-Long Education   323
   - Models of Management Education   328
   - Higher Education in National Development   330
   - Revamping the Colleges and Universities   341

7. **Higher Education in Tamil Nadu**   **356**

8. **Conclusions, Recommendations and Suggestions**   **367**
   - Solutions for Effective Functioning   367
   - Role of NCHER   375

9. **Community College**   **376**

   Bibliography   380

Foreword

Learning is a weapon to guard against ruin
And a fort indestructible by hostile men

– Kural 421

The education system has a tremendous responsibility to transform the youth into leaders. The most important part of education is to inculcate in the students the spirit of "We can do it." Education of the youth is a sacred trust; it is the supreme duty of all concerned to preserve it with utmost care and guard it vigilantly.

Higher Education for a better tomorrow by Dr. M. Rajaram provides a panoramic view of the challenges, environment, constraints, role of universities, mobilisation of resources, curriculum patterns, systems of education prevailing in other countries, quality enhancement, etc. It gives an insight into the priorities in the 21st Century.

The book serves as an important tool for those who have a quest for knowledge on higher education in its totality.

I am sure the students, teachers and public at large can benefit a lot from this book.

Dr. A.P.J. Abdul Kalam
Former President of India

Preface

The words of Dr. A. P. J. Abdul Kalam (Former President of India) below aptly sum up the importance of education in a country.

When learning is purposeful, creativity blossoms,
When creativity blossoms, thinking emanates,
When thinking emanates, knowledge is fully lit,
When knowledge is lit, economy flourishes.

Over the past 30 years higher education has grown very rapidly in India, but some issues remain strong and hinder further progress. A study of the complex structure of higher education and its challenges, problems and prospects in India with a copious reference to the state of higher education in foreign countries is of paramount importance in serving as an effective vehicle to bring about a radical change in the system. This will ensure comprehensive growth where everyone will get opportunity to grow and in the process contribute fruitfully to the society.

Higher education today has seen a quantitative growth in institutions of higher education and number of student enrolments but the core issue of quality has taken a backseat. To achieve the future requirements we must relook at the overall education system to demonstrate more positive results in the future. For accomplishing India's economic and technological development education, in general, and higher education, in particular, plays a significant role. The universities must be metamorphosed into sunny seed-beds wherein youngsters can blossom into professionals of wisdom, character and strength.

I have made earnest efforts to write this book based on my experience in the Department of Education and various other departments in Government of Tamil Nadu in the last three decades and have tried to identify problems that plague higher education in India. I have also attempted to provide suggestions for how these problems can best be tackled. The solutions offer a perspective bereft of any bias and but reflect my commitment towards social responsibility.

In recognition of the hard work that has gone into writing this book, I would like to thank my dearest friends Mr. S. Velliyangiri, Dr. P. K. Natarajan, Mr. J. Narayanaswamy, Mr. B. S. Chandrababu, Mr. C. S. Kalyanasundaram, Mr. P. Jeyaraj, Mr. D. J. Bethelraj, Mr. S. Jayabaskaran Charles, V. Rajagopal and others for all their kind support.

Dr. M. Rajaram

1

Higher Education
A Panoramic View

Structure

There are three types of educational institutions in India engaged in higher education: unitary universities, affiliated universities and deemed universities. Unitary and deemed universities are few in number, while the affiliated are in a majority. They have grown in numbers consequent to the developmental efforts of Central and State Governments and private entrepreneurs.

Education is a national investment in human resources development. Hence the question of accountability needs very special attention of Central and State Governments, students, teachers, administrative staff and general public. Lack of such accountability has led to wastefulness, mediocrity and indiscipline and even demoralisation, not only among teachers and administrators but also among students.

From 1857, the year in which the first three universities were established in India (Calcutta, Bombay and Madras), to the present day, most of our universities have been following the old pattern of affiliation.

Examining Affiliation

Affiliation is to be re-examined in today's context for the following reasons:

Centralised System

At the time the British established affiliated universities, there were only a few colleges in and around the provincial capitals and communication between the university and the affiliated colleges in the same area was easy and smooth. Today we have colleges in remote areas affiliated to the university and for everything the affiliated colleges depend on a distant, impersonal and centralised system. Catering to the needs of students in remote corners of the country was not a major concern during the 19th and early 20th centuries.

Increase in the number of universities

The number of universities was less in those days and so was the number of colleges affiliated to them, since students going for higher education were meagre.

Today we have universities that have 100 to 500 colleges affiliated to each of them. Efficient management of such universities is next to impossible because of the sheer number of colleges and students to be managed.

Infrastructure

The sudden expansion of higher education has lowered the quality of educational services provided to the students, shortage of quality teaching staff, outdated or lack of proper library and lab facilities, etc.

Special Relevance

Although affiliation is an idea that originated in Briton, especially in London University which was established in 1836, neither London nor other long established universities such as Oxford and Cambridge had colleges other than their constituent colleges on the same campus affiliated to them. This has special relevance to the educational planning in India.

Student Population

The number of students in the affiliating universities in India is unwieldy, enrolling more than 20 million students. These universities are unable to provide adequate services to these colleges and their students. Based on the student population, India needs at least a thousand universities and fifty thousand colleges. Currently there are 693 universities and about 35,500 affiliated colleges.

Cost

Since the establishment of such a large number of universities and colleges is cost-prohibitive (in terms of space, infrastructure in buildings for class rooms, laboratories and equipment, common facilities, hostels, staff quarters, extra-curricular activities, and in the context of modern on-line communication facilities, where the best of faculty skills will be easily available for all as in UGC on-line classes), we have to think in terms of:

- taking measures to curb the large influx of students into colleges where they are not trained for anything except unemployability
- starting Open Universities in every State where there is a large demand for college education
- strengthening the distance education mode by reviewing the work of institutes of Distance Education now operating in some universities
- vocationalising high school and college education to the extent possible to make education socially relevant and productive
- establishing new autonomous institutions under people's initiative in each locality and catering to the special needs of the region through provision of training, practical and field work and
- de-linking the degrees from jobs.

Revising Admission Procedures

Many students enroll in colleges today because they have nothing else to do. They are not there primarily for the pursuit of knowledge but because of the force of circumstances. Higher education should revise admission procedures to admit sincere students who are seriously interested and competent to deal with the matters of higher intellectual exercises and research. Autonomous institutions of higher learning have to streamline their academic programmes as well as their policy of recruitment of teachers and students.

Restructuring

Affiliation

Affiliation is an anachronism and the first thing to be done while restructuring higher education is to repeal the affiliation system and make colleges autonomous so that they can devise their own courses of study that are region specific and on the special needs and talents of the young people of the region, while keeping the national priorities in view. There should be academic, financial and administrative autonomy.

Centralisation

Universities and colleges are to be decentralised so that each educational institution can evolve its own programmes in keeping with local, national as well as global needs. At present there is no initiative to innovate and make the courses socially relevant.

The Syndicates, Academic Councils and the Senates of various universities and governing councils of colleges should spend sufficient time in planning so that the courses taught are relevant to the current professional world, the syllabi are so tailored and the students are given all the necessary facilities as well. The decisions of the various academic bodies must be based on academic considerations only.

Rigid Management Structure

The UGC committee that analysed various University Acts and Statutes in 1990 arrived at a significant finding that the Acts "Create rigid management structures with least provision of flexibility."

It also said that the Acts did not enable or require the universities and colleges to have innovations in teaching, research evaluation and extension to bring relevance and excellence to academic programmes.

Aim

The four fundamental aims of a university can be summarised as follows:
1. To advance the frontiers of knowledge by teaching, research and training.
2. To extend the benefits of such knowledge to all sectors of society.
3. To create an atmosphere where the teachers recognise their interdependence and the need for mutual help.
4. To publish the research findings of the academic community so that more people outside the university system including business and industry can be enthused to participate in a genuine collaborative venture that will benefit everyone.

Evaluation by Teachers

In the present system of higher education, the component of evaluation is not properly taken care of. The basic principle to all teaching is that evaluation should not only be simultaneous but carried out by the teacher who teaches it. The present evaluation system is three or four steps away from the real scene of teaching. One teacher teaches, another sets the question papers, a third teacher evaluates the answer papers and a fourth does the revaluation. This system has to be done away with. Teaching and evaluation should proceed simultaneously and continuously. The best evaluator is the teacher who teaches a particular course, which is beneficial to the students and the teacher. To prevent favouritism or nepotism, if any, the answer paper should be returned to the students and the whole system of evaluation should be transparent.

Different Treatment of Regular and Private Students

There should not be different criteria for regular student and private registrants in admission, evaluation, etc., when the same diploma or degree is awarded to both.

The huge number of private registrants is due to the result of vague admission standards, inadequate instruction procedures and learning facilities, and unscientific evaluation.

Academic programmes, time-tables and exam schedules

There is nothing as sacred as education. Teaching, research and academic work in general must be considered more important than other activities which upset educational planning and administration.

Every institution of education should insist on following the academic calendar prepared in advance, at least a year in advance, and meet the academic standards.

Quality versus Quantity

One of the legitimate requirements in the post-Independence era has been the education of a very huge number of young people who aspire for college education. In one way, this is good, as compared to the traditional education prevalent in pre-Independence period. Educational planners have to introduce vocational courses (industrial, non-industrial, job-oriented, entrepreneurial and innovative) even at the higher secondary level. This will give a practical orientation to all students with better preparedness for their future professional roles and, help to eliminate prejudices that young people often have towards certain activities and inculcate dignity of labour. This will also give confidence to youth to face life's challenges and give proper direction to them about future jobs and courses of study.

Above all, this will reduce the present practice of sending boys and girls to college just because they have nothing else to do.

Lack of suitable courses for Girls

There are women's colleges in India right from the second decade of the 19th century, but most of them are following the course pattern of general colleges. With a rise in the number of girls going for higher education, there should be courses designed especially for them depending on the job options available today. Many girls become home makers after completing postgraduate degrees in conventional areas of study or even after professional courses. This becomes an unproductive system of higher education.

Annual System versus Semester System

The majority of colleges and universities are following the annual system where the academic sessions are spread over 10 to 12 months. A few sections of a particular subject area are taught for one to two years in the conventional manner and the testing of memory is conducted at the end of second or third year. The latest aspects and developments in any particular discipline are not introduced to the students. While the semester system focuses on learning on continuous and in depth learning that aims at capacity building of students.

Fossilisation of Knowledge

The teachers have no desire to include the latest aspects of knowledge in the syllabus of various courses because it is not revised frequently. Very little freedom is there for innovation in teaching. This leads to freezing and fossilisation of knowledge.

Changes in Courses

The best remedy is to give freedom for every teacher to frame the contents of a course he/she teaches for a semester of 15 or 16 weeks. The responsibility of revising the contents of courses and evaluating the students must rest on the shoulders of teachers. There can be occasional academic meetings where teachers of similar courses get together and discuss the contents of the course unit and revise them wherever required.

Higher education will become more socially relevant and job-oriented only when changes or revisions in courses are made from time to time depending on national, regional and local needs.

Different Areas of Knowledge

To be a graduate, a student of science must also have exposure to areas other than science, particularly social service courses.

The students of social sciences must have the opportunity to choose certain basic courses in physical, mathematical and life sciences at their undergraduate level so that all students get a fairly comprehensive view of the interdependence of different areas of knowledge.

Holistic Point of View

Educational planners have to change their mindset about the rigid systems which are being followed. They have to give serious thought to the principle that everything is relevant to everything else and one should be prepared to look at education from a holistic point of view.

Quick Glance as on 2014

- There are 693 universities in the country.
- Out of 693 universities, 154 are private universities.
- Tamil Nadu leads the chart with 59 universities followed by 58 in UP and 48 in Rajasthan.
- Out of the total number of universities 47% (297) are State Universities followed by Deemed Universities with 20% share (129).
- Among 35,500 Affiliated Colleges, the top 4 fields of study, 37% Arts, 19% Science, 18% Commerce & Management and 16% Engineering & Technology.

(*Source: UGC Report*)

*****

Religion and Higher Education

Quality Literature

Universities and other bodies of academic excellence should produce high quality literature, i.e. books and journals on comparative religious education and libraries should be enriched with such materials.

Daily Prayer

Every institute of higher education should start the day with a common prayer every morning and attendance should be compulsory.

Academic Courses

Varied types of certificate, diploma and degree courses in Comparative Religion should be introduced in correspondence courses, Open Universities, etc., so as to inculcate moral values in the minds of students.

All techniques of non-formal education, i.e. T.V, radio, libraries, films, film strips and video libraries should be utilised to spread the message of non-controversial comparative religion.

Student-Centered Projects

The areas of interests and problems of the students at different levels of education and in different disciplines should be identified. On this basis the teacher can formulate religious education projects by identifying passages from different religious scriptures, stories of religious leaders and saints so that conflicts in the minds of the students are solved.

Religious Education

We are leading towards intellectual development but due to moral, legal, ethical, spiritual and social degradation, the society is full of corruption. Hypocrisy is on the increase, adulteration is the order of the day. So much so that even places of worship have been used for political and fanatic purposes without regard for any ethical standards. The only way to save the Indian Society from further deterioration is to introduce meaningful, non-dogmatic, positive comparative religious education sans casteism, communalism, obscurantism or blind beliefs obstructing the scientific bent of mind, in colleges and universities (also subject to the prohibition in Article 28 of our Constitution regarding 'religious instruction'). However, caution will have to be exercised so that real intellectuals with broad outlooks and specialised degrees undertake to teach it so as to get the right message across and show no religious biases.

Research in Social Science

The emphasis on social science research in the higher education sector has often been halting and hesitant, with inadequate financial support, though there are many higher education research institutions in the country. There is a need for promoting orderly growth of higher education research in social sciences.

*****

Higher Education and Indian Constitution

Constitutional Provisions

- Shared responsibility of Union and States.
- Values of equity, equality and social justice set parameters for reform.
- Right of minorities to establish and manage educational institutions.
- Higher education is a part of Concurrent list in Seventh schedule.
- Coordination and determination of standards of higher education and research, a subject in the Union list.
- In the scheme of things, reform of higher education is a national concern in which the Union has special obligations.

Governance of Higher Education

- Universities can only be established by a Central or State Act or as a Deemed University under Section 3 of the UGC Act.
- Six types of organisational models are involved in imparting higher education in India – Central Universities, State Universities, Deemed Universities, Private Universities, Institutions of National Importance, and higher education Institutions set up by States with degree awarding status.

- There are 693 Universities and 35,500 affiliated colleges.
- Governance of Universities is determined by the Acts and the Statutes under which they are created. Statutes include Ordinances, rules and regulations.
- Studies show that central acts are little more liberal in respecting university autonomy as compared to most of the state acts.
- Experience shows that if given autonomy, academic institutions perform better in all parameters. Universities should be self-governing institutions under clear mandate
- State universities are burdened with affiliated colleges offering varying standards of education with indifferent managements and accountability records.

Quality in Higher Education

- Over centralisation and low involvement of faculty and students in governance.
- Low autonomy and lower management skills with administrators of universities.
- Too many nominees of government and practicing politicians in the governance structures leads to politicisation of university administration.
- Multiple regulatory bodies distort efficiency of governance stifling innovation and breeding malpractices and corruption.

Improving Governance

- A package of six pieces of Legislations is now pending before parliament.
- Object is to increase access, ensure quality and promote inclusiveness in higher education.
- To increase GER from 13% to 30% by 2020.
- One over-arching regulatory authority for the entire higher education – National Commission for Higher Education and Research (NCHER)
- Full autonomy for higher educational institutions through restructuring governance systems

- Learning across disciplines, increasing choices of learners, promoting research and innovation.

National Accreditation Regulatory Authority

- Separation of standards setting function from implementation function.
- Accreditation through independent and registered accreditation bodies based on prescribed parameters.
- Accreditation of institutions and programmes to be mandatory.

Constitutional Provisions for Education

- The Constitution guarantees that "no citizen shall be denied admission into any educational institution, maintained by the State or receiving aid out of State funds, on grounds of religion, race, caste, language or any of them."
- Article 29(1) provides "Any section of the citizens, residing in the territory of India or any part thereof having a distinct language, script or culture of its own shall have the right to conserve the same."
- Article 350 A of the constitution states, "It shall be the endeavour of the State to provide adequate facilities for instruction in the mother tongue at the primary stage of Education to children belonging to linguistic minority groups."

Constitution of Minority Institutions

Article 30 of the constitution facilitates that "all minorities, whether based on religion or language shall have the right to establish and administer educational institutions of their choice." It has been further guaranteed that "the state shall not, in granting aid to educational institution or discriminate against any educational institutions on the ground that it is under the management of a minority, whether based on religion or language."

Freedom of Religion

Article 28 guarantees freedom of religion. It declares that, "no religious instruction shall be provided in any educational institution wholly maintained out of State funds."

Article 28 also provides that, "no person attending any educational institution recognised by the State funds, shall be required to take part in any religious instruction that may be imparted in such institution or to attend any religious worship that may be conducted in any such institution or in any premises attached there to unless the person or, if such person is minor, his guardian has given his consent thereto."

Constitution on the Advancement of Weaker Sections

Article 46 of the Constitution declares that, "the State shall promote with special care to the educational and economic interest of the weaker sections of the people and in particular, of the Scheduled Castes and Scheduled Tribes and shall protect them from social injustice and all forms of exploitations."

Article 15 of the Constitution has banned all discriminations against citizens on the grounds of religion, race, caste, sex in order to promote advancement of the socially deprived persons.

List of State Subjects

Education including universities, subject to provision of entries 63, 64, 65 and 66 of list I and Entry 25 of list III.

Entry 12

Libraries, museums and other similar institutions controlled or financed by the State, ancient and historical monuments and records other than those declared by or under law made by parliament to be of national importance.

List of Concurrent Subjects

20: Economic and social planning
25: Vocational and Technical Training of Labour

*****

Challenges in Higher Education

- Mushrooming of ill-equipped, ill-provided and inadequately staffed colleges and universities.
- Admission of undeserving students into the institutions, resulting in a large scale creation of poorly equipped graduates who remain unemployed or unemployable resulting in consequences like social problems (tensions) and so on.
- Collection of capitation fee for admissions.
- Politically oriented student-unions that pose a threat to campus peace.
- Loss of working days due to strikes and agitations.
- Considering other factors than merit for appointing teachers is a common trend. Affluence, caste and religious biases are factors that are often given preference.
- Prevailing teacher indiscipline.
- Poor quality of performance by teachers due to lack of motivation.
- Lack of research orientations.
- Unionism among teachers.
- Poor quality of evaluation and its inherent vulnerability to corruption.
- Examinations are not conducted as per schedule and delays in the announcement of results.
- Conduct of examinations is affected by many inefficiencies and malpractices.
- Poor financial status of colleges and universities means lesser resources for laboratories, libraries, playgrounds, hostels and so on.
- Political interference in educational institutions, e.g. in the appointment of the Vice-Chancellors and other top functionaries of Universities and the constitutions of different authorities and bodies in universities.
- Lack of will to address these problems with conscious strategies.

In spite of strenuous efforts in the past 66 years none of our Universities, IITs or IIMs could find a place within the first 200 universities of the world, in terms of total content, as assessed by London QS ratings. In 2014 rankings, the top-placed Indian Institution is 222nd in the world — IIT, Bombay and IIT Delhi ranked 235th.

- Some fresh thinking and basic changes are essential for overcoming this defect.
- Of the five cognitive skills: thinking, analysing, synthesising, integrating and innovating, our higher education is lagging behind in basic and applied sciences and innovation as evidenced by the rare and few Nobel Prizes won by Indians in India, in spite of our rich, ancient and scientific heritage and culture. Awareness and initiative are essential needs.

Devaluing Indian Degree

Declining standards manifest themselves in many forms, chief among them being the devaluing of Indian college degree, which many students realise to their mortification at some critical stage in their career when it is too late to make any course corrections. Therefore, the primary objectives of a national policy on education are to enhance quality of education, maintain national and international standards and establish relevance of education to social needs.

Four Goals

The Higher Education Policy and the program of action have mainly focused on four goals, which include Greater Access, Equity, Quality and Excellence (This is the priority as per the XI Plan period).

Enrolment Ratio

The enrolment ratio in higher education has increased from 7% in 1950 to 9.39% in 2003. This compares adversely with enrolment ratio in other countries , i.e. 100% in Canada, 80% in USA, 50% in France, and Thailand 19% show better ratio than India.

Resource Crunch

The resource crunch is the key factor with only 6% of GDP being allocated by the Government for the education sector while effective allocation hovers around 3% in stark contrast to the Kothari Commission's recommendation in 1966 at least 10% of the budget be reserved for education.

Disparities

Typical disparities found in respect of the enrolment rate include inter-state, rural/urban, inter-social group, male/female and poor/non-poor disparities.

Rural Student

Effectively, only half of the rural student population that completes its higher secondary education attends college.

Gross Enrolment Ratio

The Gross Enrolment Ratio (GER) varies from 21% in Kerala to 6% in Bihar. The GER is 5.09% for Schedule Castes, 6.43% for Scheduled Tribes, 7% for other Backward Castes with further gaps in rural areas, as compared to the national average of 10.10%. The GER for girls is only 8% against 12% for boys. With the GER for the poor at 2.41% as against non-poor at 12.8%, only 2.4% of economically disadvantaged students get admission into institutions of higher education.

Public Demand

The social demand for higher education exceeds the public supply; the private market seeks to meet the unsatisfied demand apart from demand against the public supply; and the demands for high quality and content in education also contribute to the growth of privatisation.

The private entrepreneurs are ready to provide higher education either for philanthropic or other altruistic motives or profit. The dividends could be social and political gains, or quick economic profits.

Public and Private Sectors

In the mixed higher education system, there is significant diversity from country to country. Some systems are dominated by the private sector, which can be termed as mass private and restricted public sectors, e.g. Japan, Republic of Korea, Philippines and Colombia, etc. There are mixed systems dominated by the state sector, as in several developing countries of South Asia, Africa and Western Europe. These systems can be described as the 'parallel public and private sectors'.

Privatisation of higher education may be noted and classified into four categories.

Total Privatisation

This is an extreme version of privatisation implying total privatisation of higher education, colleges and universities being managed and funded by the private sector. These unaided private institutions do provide financial relief to the Government.

Strong Privatisation

This means recovery of full costs of higher education from user students, their employers or both. This system is not empirically feasible.

Moderate Privatisation

This form of privatisation implies public provisions of higher education but with a reasonable level of financing from non-governmental sources.

Pseudo-privatisation

There is what can be termed a Pseudo-privatisation, which cannot be really called privatisation, higher education institutions under this category are private but Government 'aided'. They are originally created by private bodies, but receive nearly the whole of their expenditure from Government. Thus these institutions are privately managed but public funded.

Issues in Higher Education

The rapid expansion of higher education has created more problems than it has solved. The important among them are:

- The institutions of higher education in developing economies have been set up mostly in the pattern of developed industrialised countries with completely different economic conditions and hence the content and method of curriculum have been sharply irrelevant to the actual national economic needs.
- The unit cost of higher education has been comparatively high within the inherited model of education involving a very high private cost creating high social demand.
- The production sectors of the economy are not involved much in the existing system of higher education, implying that the institutions of higher education are not producing the types of graduates they needed.
- There is a marked mismatch in terms of the field and specialisation of graduates and the absorptive needs of the labour market. In the case of employment, the planners of higher education are handicapped in the assessment of the actual labour market needs for skills in various sectors of the economy.
- There has not been any serious attempt to regionalise higher education in respect of objectives, content and method of instruction in rural areas and the neglect of their needs resulted in rural exodus for higher education and in search of jobs in urban areas created the problem of unemployment and related problems of urbanisation of cities.
- Even though empirical evidence justified investment in higher education for economic growth, except for direct self-consumption, higher education per se, failed to create additional employment since the type of education offered restricts the entrepreneurial spirit and initiative and discourages self-employment.
- The higher education affects the labour market, disappointing the graduates, and results in political crisis, involving huge national costs.

- The present labour market pricing mechanism based on the performance in examinations has very weak association with the job performance or the world of work.
- The higher educational objectives in most of the developing countries are restricted to the changing needs of the economy.
- The present system of higher education is very rigid and structurally formal, perpetuating social disparity, discrimination and economic inequality.
- There is no correlation between the extent and bulk of seats provided for research, high-tech jobs and mechanical field work jobs; the imbalance between demand and supply in various fields accentuates unemployment and underemployment.

Higher Education and Labour Market in India

Our educational system appears to have been created primarily to meet the socio-economic needs of urban centres and their metropolitan peripheries by a vested interest group. On one side, National Government seems to be attracted by equitable distribution of means of production and fair means of distribution of education and employment and thereby to create economic opportunities to attain social equality. But in certain quarters especially among economically privileged groups, employment expands very rapidly, whereas education is crippled. Among the under-privileged and weaker sections, education expands very rapidly but employment potential is crippled. This functionally contrasting phenomenon has much to explain in the present state of higher education and labour market in India.

The relationship between education and labour market is of considerable significance in a free market economy. This involves a considerable amount of complexity, it defies simplified theoretical explanation based on the functional relationship between educational output and labour market intakes. Besides the perceptions and expectations of individuals, the attitudes of employers and the nature of socio-economic system also plays an important role in the functional linkage between higher education and labour markets. Education is merely academic in nature without appreciation and involvement in the needs and problems of society.

Goals of College Level Education

- To establish dynamic and beneficial linkage between education, employment and development with due regard for the economic and social aims of the country.
- To promote respect for and belief in values of national integration, secularism, democracy and dignity of labour.
- To sensitise academic communities to the problems of poverty, illiteracy and environmental degradation through extension services and organised participation in poverty reduction and environment improvement programmes, and to facilitate development, mobilisation, organisation and utilisation of the youth to involve and participate in the process of national development.
- To encourage colleges to get involved in the development activities in the community and provide requisite support through extension services of students and faculties.
- To follow the system in some educational institutions of the West that insist on field experience for at least one year after basic degree/diploma, before a student is considered for admission to postgraduate courses.

The Principal as Learner and Leader

While it is impossible for any Principal to be thorough in all disciplines, he must be an academic leader with genuine interest and involvement in the developments taking place in various disciplines, at least in a general way so as to be able to talk intelligently to the staff of the institution and to others outside the institution and to raise the right type of questions. He must, therefore, continue to read current educational literature. He must find time to join meetings, seminars, etc, as well as engage in explorations with professional people regarding possibilities of advances in various subject areas in the college. He must find time to visit other schools so as to learn from them. He must interact with like-minded people, especially professionals acquainted with developments in various fields or who will give constructive feedback on the quality of learning and education that is imparted in other institutions. He must be open to ideas, open to people, open to change, open to experimenting and innovating. Playing safe by maintaining of status quo will be against the very spirit and demands made on him as an academic leader.

It is the responsibility of a Principal to create a healthy academic climate in the institution.

Accent on Learning

One way to bring about a revolution in education is to change the accent from teaching to learning. This will ensure that the student becomes the focus; learning outcomes are emphasised and through classroom tests and periodic assessment the quality of learning is assessed rather than only the quantity of marks obtained. This will also mean that the students will be sequenced to learn with understanding, will be allowed to explore, to apply to relate as also learn to think, to question, namely relate facts into meaningful wholes, leading to new knowledge.

The accent on the student and on every student will shift focus from the exceptional achievement of one or a few students be it in sports field or in the university's examinations, or in intercollegiate contests, to the high achievement of all or most of the students. The aim would be to help them discover themselves, their talents, abilities and interests and develop them to an optimum level by making use of the many opportunities that the institution provides within the classroom and outside.

This will mean that teachers also read books and periodicals, engage in professional dialogues so as to learn from one another and in general become motivated to go beyond the immediate and narrow requirements of the classroom and the syllabus. The object would be to gradually make the teaching community a learning community. As mentioned above, this will not take place at the level of the entire staff unless the Principal himself remains a learner and motivates others to follow suit.

Dealing with Living Component

Education is concerned with the development of the human mind, its critical faculty, objective approach, scientific temper and analytical reasoning and, therefore, educational administration should concern not only in matters of details but in regard to fundamentals as well. Education administration has to be dynamic and evolving in order that a university, college or school may respond adequately to the changing educational needs of the society and its general ethos. An institution that does not recognise the dynamics of education is doomed to stagnate and this is what happens when the administration of a university functions like a bureaucracy. The procedures become self-defeating to such an extent that no new institution can be set up, no department can grow and no innovation can be tried out. It is obvious that the management of a university or a college cannot be cast in the same mould as management of an office or a private or public sector enterprise for the simple reason that an institution deals with living components rather than raw materials and capital goods.

Updating Courses

A university in modern times cannot discharge its responsibilities unless it has an inbuilt mechanism for the revision and updating of courses on a continuing basis. In the absence of mechanism for the improvement of curricula and restructuring of courses, a university merely degenerates itself into what may be called academic 'book-keeping'.

Orientation Programmes

If a university or college has to fulfill all its functions, it would be necessary for it to pay adequate attention to the training and orientation of those entrusted with the task of its development. This task cannot be fulfilled just by the introduction of an optional paper on educational administration in the M.Ed., courses or by a workshop or two, organised as a kind of sporadic activity. This would have to be planned through a series of workshops with well-defined objectives and a comprehensive idea of learning outcomes. All administrators from the lowest to the highest echelons would have to be brought within the purview of these orientation programmes.

Streamlining Administration

In modern times, no system of administration can function effectively unless it is open and the administrator has an open mind and a certain degree of intellectual resilience. There should take place a continuous dialogue among the various components of the university system so that our antediluvian administrative procedures can be thoroughly streamlined. It is also necessary to devise such structures, so that administration does not carry an army of clerks as a millstone around its neck. Finally, it is of the utmost importance for the administration that it should carry out internal as well as external economies by examining a number of important questions such as the effects of changing the structure of courses, varying the mix of teaching and research, use of buildings, savings in buildings costs, faculty time, etc. In other words, financial management should become an ally rather than a bug-bear for the academic community. The system of higher education in India indicates that improvements can be brought about only with the active collaboration of the universities and the state governments concerned. Such a collaborative effort is crucial for the implementation of various developmental activities and maintenance of standards.

Human Organisation Procedure

Administration of today is a challenging task. It not only requires technical 'Know-how' but also some practical human skills. There are detailed volumes written on the scientific analysis of administration and technical functions of an administrator but every administrator knows that there are some practical human qualities needed for successful operation of an organisation. Hence, administration is an art for everyone has to learn on the job. Mere application of standard operational procedures (S.O.P) neither brings success nor happiness. It is Human Organisation Procedure (H.O.P) which helps in the effective administration in any situation where humans are involved.

Qualities of an Administrator

There are a few important assumptions of Human organisational procedures:
- Organisation consists of human beings with human feelings.
- Every human being is unique and likes a personal approach from the superiors.
- Every human being is worthy and has some strengths and weaknesses.
- Administrator is a trustee with powers and privileges to be used for the institution and for the benefit of fellow workers or subordinates.
- Administrator obtains more co-operation and efficiency from the subordinates if he draws on their strengths and overlooks their weaknesses.

The modern administrator needs certain human qualities and skills as a leader of human organisation. Truly speaking, educational organisations are more than human in nature than many others, as they prepare and train human materials for the society at large. The most essential qualities of an educational administrator are:
- Administrator must have the quality of 'love'
- Administrator must be 'enthusiastic'
- Administrator must be 'action-oriented'
- Administrator must be 'decisive'
- Administrator must be 'energetic'
- Administrator must be 'resourceful'

The human qualities in the administrator are denoted by the word LEADER. This has to grow everyday in competence and efficiency, courage and confidence, personality and achievement.

*****

Environment of Higher Education

Four assumptions reflect the environment in which higher education operates, now and for the future:
- Conditions and conventions within the environment are changing.
- They are changing faster than they did in the past.
- Changes will continue to rapidly occur as we progress in the twenty-first century.
- Sensitivity to these changes is imperative and their implications for colleges and universities must be anticipated.

Why should someone read a book about quality in higher education? Those involved in higher education believe that quality is already being practised. However, there are at least six factors within higher education which question the assumption that it is quality driven.

Providing Employees to Employers

More than any previous point in history, the perception of quality in higher education today is increasingly becoming a problem for many outside the academy. Within higher education a tradition prevails that colleges and universities are the preservers, transmitters, and generators of knowledge and that, except for a few established professions such as law, medicine, the clergy, and more recently the arts and sciences, higher education should not directly relate to the world of business and provide employers with employees. Many members of the academy — perhaps most members — still hold this view.

Buying Instruction/Selling Research

This view, however, conflicts with the opinions held by some involved in higher education. At the most basic level there is disagreement over the priorities assigned by the academy to the traditional trial of teaching, research, and service. At a recent conference, Elaine Hairston, chancellor of the Ohio

Board of Regents, summarised the situation as, "We are buying instruction and higher education is selling research." Chancellor Hairston's assessment is shared by the governing bodies of other States' higher educational systems and many private institutions.

Getting a Job

The general public also seems to have greater expectations for the job-related value of higher education than is recognised in the traditional view. According to policy analyst Daniel Yarikelovich, 88% of the people feel that "a high school diploma is no longer enough to qualify for a well-paying job, and 73% agree that having a college degree is very important for getting a job or advancing in one's career."

Budget Deficit

Commenting on the relationship between the products of colleges and universities and the expectations of employers, Seymour concludes, "the disconnect is real between what our colleges and universities produce in terms of learning and outcomes in their graduates and that industry requires. And the longer we refuse to address the gap, like the budget deficit, the more we drag it that will reflect on our economy and global competitiveness."

Economic conditions in the United States have generated increasing concern about career opportunities and economic well-being. According to Yankelovich, the historical trend of increasing economic well-being has been reversed. "Today we are a people who are living at the 1965 level, in terms of real wages."

Consumer-Oriented Assessment

Students, parents, legislators, and employers have increasing expectations of higher education and are willing to commit funds to evaluate the performance of colleges and universities in the light of these expectations. Many believe that these constituent groups are bringing an educated consumer orientation to their assessment of higher education. While the following statement focuses on students, it is applicable to all constituent groups.

Today's students expect from colleges and universities what they could get elsewhere: better service, lower costs, higher quality, and a mix of products that satisfy their own sense of what a good education ought to provide. They want the enterprises that serve them to be efficient—not for efficiency's sake, but because efficiency promotes the flexibility and adaptability they seek in the marketplace.

*****

Regulatory Authority

It would be better to have a two-tiered regulatory authority for higher education.
- There will be a National Higher Education Regulation Authority at the central level and a State Higher Education Regulation Authority set up at the State level.
- Universities and all other Institutions of Higher Education to continue with their activities but they will come under the ambit of the regulator and function in accordance with the guidelines as per the law laid down.

The regulatory framework would have a more rational and coordinated architecture for the system as a whole. This will eliminate unnecessary duplication of effort, and cater to the neglected social interests in areas such as curriculum, teaching materials, admission processes and information systems.

The regulator will make the Indian higher education system in respect of the framework that will directly impact the systemic climate or educational eco-system. This in turn, along with the Developer and Assessment and Accreditation agencies will lead to tremendous improvement in the following:
- Curriculum
- Infrastructure and training Equipment Technology and ICT in Education
- Faculty Quality

- Employability and relevance to society
- Equity and Access
- Evaluation and Research output

Regulation coupled with focused efforts in Development, Assessment and Accreditation will impact the system in the following way:

Educational Eco-system

- Strengthening their internal governance.
- Developing the architecture of a rational system of higher education and orchestrating its smooth operation in a manner that promotes both mass education and excellence. This along with autonomy will lead to competition and legal enablers like faculty mobility for intellectual cross fertilisation with some checks for ensuring educational/ academic stability.
- Protecting higher education as a venue for free and open discourse on a range of matters, even if the subjects are sensitive from society's point of view.
- Addressing all planning issues in a global context and considering how their systems can be linked to the wider world.
- Regulating the private portion of higher education so as to encourage high standards while deterring abuses.
- The regulator could address the issue of foreign Universities setting up their campuses in India and lay down clear provisions for international collaborations and degree programmes.

Curriculum Related

- Improving the quality of existing academic programmes such as those involving science and technology, and developing new programmes, especially for the provision of general education and for helping bright and motivated students from disadvantaged backgrounds to overcome their academic deficits.

- Establishing new types of higher education institutions that are modified, innovative and focused on serving local development needs of the community especially in the areas of agriculture, health and industrial development.

Infrastructure and Technology

- Investing in the establishment of learning common things through which students from many institutions gain access to educational resources such as Internet, libraries and laboratory facilities.
- Categorising institutions based on the level of their infrastructure, prescribing and mandating the minimum norms in terms of the physical infrastructure, ICT facilities, libraries, laboratories, play ground, sports facilities and so on.
- Put in place a system of calibrated penalties and interventions for institutions which are defaulting in terms of minimum mandated quality and process norms.

Quality of the Faculty

- Laying down minimum standards of academic qualifications and other competencies for faculty recruitment.
- Laying down the standard processes to be followed for teacher recruitment based on principles of transparency, merit and equity.
- Mandating regular capability-building exercises for all levels of teaching and non-teaching staff.
- Prescribing the performance indicators and the processes for disseminating these on an annual basis at the level of each district.
- Instituting a set of awards for the best performance in each district based on objective measurable criteria and link this to incentives.

Employability and Relevance to Society

- Investing in the establishment of learning common things through which students from many institutions gain access to educational resources, i.e. Internet, libraries and laboratory facilities.
- Protecting higher education as a venue for free and open discourse on a range of matters, even if the subjects are sensitive from society's point of view.

Equity and Access

- Prescribing the norms for all institutions to give access to deserving students.
- Special provision for every institution to have diversity and for meeting the particular needs of students from special and marginalised categories.

Evaluation and Research Output

Laying down minimum norms for student evaluation including common testing mechanisms that use a countrywide pre-metric testing supplemented by internal assessments of competencies, project work, aptitudes and special abilities.

Involvement of State Government

An effective system of higher education relies mostly on the State exercising active involvement. The government must ensure that the system serves the public interest, provides at least those elements of higher education that would not be supplied if left to the market, promotes equity, and supports those areas of basic research relevant to the country's needs. The State must also ensure that higher education institutions and the system as a whole operate on the basis of financial transparency and fairness. With a view to ensure this, the government should enact and lay down the rules and guidelines to be followed by the regulator.

A Regulator Framework for Governance should be put in place that actively promotes and mandates:

Academic Freedom	Shared Governance
Clear Rights and Responsibilities	Merit-Oriented Selection
Financial Stability	Accountability
Regular Testing of Standards	Mechanism for Close Cooperation
Processes and Tools for Achieving Good Governance	Transparency, Equity
Research Rigour	Faculty Councils
Governing Councils	Budget Practices and Financial Managements Data for Decision Making
Appointment or Election from Amongst Selected Meritorious Candidates	Merit Based Faculty Appointment and Promotion Decisions
Faculty Compensation with Measurable Responsibilities	Provision for Visiting Committees and Accreditation
Institutional Charters and Hand Books for Institutions	Faculty and Non Faculty Staff and also Students

National Higher Education Regulation Authority

The National Higher Education Regulation Authority which will primarily be concerned with laying down standards for establishing new universities and colleges as also monitoring the quality and processes followed by the existing institutions of higher learning including Universities and colleges. The regulator can focus on deliverables of the institution offering higher education, the fees charged by it, the inputs that go into the process of delivering higher education like minimum qualification of the teacher, the basic curriculum framework, minimum infrastructure required by the institutions and other yardsticks defining quality.

The regulator would protect the interest of the students with respect to fees, quality of education, research and development, imparting of skills needed for employability, all-round development of students, provision of good quality teaching–learning materials and textbooks as also multimedia education aids. The regulator would also protect the interests of the self-financing institutions, government-run institutions and Grant-in-aid institutions in respect of fees and such other charges levied by them for imparting quality of education depending on the infrastructure available as also the differentiation of higher education institutions horizontally and vertically.

Regular Framework

For quality in higher education, the regulatory framework, to be truly effective will be supplemented by a development agency at both the Central and State Levels and an Assessment and Accreditation Agency at the Central and State Levels. This strategy will, inter-alia, address issues of flexibility and quality of curriculum, teacher quality, issues of using technology-aided education, employability, accreditation, educational infrastructure, research, performance as also evaluation primarily by putting in place a two-tiered regulatory framework with well-defined roles and authority. The issues are taken up across the country in a time-bound manner.

National Asset

The demographic dividend is one of the noteworthy aspects. With 550 million young people in the age group below 25 years, it is going to be a challenge to provide educational and employment opportunities for them. The kind of training, skill development and vocational education programmes we plan today will determine the social and economic status of India's population in the times to come. This enormous demographic dividend is India's greatest potential opportunity and, simultaneously, her biggest challenge. We have to wake up to the challenges and constraints that these huge numbers represent at least from now. We have to work on them through the education system to convert this opportunity into a national asset rather than a liability.

Economic Growth

Higher education is of permanent importance for economic and social development. Institutions for higher education have the responsibility for equipping an individual with advanced knowledge and skills required for positions of responsibility in government, business and the positions. It adds, "Higher Education investment is important for economic growth."
It is indeed a fact that many years of lesser investment in education have created gaps in infrastructure—classrooms, laboratories and libraries and so on.

International Educational Exposure

There is a need to make courses modular and flexible to help institutions attain international standards. The linkages with other countries through exchange programmes have to be stressed enough. International educational exposure expands horizons and instills cultural competence and understanding of global realities and problem solving skills.

Quality Assessment and Accreditation

It is important to recognise that a substantial portion of colleges and universities are not assessed for quality and therefore, we don't have a full picture of the quality and excellence of universities and colleges engaged in Higher education. Of the total 18000 colleges only 20% are accredited colleges and most of these colleges are self-financing colleges without permanent affiliation. It is therefore necessary to bring these colleges under the fold of quality assessment to improve the standards of college education in the country.

Disclosing Relevant Details

The price of not having a proper accreditation and regulatory body is far more than the cost of having it. In a democratic society like ours, the regulatory functions should be of the nature that force the institutions to disclose all relevant details and thereby allow students to take decisions.

Social Benefit

The level of development in a country is directly correlated with the gross enrolment ratio at higher education levels. However, it will not serve anybody's purpose to have the numbers without quality. It is presumable that the more effective the regulations for implementation of quality higher education, greater will be the social benefit to the cost invested by the state and the individual especially, in a situation where more and more higher educational institutions are owned by private sector.

Buffer Mechanism

A system based on strict state control has many advantages:
A framework having provisions of development, accreditation and regulation may be the best option or strategy. State supervision needs a precarious balance with issues of autonomy and accountability, which is best achieved by buffer mechanisms, which are distanced from the government. Buffer mechanisms generally consist of statutory bodies that include representatives of the government, institutions of higher education, the private sector, and other important stakeholders such as student–parent organisations.

Examples of Buffer mechanisms would be:
- Councils of higher education that advise the government on the size, shape and funding of higher education, and are also

responsible for quality assurance, promotion mechanism and accreditation.
- Research councils or agencies that fund and promote research.
- For the effectiveness of Governing Councils (or boards of trustees) require clear mandates, well established operating procedures and full autonomy from both government and academia.

Advantages of forming a Regulatory Commission

- The Regulatory Commission will standardise the quality parameters in Higher Education sector through transparent methods and this will lead to the promotion of quality environment.
- The power of appointment of the members lies with the State Government.
- Establishment of the Commission may enhance the confidence levels of private sector thereby attracting more investments on private-public partnership mode.
- More investments will provide better access and equity and this will lead to improved employment levels.
- Obtaining large scale funding from government of India will be possible.
- Since large benefits are expected to flow through the policy, the society will wholeheartedly welcome the proposal.
- The rural areas would get fillip as the rural infrastructure will be strengthened.

Higher Education Council

The University Grants Commission (UGC) must ensure that its funds are not wasted but functionally and optimally used by universities and colleges, by implementing the educational policies laid down. Even though the UGC streamlines, strengthens and expands its monitoring system for periodical appraisal of the performance of universities, an inter-university coordinating council or a state council of higher education has to be set up in every state for the specific purpose of maintaining quality control in the administration and management of higher education.

The higher education council can play an effective role in guiding universities in their proper functioning, academically and administratively. The council should be vested with powers to oversee and monitor the implementation of all educational programmes, as per the guidelines laid down by the UGC. The higher education council should have powers to make appropriate recommendations to the State Government as well as the UGC for sanction of grants not only for maintenance of administration but also for development schemes geared for promotion of the academic quality of teaching and research.

Planning

The Higher Education Council can extend its services to the universities in the matter of scientific and professionalised management. It can undertake detailed exercises in man-power-planning, coordinated with educational planning. The council can induce the State Government to refrain from permitting the unrestricted and unplanned expansion of higher education.

*****

University Grants Commission

Formation of University Grants Commission (UGC)

The UGC owes its existence as an autonomous statutory body to the recommendations made by the University Education Commission of 1948-49. On 3rd November 1952, the Government of India resolved to create a University Grants Commission which started functioning in 1953. The UGC Act was passed by the Parliament in 1956. Although the UGC has been designated as a grant-giving body, its main functions are related to the maintenance and co-ordination of standards.

The measures to rescue universities from financial crisis have been gaining more importance in recent years than real academic activities in many states. The UGC is mostly bogged down with problems of central universities and their colleges and have no time for state universities although a larger proportion of enrolment in higher education is in these universities vis-à-vis central universities. These institutions, particularly the older and larger ones, certainly deserve larger maintenance and developmental grants.

The intention of Entry 66 of the Union List of the Seventh Schedule of the Constitution of India as well as placing 'Education' under the 'concurrent list' in so far as it is related to university education was to regard all universities as national institutions irrespective of the source of their creation. But, the HRD Ministry/UGC is still treating the State Universities as just local entities and not as an integral part of national university system.

State Level Council for Funding

Presently, the sources of decision making and funding, as far as State Universities and their colleges are concerned, are found in a loose series of interrelationships among the Union Ministry of HRD, the Planning Commission and the UGC at the centre and the Ministries of Education and Finance in the States. The entire situation is that there is a lack of coordination between these agencies.

Therefore, it is desirable to have a state-level body or a council, as a channel of communication between the State Government and the UGC on the one hand and between these agencies, institutions and faculty on the other. The choice of members to serve the council is very crucial; the duties and obligations of the Council should be clearly defined. It should be free from the different pulls which dominate the higher education scene today.

Perspective Plans

The Council could assess periodically, the financial needs of universities and their colleges, determine the quantum of grants from various agencies and ensure its timely flow. It could also advise the State Government and institutions on enrolment policy, provision of adequate infrastructural facilities, fixation of fee rates for different courses and measures to augment additional non-governmental resources. It could help in preparing perspective plans for the overall development of higher education in the State. It could also see to it that higher educational perspectives form a national and international angle, get due importance at the State level that rules are used as an aid and not as an obstacle to research and development, experiment and innovation, and the vast administrative machinery in the universities becomes an instrument of progress rather than halting it. The UGC itself can discharge its function more effectively with the help of State councils.

*****

University–Government Relationship

Universities in the country are established under Acts of Legislatures. They are set up by Acts of Parliament; the remaining 150 or so of the Universities are all functioning under Acts of State Legislatures. The maintenance expenditure of these universities is provided for by the respective governments – the Central Government in the case of Central Universities and respective State Governments in the case of State Universities. Since all these universities are creations of the legislatures and most of them largely depend on funds from the public exchequer, the universities have to remain accountable to their respective legislatures and Government.

Role of Government towards Universities

The concerned governments also have the responsibility to ensure that the grants provided by them are utilised properly and that the Universities which are funded by them function at a high level of efficiency and effectiveness. The role of governments is thus broadly that of a partner in enabling the universities in the achievement of their goals.

Universities on the other hand, are vested with the responsibility to perform certain specific functions mentioned in the Acts of their incorporation. Performance of many of these functions requires exercise of academic judgement, which lies exclusively within the domain of the universities. In the performance of these functions autonomy is vital; the process of education cannot and should not be left to the external influences that are beyond the academic fraternity.

Central Universities

The President of India as the visitor of central universities is not an officer of any of them; he functions outside the normal decision-making processes within the universities. The powers vested in the visitor are the appointment of the Vice-Chancellor; appointment of certain members on the Court, Executive council, Finance Committee, Selection committee, etc.; ordering enquiries and instituting inspections; giving or withholding assent to the statutes; arbitrating in disputes between selection committees and Executive councils on the appointment of teachers; and annulment of any proceedings of the universities which are not in conformity with the Acts, statutes, ordinances, etc. In exercising all these powers, the President of India as the visitor of the Central Universities, is advised by the minister-in-charge of higher education at the Centre.

State Universities

The position in respect of Governors functioning as Chancellors of the State Universities is however different. He is an officer of the University. Most University legislations provide that the Chancellor, Vice-Chancellor and the members of the decision-making bodies are all constituted into a corporate body. The implication of these provisions is that the Governor is statutorily a member of the University and is a participant in the internal decision-making process.

Universities and National Institutions

The University system in India is more than a century old. The setting up of national laboratories by the Government to tackle specific industrial or technical problems in areas of science, engineering, agriculture, medicine and social sciences is of a more recent origin. Agencies like the CSIR, DAE, ICMR, DRDO, ISRO, DOE, DST, DOO, ICHR and ICSSR have huge sums of money at their disposal. Their laboratories and institutions have a highly developed infrastructure. Many of these institutions have talented scientists who could assist the university system in teaching R&D programmes, bringing greater relevance in their working. On the other side, these institutions depend critically on the University system for their intake of qualified manpower. They also require continuing education programmes for their staff by way of refresher courses and advanced degrees, which could be provided by the universities.

The state of interaction and co-operation between the universities and these agencies unfortunately is not satisfactory, except in a few universities. There is no evidence of organised programmes whereby staff from national laboratories come and spend some extended periods of time in the universities and vice versa. A few university research scholars utilise the facilities of the national laboratories to a limited extent. Similarly, some of the younger staff of the national institutions works part-time or otherwise for advanced degrees in the universities. Participation in conferences and symposia, however, takes place to a sizable extent. Moreover, the staff members from both sides participate in a few national projects. Considering the size of the university system and national laboratories/institutions, the magnitude of the collaborative effort is, nonetheless, very small.

Strength of Students

With a student population of about 315 million, India has the third largest system of higher education in the world. The magnitude of largeness can be gauged from the fact that nearly 150 new colleges are established every year. Out of this student population nearly 33% are women and 15% are from Scheduled Castes and Scheduled Tribes.

Strength of Teachers

On an average for every sixteen students in an Indian University there is one teacher. The teacher-student ratio is favourable in the institutions, Departments of science and technology, agriculture, medicine and other professional courses than in arts, humanities, law and social sciences.

Non-Teaching Staff

The non-teaching staff consists of technical staff, administrative staff, ministerial staff, service staff, etc. Their number is quite large especially in the institutions of science, technology, medicine and agriculture. In the Central Universities the number of non-teaching staff is about four times that of the teaching staff. More or less the same ratio may be there in other Universities as well.

Important Features

Some of the important features pertaining to higher education in the University system over the last few decades are:
- Large scale entry of first generation students to institutions of higher education.
- Unusual expansions, including that of professional and technical education.
- The rise of regional universities, a new phenomenon having its hold on their areas of jurisdiction.
- Realisation of the need for correspondence courses.
- Vociferous demands made by students' organisations, seeking participation in the administration of the universities and colleges.
- Teaching staff organisations and the non-teaching staff organisations of the institution becoming stronger day by day.
- The gradual acceptance of the concept that a college should play an important role as an 'area institution' in the development activities of the areas is slowly taking roots.
- Air-tight compartmentalisation is giving way to the basic need of interdisciplinary functioning in applied research.

- Establishment of single-discipline universities particularly in the field of agriculture, medicine, engineering and technology.
- The proposal for giving autonomous status to the colleges is being implemented.
- Existence of a large number of small colleges in several states that have enrolment of less than 500, generally set up in response to popular demands.
- The average number of affiliated colleges per affiliating university in most of the states is quite high as compared to the number of 30 affiliated colleges recommended by the Kothari Commission. Some States have an average number of affiliated colleges per University ranging from 90-140.

*****

Autonomy for Central Educational Institutions

The recommendations of the expert committee appointed by the Ministry of Human Resource Development (MHRD), Government of India are:

- Governance and reforms of universities depend on power (autonomy) with responsibility.
- Contemporary developments in technology and management demand flexibility in structures and procedures of higher education institutions.
- IIT/IIM models recommended for Central Universities as well.
- Simplified three level governance structure—IIT Council, Board of Governors and the Senate supported by Committees for special tasks.
- The IIT act provides a simple structure of council, Chancellor, Board and Senate leaving the rest to the statutes framed by the Board of Governors of each institute.
- Chancellor of the university can very well perform the duties of the visitor and the head of state can be spared of this burden.

- IIMs enjoy still greater autonomy as they are not established by government and there is no Act governing them at all. IIMs are governed by the statutes of their respective sponsoring societies. Their relationship with government is based on MoUs — IIMs are therefore largely faculty managed institutions enjoying full autonomy.
- The National Law Schools established under different State Acts provide yet another model of full functional autonomy with marginal government control showing better governance and outcome in terms of academic quality.
- Apart from structures and procedures, consistent good performance is a guarantor of autonomy.
- Funding to be norm-based and under block grant arrangements revised on performance basis.
- External peer Review Board to evaluate universities at periodical intervals and its suggestions to be acted upon by the executive Council/Board of Governors.
- Affiliation system to end with promising colleges or cluster of colleges being given university status and others to be given administrative autonomy and brought under examining Universities for temporary periods.
- Autonomy is the key for better performance of higher educational institutions.
- Autonomy is, to a large extent, the function of legal framework, structures and procedures.
- The IIT, IIM or the NLS models can mutati's mutandis, be adopted for universities as well.
- Affiliation system should be discontinued and the colleges be made autonomous, eventually giving them the status of universities if they meet minimum standards.
- Funding pattern has to change towards norm-based block grants with performance-based increments and freedom to generate resources outside Government.
- Expert Peer Review of institutions and performance audit of individuals should be mandatory.

Objectives of Autonomous Colleges

The scheme of autonomous colleges was conceived with the following objectives.
- To reduce the load in the university system.
- To reduce the high degree of centralisation in the system of higher education and to bring about decentralisation in the system.
- To promote creative innovations in the system of higher education.
- To provide freedom to the colleges in having their rules of admission, courses of study and syllabi and system of examinations.
- To insulate or protect the better educational institutions from the evil influences of the bad and mediocre colleges.

Essence of Autonomous Colleges

Freedom is the essence of autonomous colleges. All the salient or distinguishing features of autonomous colleges are linked to freedom of the institution. Instead of being dependent on a university, the autonomous colleges have their own rules of admissions, their own curriculum and courses and have their own methods of evaluating the students. Instead of being affiliated to a university, the autonomous colleges function as independent units. The autonomous colleges have their own boards of studies to take decisions on academic matters. They have their own question papers for the examinations instead of having the question papers prepared by the university. Evaluating the students through an internal assessment system, publication of examination results independently and following new and innovative programmes in teaching and evaluating process, are also the important features of autonomous colleges.

Central Universities

The setting up of newer Central Universities and with many more universities (Private and Foreign) in the pipeline is going to pose a serious challenge to the existing state Universities. Not only will the new universities attract good students but they will also attract good faculty from other universities.

Importance of University Location

This is not to say that all Central Universities attract good students and faculty. For a variety of reasons, barring some really well-known and well-established ones, a number of them are still struggling to attract the very best. In some cases, those (especially in the north-eastern region) have not been able to attract a mix of Pan-Indian students and faculty due to problems of bad/remote locations and the lack of adequate facilities in terms of schooling/medical aid/travel/stay. This trend will be replicated if the newly established Central Universities are not location friendly. In fact many of them are still struggling to find land.

Local Economy

On the other hand, despite all the ills that affect state universities, a number of students from rural, and mofussil areas and even from the north-eastern states join the ones located in urban areas. This is not only due to their past glory, but also because they are located in well-connected areas. It has to be recognised that universities play a very important role not only in quality education and employment but they are also laboratories of advanced research and play an important role in influencing and affecting the local economy. This is why the states need to pay them adequate attention.

"Universities", a unique combination of autonomy and decentralisation create exactly the modern type of institution which is able to innovate in a far more effective way than either government, bureaucracy or corporate.

Innovation

The expansion of higher education is characterised not just by the linear growth of existing institutions and systems, but also by innovations in curriculum, institutional structures and in the use of technology. One important innovation which is being widely adopted by most countries is the use of distance education techniques for teaching. Distance education has immense potentialities, particularly as a means for broadening access to higher education and knowledge at a relatively low cost.

*****

Constraints in Higher Education

The main constraints in the way of fulfilling the objectives of Higher education are:
- Out-dated curriculum and resistance to adoption of new curricula by various stakeholders;
- Inflexibility of choice options, often irreversible, life determining career decisions being made at the 10th standard itself;
- Unhealthy heterogeneity of curriculum across various universities and states;
- Poor infrastructure;
- Archaic resources of teaching and learning;
- Poor quality literacy, laboratory, playground and other facilities for students;
- Lack of commitment of faculty;
- Unqualified or incompetent teachers;
- Faculty recruitment practices leading to corruption and poor quality teacher recruitment;
- Lack of qualitative refresher training options for teachers on regular basis;
- The complete lack of orientation of courses to deal with employability of students;
- Soft skills, ICT skills, Functional English skills and other job-oriented competencies not incorporated in the curriculum;
- No initiative or effort on the part of colleges to provide for counselling or orientation to students in terms of career paths available and vocations;
- It is important to draw a distinction between 'qualified and employable'. The talent for many segments and aspects of various industries are required to possess certain basic technical and behavioural skills to be considered employable for the industry:
- Out of the 5 million graduates produced annually in India only about 15% are readily employable and can be absorbed directly by companies. Within the remaining 85%, a further 20% can be made employable through intensive training and the rest of the graduates are deemed unemployable;
- Lack of transparency;

- Unwieldy and messy governance structure in universities;
- Poor quality students coming into higher education;
- Prevalence of ossified mindsets with parochialism with lack of exposure visits and exchange programmes is another constraint;
- Lack of rationalisation of tuition and other fees leading to various distortions;
- Corruption at various levels in the administration;
- Politicisation of campuses;
- Indiscriminate expansion dilutes quality results — deterioration in average quality, increased profit provision all have serious consequences.

Evaluation of Research output

- Lack of linkages of universities with research laboratories and industries is another impediment that could otherwise lead to public good, which could be freely shared internationally as against pure commercial approaches and profit minimisation.
- Poor conduct of examination to faculty methods used to gauge and evaluate student learning, which at best tests repetitive learning.
- Lack of project work or creative works for evaluating students.
- Research is mostly pushed down as a priority due to lack of sensitisation, mentoring and orientation.

Deterioration of Standards

The play of sociological and political forces that make a compelling demand on the system of higher education to inflate quantitatively without effecting any fundamental change in its objectives, improvement in management and efficiency in performance. The colleges and universities have been allowed to expand with mindless haste to accommodate a bulk of ill-motivated, ill-prepared students from urban and rural sectors with the attendant deterioration in standards. Interpersonal contact between the teacher and the taught is hardly possible where the strength of the class is huge.

*****

Institution–Industry Interaction

Engineering colleges and polytechnics started functioning in the country in isolation, without any linkage with industry since inception. As a result there is a churning out of thousands of so called 'theoretical' graduates and diploma holders whose performance in job positions leaves much to be desired. Continuous and intensive industry–institute interaction is necessary to tide over the situation and it assumes special significance at this juncture due to the recent moves of restructuring and globalising our economy and signing of the GATT.

Practical Skills

Practical content in technical education should be deep rooted. If the foundation is strong then the super-structure can be expected to stand well. Technical education cannot grow in isolation away from practical skills. They are inseparable.

The practical training should be an integral part of technical education and can be gauged well if one takes a careful look at the engineering profession. The ultimate test of success or failure, of an engineer's product takes place in its actual use. It may bring happiness if it is successful or disaster if it is failure.

Lack of Foresight

Though India has the third largest manpower pool in science and technology in the world, its contributions in these areas are insignificant. The country could not plan, train and harness the huge pool of manpower effectively for economic growth. The present picture in the country is that in certain areas there is surplus of trained manpower while in others, a shortage or the level of skill and knowledge attained is far below the desired level. This pathetic scenario is the result of wrong planning or no planning at all. This is due to the facts that in many areas the intake capacities in institutions are fixed arbitrarily without having any linkage with the demand in the industry and other fields; lack of foresight in starting new courses as the situation demands; training confined to traditional and obsolete technologies that has no linkage with advanced technologies, which might have been developed in certain areas; and also lack of industry institute interaction.

Scarce Resources

Thus scarce resources are being wasted and there is widespread discontentment, uneven distribution of wealth and erratic growth resulting from unemployment, under employment or failure on the part of the technically qualified persons who are the products of a defective education system to optimise production.

Corrective Measures

The country realised its mistake only in the early seventies, but it has done pretty well for implementing corrective measures that have been already identified through numerous seminars, workshops and high-level discussions. The result of this lackadaisical attitude and vacillation are not far to seek. Year after year thousands of graduates and diploma holders come out of engineering colleges and polytechnics whose capability to deliver the goods is evidently questionable and as a result economic growth suffers. Again to sustain this defective education system a good chunk of money has to be diverted.

Apprenticeship Training

It is not that the entire lot of elites involved in the system are apathetic to the need of the hour. There are willing workers, though extremely limited in number, from the industry too, who spurred by their conscience of the prevailing situation have come forward to contribute in a meaningful way.

In the statute book there is an act known as "Apprenticeship Act" providing post-institutional practical training of technically qualified persons in industry and government departments. But these provisions are mostly violated than obeyed. Intensive and continuous industry–institute interaction that is mutually

beneficial to both is necessary to tide over the situation. Some of the activities under this may be as follows:
- Experts from industry may be associated in formulating a viable curriculum, which should be updated to include technological development in industry.
- Experts from industry may be invited to address the students and industry.
- Experts from industry may be associated with examination systems.
- Faculty may be allowed to undergo practical training in industry.
- Students may be allowed to undergo training in industry during institutional studies or immediately thereafter on passing.
- Students may be encouraged to take up project works related to industry.
- Institutions may offer tailor made continuing education programmes to meet specific needs of industry which may also provide for horizontal deployment as well as vertical mobility of personnel deployed in the industry.
- Industry may engage students for production of those items which do not require much skill outside the normal working hours in the workshop of the institutions.
- Industry may assign problems to institutions for viable solutions in which, faculty as well as senior students may be engaged.
- Industry may assign relevant research projects to institutions that are necessary for meeting their future needs, in which senior faculty of high academic and professional attainments may be engaged and faculty at lower level and senior students may also be associated.

Liberalisation and Globalisation

Now that the country has embarked upon an ambitious programme of Liberalisation and Globalisation it has become incumbent upon the industry and technical education system in particular to gear up efforts and make good the deficiencies to join the mainstream of global economy.

*****

Orientation Programme – Objectives

The university/college teachers should perform better in their crucial role in the delivery system of higher education. For attaining this objective, their enhanced motivation level, their better skills and knowledge and their thorough grounding in the latest teaching techniques and methodologies, including information technology are essential. Accordingly, the UGC vision statement about the Orientation Programme organised by Academic Staff colleges spells out its following objectives, which enable the newly appointed university/college teachers to:

- understand the significance of education in general and higher education in particular, in the global and Indian contexts;
- understand the linkages between education, economic, socio-economic and cultural developments, with particular reference to the Indian polity where democracy, secularism and social equity are the basic tenants of our society;
- acquire and improve the art of teaching at the college/university level to achieve goals of higher education;
- keep abreast of the latest developments in their specific subjects;
- understand the organisation and management of a college/university and to perceive the role of a teacher in the total system;
- utilise opportunities for development of personality, initiative and creativity; and
- promote computer-aided literacy as well as ICT in teaching and learning process.

By equipping teaching with better skills, sensitising them to the socio-cultural issues and challenges of the day and by providing them with this positive orientation it is expected that they, in turn, should be able to mentor their students in order to become better citizens and more conscientious members of community. The recent knowledge explosion has justified all the more need and relevance of Orientation Programmes for teachers for they cannot cope with the ever-increasing mass of information and knowledge, without assimilating it as part of participation in systematic and organised Orientation Programme.

Continuous Internal Evaluation

Continuous internal evaluation is an ongoing process of gathering such information about students by their teachers throughout the course of instruction, as if could provide feedback for improving the efficiency of learning and making long-term decisions about the students.

The above definition leads us to the list of a few characteristics of continuous internal evaluation, which are given below:

- It involves both ongoing observation and periodic testing of students by teachers who teach. The planning for such assessment should be made at the beginning of the course itself. It is a continuous process of updating judgement about performance in relation to certain criteria that may allow cumulative judgement at a later date. Its main purpose is to provide feedback to both teachers and students for improvement of teaching-learning process.
- It serves both formative and summative purposes, formative in the sense that it is used to improve instruction, and summative because it is used to supplement or complement the final examination results. Its contribution to the final examination results makes it more reliable and a valid measure of student performance.
- It is not a substitute for the final or terminal examination. It only acts as a supplementary means to improve the dependability of final examination organised by the university/board at the end of the course, even though its effectiveness in this regard depends on the way it is organised.
- It is a process of management of instruction. Both, the teachers and students become aware of their progress when they receive timely feedback signals. It reduces anxiety, stress and tension usually felt by the students at the time of final/terminal examinations as both the teachers and the students feel greater sense of responsibility.

Internal Evaluation Weightage

The decision about the relative weightage of external and internal evaluation is taken by the teachers and the examining bodies and may vary from place to place. In some universities, these weightages are in the ratio of 75:25, while in certain others they are in the ratio of 60:40. Some universities have adopted the 50:50 models. One institution of higher education for women has adopted 100% internal evaluation system. The assessment is made keeping in view various aspects of students' behaviour. Some of these are class attendance, assignments, periodic tests, classroom observation, practical/laboratory work, library work, term paper and community service.

Question Bank

A question bank is a large collection of test items developed by a group of trained and experienced professionals (teachers, psychologists, subject experts, testing specialists, etc) and printed on index cards or stored in the memory of digital computers, along with certain supporting data (such as default value, discriminating power, time required for attempting each item, subject matter component, etc.) and capable of being reproduced or retrieved whenever needed.

Objective Type Testing

During the second half of the 20th century, testing technology has made considerable headway, not only in the advanced countries, but also in the developing countries of the world. The traditional essay type examinations are losing their popularity in favour of objective type tests, which are increasingly being used in large-scale public examinations conducted by the employing bodies as well as by educational institutions. A large body of tests has been developed by bodies like the NCERT, UGC and the UPSC for being used in various public examinations conducted by them from time to time. Some of the prominent institutions of higher general and professional/technical education are using objective tests for making admissions to various courses of study.

Question Bank and Objective Type Testing

- The availability of question bank encourages the teachers to use large tests consisting of various types of questions covering all aspects of subject matter or curriculum. This improves the overall validity of the examination.
- Since the scoring techniques of test items of the question bank are standardised and most of the items are objective type, the reliability and objectivity of the resulting test may be improved.
- When the question bank is large enough and covers a wide range of the subjects, each sample test drawn (at random) is a cross-section of the prescribed course content. Thus, all possible sample tests drawn from the bank may be safely assumed to be parallel or equivalent in all respects, and the problem of non-comparability of examination marks is solved.
- The size of the question bank can reduce the anxiety about the secrecy of the question papers, the larger the size of the question bank less the chances of guessing the probable questions by the students. Remembering the answers to all the questions without acquiring required knowledge (Millman and Arter 1984) and skill is extremely difficult, if not impossible.

Computer Based

The question banking system is becoming increasingly computer-based and subjected to automation. This will lead to increased economy of instructor time and cost in assembling the tests error free. With the help of computers, several operations such as computing and maintaining item-wise statistics, tailoring test forms to suit specific requirements, scoring of test booklets in smaller period of time, and recording test performance to be used by teachers for feedback for improvement of instruction, are simplified.

Teaching Programmes

Broadly speaking, there may be two kinds of teaching programmes, micro and macro.

Micro Teaching

Short skill teaching programmes of around 10-15 minutes, e.g. questioning, explaining with examples, stimulus variation skills and reinforcement.

Macro Teaching

Long Teaching programmes, e.g. lectures, seminars, symposia and conferences.

Lectures

The oldest and most popular method of teaching being lecture, lectures are so common at the university level, throughout the world, that university teaching has become almost synonymous to lectures and lectures are supposed to be continuous exposition of things, i.e. subject matter. However, lectures have undergone certain changes by incorporating certain teaching skills as questioning, explaining with examples, focusing and highlighting important issues, ignoring insignificant points, hinting at things for the curious and intelligent and summarising at certain crucial points. Thus a lecturer now plays the important role of an intelligent guide helping the new visitors and tourists of the world of knowledge and experience. Lectures have certainly become indispensable at the university level not because they are taken to be the best method of teaching but because of their peculiar benefits which can never be accrued from any other methods of teaching.

Benefits of Lectures

- Lectures provide opportunities for the students to share 'a joint corporate venture' and participate enthusiastically in a group activity (as against the solitary reading programmes).
- Students sometimes learn better from oral explanations and guidance, i.e. through ears than through self-study programmes where the difficulties dampen the enthusiasm as well as understanding of the subject matter.
- Lectures serve best in introducing the target content (which becomes a very cumbersome task for student depending on bulky books only).

- Lectures are as good as honey, which the bee (teacher) prepares nicely and naturally by sucking the nectar from innumerable buds and flowers (books and journals).
- Lectures fill minds with enthusiasm to learn more and work harder to discover new vistas of knowledge (which no books replace).
- Then there is personality of the teacher that serves as a model for the students. Here again books fail to replace a live lecture.
- A teacher keeps on relating the core issues with the current scenario and topical problems for making his points more understandable — what we call driving home the target point.
- A really effective lecturer is like a good guide drawing your attention to the crucial points, overlooking the insignificant and always presenting the difficulties as never insurmountable.

Symposium

The word symposium is derived from the Greek words sum (together) and posies (drinking). Originally, symposium refers to any gathering at which interchange and discussion of ideas take place. It may also serve as a platform for presenting short articles and papers dealing with a common topic.

Seminars

(From Latin word, semen: seed). Seminars represent a group of advanced students pursuing high-level research programmes in a specific subject under the supervision of experts in the field. Here again ideas may be exchanged orally as well as in paper form.

Conferences

(Taken from Latin word conferee that means to bring together). These are broad spectrum programmes of discussion and paper readings allowing a full-fledged interchange of ideas and views and consultations revolving round different aspects of a broad field of problems.

Benefit of Information/Communication Technology to Teachers

- ICT allows engaging and motivating students to a great degree.
- The Internet increases access to authentic data.
- Simulations enable teachers to show experiments that would not otherwise be possible.
- Data logging and digital video recording allow access to new resources of data in a wider range of experimental settings.
- ICT is quicker and more accurate data collection, saving lesson time and giving better quality results.
- Teachers can spread the support time more evenly rather than attempting to give all support to individual students.
- They can set assignments online, view the work submitted by students and give instant feedback.
- Initiate discussion about topics.
- Provide resources online, such as documents, presentations date or give direct links to website on the topics of study.
- It helps in tailoring resources to meet the needs of the students.

Teacher and New Technology

In this advanced era the teachers cannot remain immune to the increasing technology spread in the market. They being in the forefront of the society have special duties and responsibilities than in any other profession. They being the creative heads of the society need to learn and imbibe newer techniques and methodologies so as to increase the retaining understanding and learning capacity of their students. The teachers of the new breed should be technologically aware and should possess quality of knowledge management so that they can integrate technology in their pedagogy, present content in a different style by different teachers and they can manage the whole process of planning organising and implementing the content in an integrated approach in an appropriate manner. The new trend in education requires well-equipped and technologically trained teachers and learners to meet the challenges of future education.

Definition of Education

The word 'education' has very wide connotations. Depending upon the context it has assumed several meanings. Scholars have defined it in a variety of ways. Whereas no single definition can be taken to be perfect, each definition does underline a particular approach and signify some essential aspects of the subject. Some of these are as follows:

Education is a quest for vision.
Education is a crucial factor for survival.
Education broadens our look.
Education sharpens our mental faculties.
Education teaches tolerance.
Education is the basis of a dignified existence.
Education is fundamental to all-round development.
Education is a unique investment.
Education is a guarantee for national self-reliance.
Education is a tool for self-empowerment.
Education leads to dignity and prosperity.
Illiteracy is the highest form of poverty in the life of a nation.

These insightful definitions must be carefully examined and then must be elaborated upon in order to evolve relevant strategies for the realisation of the objectives signified by them.

Learning

The UNESCO document underlines three kinds of learning:
- Learning to know, i.e. acquisition of knowledge/facts/ideas.
- Learning to do, i.e. acquiring skills and application of knowledge to occupational needs.
- Learning to be, i.e. to live and let live, which is learning to coexist,

Four Pillars of Higher Education

After the long scholarly debates on the goals and functions of higher education, four pillars of equal significance have been identified upon which the edifice of higher education can be erected. They are:

- Knowledge, i.e. the storehouse of the present state of our knowledge (in any specified area/areas).
- Concept, i.e. creation of knowledge, making useful addition to the current state of knowledge.
- Skills, i.e. application of knowledge in diverse fields of human activity, like occupation and professions.
- Value, a system which provides safeguards against misuse of knowledge for selfish ends.

University vs Industry

The difference between a 'University' and an 'Industry' is that the 'University' produces trained human beings of all kinds and trains them to accept various challenges in different fields, while the "Industry" produces homogeneous goods that are identical in shape and quality and are not living beings. But both the University and the Industry have one thing in common, i.e. management of employees who work for achieving a common goal with a common objective in their organisation but they have their own personal, mental and societal needs. When these different needs are not fulfilled and the person experiences obstacles or barriers from the superiors or fellow workers, he becomes depressed and does not work more sincerely. Finally, he/she develops apathy towards the work as well as the organisation. It slows down the production rate both in quality and quantity and finally affects the whole organisation adversely. This phenomenon is common to all types of organisations irrespective of their type of work, objectives, type of product and number of employees working in the organisation. Development of human resource is thus a desired need of any kind of organisation.

Faculty Development Efforts in India

In the light of the National Policy on Education, 1986, steps have been taken to protect the higher education system from "degradation". Courses and programmes of study have been introduced and designed to meet the demands of specialisation better. Co-ordinative methods have been developed by the

UGC to keep a watch on standards. The Scheme of Academic Staff Colleges, developed with care and extended with caution, has been introduced to provide training to college teachers on an ongoing basis throughout the year. Forty eight such Academic Staff Colleges (ASC), currently 66 ASCs, were set up throughout the country in 1987 and it is about 25 years now that programme of development of academic staff through the institutional mechanism of ASC's has progressed steadily and systematically. Until 1987, no mechanism was there for the professional development of teachers.

Faculty Development Efforts in the USA

Faculty development is largely a self-regulated phenomenon in the United States. There are a number of private institutes that have come up to provide training to college teachers. A teacher strives to grow professionally, attends summer schools, seminars, and workshops in his discipline to update his knowledge and learn new skills, not at the cost of an institution but at his own initiation.

Three Basic Capabilities of a Graduate

Acquisition of knowledge

This indicates not only knowledge that is adequate and relevant to the appropriate level of study, but also the capacity to gain and innovate new knowledge in response to the emerging situations and circumstances.

Personality Development

It is a process of natural flowering of all the inherent individual talents of the young person in full harmony with his fellow human beings. While acquisition of knowledge opens up limitless horizons of ever expanding enlightenment; it is the personality formation that guarantees a sound mental equilibrium and healthy social acceptability to the growing youth.

Development of Productive Activities

The fundamental attribute of graduate-level education is the development of the ability and willingness in the students to engage themselves in some productive activities after completion of the study.

The important part to be noted here is that this third component of preparing students for some productive engagement has never been adequately stressed in the Indian higher education system.

The objectives of vocational education at +2 level are:
- To fulfill the national goals of manpower development and all removal of unemployment and mal-distribution.
- To impart education relevant to productivity, national development and individual prosperity.
- To meet the need of middle level manpower for growing sectors of economy.
- To divert a sizable group of students to various vocational courses.
- To prevent a rush to general education at higher level and attract to attach the student to various vocational traders.
- To prepare students for self-reliance and employment.

One of the major objectives of vocationalised restructuring of first degree courses is to reorient the graduate education in such a way that students are given appropriate theoretical knowledge and practical training in at least one subject area, which promises employment possibility after graduation. As for the restructural vocationalisation, now introduced by the UGC, nearly one-third of the subject content of the traditional first degree courses is replaced with vocational components related to the remaining subjects taught.

Purpose of Higher Education

- To help individuals and society to understand and adapt to the implications of change, while maintaining the values which make a civilised society.
- To inspire and enable individuals to develop their capabilities to their highest potential levels throughout life,

so that they grow intellectually, are well equipped for work, can contribute effectively to society and achieve personal fulfillment.
- To increase knowledge and understanding for their own sake and to foster their application for the benefit of the economy and society.
- To serve the needs of an adoptable, sustainable, knowledge-based economy at local, regional and national level.
- To play a major role in shaping a democratic, civilised and inclusive society.
- To develop total quality of people with vision, values, skills and positive attitude.

Traditional and Contemporary Educational Settings

Sl. No	Subject	Traditional setting	Contemporary setting
a.	Student role	Store information	Create knowledge
b.	Teacher role	Present information, information giver	Facilitator, guiding students in active learning
c.	Curriculum design	Breadth, Fact retention, fragmented knowledge, disciplinary separation	Depth, multidisciplinary themes, knowledge integration, application of knowledge
d.	Learners characteristic	Independent learning	Collaborative learning
e.	Role of technology	Direct instruction, drill practice, tutorials, etc	Collaboration, exploration, research, etc

Transformative Changes for Quality Higher Education

Sl. No.	Area	From	To
1.	Business approach	Competitive	Co-operative
2.	Content	User	Developer
3.	Delivery	Within institution	Across the border
4.	Education Process	Discipline specific	Multidisciplinary
5.	Focus	Internal Processes	Collaborative Process
6.	Flexibility	Restrictive	Flexible
7.	IT System	Defined by producer, inflexible	Defined by user adaptable
8.	Knowledge attitude	Hoarding	Sharing
9.	Learning	Confined	Open
10.	Pedagogy	Teacher centered	Learner centered
11.	Perspective	Narrow	Broad
12.	View of other institutions	Suspicious	Trust
13.	Quality control	Internal	Shared

Educational Managers

Educational Managers are generally involved in planning, organising, co-ordinating and executing various educational activities of the institution to achieve the pre-decided goals. They are normally involved in managing men, materials and other processes of the institution. While managing materials, it is essential to know the function of knowledge of several techniques like planning, budgeting, resource allocation, etc. Management of human resource requires knowledge of human nature and behaviour. It is not enough to have a good mind; the main thing is to use it well. Any manager interested in managing human resources, must have an understanding of human nature. In order to be more effective, the manager should explicitly understand the dynamics of human behaviour.

*****

Research

Selection of Research Topics

Selection of a relevant topic for research is a fundamental rule of immense importance. For example, before selection a historian uses his imagination which differs from that of other historians. He will try to see human behaviour through his own eyes and different from those of his colleagues. He will then construct his own philosophy of history. So choosing a topic depends not only on his imagination but also on his observations.

Role of Research Guides

What role does a research supervisor play in moulding the young prospective research scholar?

Identifying Problems

Students join as research scholars with their heads full of ideas and hearts full of hopes. Soon they come face to face with the hardships. For example, every branch of science is so competitive today and many research guides take students without a concrete research plan, leaving it to the students to prepare one. The students have no experience in research and so they suffer.

The research supervisors do not help them to identify a problem or design the experiments. In case the student himself identifies a research problem, either the guide doesn't allow him to go ahead with it or doesn't really give him the due attention. The guide's presence is felt only at a time of analysing the data or writing a paper.

Regular Monitoring

The student's progress is not monitored regularly but when his tenure is approaching an end, the supervisor puts a lot of pressure on him to bring out a thesis even if it is a substandard work that has been done in a much shorter period. The student wastes much time and effort in the process and eventually loses the drive to do more work. Regarding quality of the work, there is no concept or phenomenon involved for the basis of the work.

Often, organising conferences and going abroad frequently, takes up a lot of time of the guide and consequently there is no time for discussions with the students. In some instances, the supervisor takes months together to correct either a paper or thesis. The progress often gets hindered when the guide makes a slight change in the research topic.

Remedies

Harassment and pressure are constant companions forcing some students to go to the extreme ends. (Some research scholars quit the course and a few even end their lives.)
Remedies for the above said problems are:
- Strict measures have to be enforced to look into the quality of the research work.
- The number of papers published by the guide in well-reputed journals should be taken into count.
- The particular faculty member should submit a kind of "work plan" to a committee comprising eminent professors that can look into the importance of the work and its worth.
- Periodic progress in research by the student has to be monitored in the form of presentations by the student.

Problem Areas

To begin with, a thorough knowledge of a particular subject area is needed. Hence, it is necessary to have completed a major part in the subject before plunging into research. The more one knows about a particular field, the more able one is to detect gaps in it and to reorganise problematic areas that require investigation.

Problems and Solutions

The researcher should have the ability to detect problems and find solutions to a particular problem. He must see whether he can make any contribution to knowledge on this. He must also see whether there is any problem and whether his thesis will attempt to solve the problem. For this he must have direct contact with the experts in the field, the more the problems are investigated, the more the problems emerge for further investigation. He must also go through the writings of experts in the field, and various research journals. Further, he must study the current literature in his chosen field. He must be familiar with recent doctoral dissertations in his field of interest and must be familiar with the publications regarding dissertations published by university (news bulletins).

Following are the criteria for selection of a topic:
- Is there adequate supervision?
- Does the topic interest the researcher?
- Can it be completed within the stipulated time?
- Are the necessary equipment and subjects available?
- Is the study feasible?
- Is the problem a significant one? This is a difficult question to answer as an apparently unimportant fact may turn out to be important in the hands of a scholar.
- The researcher should make sure that the area is yet untouched. If research has already been done in the area, the research must prove how it is an improvement upon the pioneering work already done in the field.
- The topic must be limited in scope so that it could be developed adequately and specifically.

Higher Education: A Panoramic View

- The topic must be acceptable to the intended readers as well or else the efforts would go waste.
- And the researcher should add new information or a new interpretation or advance a new theory. In short the purpose of research must be quite explicit and clear in his mind.

Current Live Issues

The researcher might take up currently live issues of national or international events, political, educational, religious, artistic or humanitarian movements, organisations or persons connected with them. Art forms, like architecture, picture, sculpture, ceramics, theatre, dance, music, and literature could be taken up for research. One could work on prominent personalities, of politics, business, agriculture, sports, arts, science and professional religion. One could also work on his native place or region its history, institutions, economy, outstanding persons, school, college, students' social life, organisations, ports, temples and so on.

A researcher should know more about the benefits of a library, for books are his never-failing friends. Research involves original planning. The viability of a topic depends on the availability of material and sufficiency of the subject. To avoid repetitive work, topic banks and clearing houses of research subjects should be set up.

*****

Universities

A hundred and fifty years ago, even the idea of the university as a popular institution was a new one, not only in India but also in England and in most parts of Europe. The universities were small, selective, and often reclusive places and they were designed neither to overrun the existing hierarchies nor to produce hundreds of thousands of graduates every year for employment in government and other offices. When the first universities were started in Calcutta, Bombay and Madras (Kolkata, Mumbai and Chennai), such a conception of the social responsibility of a university was still in the future.

The universities were among the first open and secular institutions in a society that was governed largely by the rules of kinship, caste and religion. In that sense they were islands of modernity in a world bound largely by tradition. Right until the time of independence, the universities were few and far between. Their influence did not reach very far or penetrate very deeply into a society that was steeped in poverty, illiteracy and inequality. But their influence, no matter how restricted, was progressive, both intellectually and institutionally and this progressive influence appeared to be spreading gradually.

Twin Objectives of Universities

The challenge before our universities in the 21st century is to combine two distinct but important objectives. The first objective is to maintain and apply strict standards of academic discrimination without fear or favour and without consideration of caste, creed and gender. The second is to make the universities socially more inclusive, in practice and not just in principle. The difficulties of keeping both objectives simultaneously in view are not given the attention they deserve. Some of our best universities still maintain high academic standards and their graduates fit easily into the best universities outside the country and perform very well there.

Impact of Universities on women

In the last century, the universities did more than any other institutions to change the role of women in public life. Their presence in the professions in administration, in management, in the media and in other areas of employment in remunerative and responsible positions would not have been possible if the universities and the colleges had not opened their doors to them. Oxford and Cambridge had been in existence for 600 or 700 years before they began to admit women to their degrees. Calcutta University admitted two women to its BA degree in 1883, and they became the first women graduates in the British Empire.

Women from Backward Communities

The routes through which sections of society earlier largely excluded from the universities and came to be gradually incorporated in them have varied from one case to another. Organised political pressure has played no little part in the slow but steady inclusion of women in the universities, first as students and shortly afterwards as teachers. Pressure from political parties in both government and opposition has been the main driving force behind the increase in the number of students and teachers from the backward communities. It is now much more widely acknowledged than 50 or 60 years ago that having more women in the universities is good not only for women, but also for universities. This acknowledgement has been won through much toil and effort and not without disappointments.

Separate Institutes for Women

Till the time of Independence, it was not considered proper in many, if not most, Indian families for mature girls to enter institutions where their fellow students and their teachers would be mostly men. Having separate institutions for women solved the problem to some extent but it was not a satisfactory solution for postgraduate study and research. It was only when women were allowed to move more freely on their own that they made their way more fully into the universities and their successful performance there led to a further easing of the bias against them.

Creation of Abilities

There is general agreement that equality of opportunity is a desirable objective and commitment that is written in the Constitution of India. Equality of opportunity depends not just on the removal of disabilities but also on the creation of abilities. Access to universities is restricted because of insufficient and uneven development of secondary education.

Diversity of Talents

The growth of knowledge is now so rapid and so extensive that some have begun to say that we are moving into a new type of society which they call 'the knowledge society'. The universities of 21st century, no matter where they are, have to adapt themselves to the requirement of a new type of society that is emerging. Not all individual members of a university, or even all individual universities, can be expected to excel equally in teaching and research, but the university system as a whole must be attentive to the demands of both. If we do not leave enough room for the diversity of talents within a university or among the different universities but to impose the same requirements on each of them, very little advance will be made in either teaching or research.

Socially Inclusive

The universities have social and not just intellectual obligations; they are both social institutions and centres of learning. Unlike the universities of past, modern universities aim to be socially inclusive and not exclusive. In India the universities made a good beginning by keeping their doors open to women and members of all castes and communities. There are two views on admission and appointments — one thing is to go by merit alone and another is accommodating every section of society in sufficient numbers.

Longer Life Span

As an institution, the university has a longer life span than the life span of any of its individual members. It was there before most of its present members entered it and will continue to be there after they leave it. This appearance of continuity brings a lot of changes both in the internal structure of the university and in its relationship with its environment.

Employable Graduates

A university cannot disown its responsibility to produce graduates but it must at least try to ensure that it is not overwhelmed by that one single responsibility. Producing employable graduates is an important responsibility of the university, but it is not its sole responsibility and not, in every case, even its main responsibility.

Individual Mobility

University degrees cannot eliminate social inequality, but they are an important aid to individual mobility. What social and political commentators usually mean when they say that they want inequality to be ended is that they want the obstacles to individual mobility to be removed or relaxed. The universities may not have brought inequality to an end, but they have acted as important catalysts for individual mobility. This may not be the same thing as the advancement of science and scholarship, but it is nevertheless an important social function in a democracy.

Cluster of Disciplines

The universities of the 21st century cannot be set up with the same objectives with which our first universities were set up in 1857, nor when set up should they be encouraged to follow the same trajectories that the earlier ones did. We have accepted the principle that a university today does not have to be universal in its coverage of disciplines in order to engage in the combined pursuit of teaching and research at the highest level of excellence. The viable university should have a cluster of disciplines with a core and a periphery. Not all universities need to have the same core or the same periphery.

The changes to be introduced to uplift the universities and colleges are:

Establish of Endowments

A system of endowments should be established for colleges and universities. The alumni and the community should be canvassed to contribute to the endowment. The endowment money should be invested and the income from this investment should be used to fund special chairs at attractive salaries and support research projects.

Classification of Faculty

A classification of faculty based on whether they do research or only instruction should be introduced. The research faculty should be provided suitable rewards. Further the staff at research institutes and universities must compete for research funds based on research proposals evaluated by peer review.

Evaluation of Faculty

A system of evaluation of the faculty, on performance over a fixed number of years at the start of the career, before awarding life-long tenure should be introduced. The evaluation should ensure that the faculty has shown enough promise in terms of research achievements to merit a permanent appointment.

Funding Formulae

The basic funding at colleges and universities should be according to an appropriate formula that takes into consideration enrollment at the Postgraduate and under-graduate levels and the nature of the programmes offered. It should be left to the college or university to raise additional resources through endowments or by soliciting research grants.

Periodic Assessment

A system of periodic assessment of colleges and universities should be introduced. This should be done both for individual programmes as well as the educational centre taken as an entity. The results of such an assessment should be made available to departments, so that they can use this criticism for improvement.

Fellowship Programmes

A system of fellowship programmes should be introduced so that college teachers can visit better institutes for a semester or a year.

Foreign Students

Revenues can be enhanced by recruiting foreign students and charging them fairly higher fees than for those of Indian origin.

Project and Contract Studies

Government users like State and Central agencies should be encouraged to contract studies and projects to colleges and universities. This would increase the proportion of directed research.

Work Study Programmes

Work study programmes should be introduced to replace the current free scholarships. Not only would this cut down in the size of the bureaucracy of the permanent support staff but inculcate the value of the work.

Sharing of Ideas and Results

Avenues for sharing of ideas and results as in conferences and journals shall be strengthened. In the past this has implied attending a few conferences abroad but there is need to reorganise more meetings within the country.

Dynamism and Responsiveness

It is believed that with changes like the above ten, without having to inject unreasonably large additional resources, it would be possible to make the system of higher education dynamic and responsive to the needs of the country and allow the renewal of our great tradition of excellence.

These changes cannot be introduced all at once in all universities. But a beginning could be attempted at select centres. The endowment idea should get the community involved, and force the administrative leaders of the universities to interface with it. Better management and more tuition fee from foreign students could raise further revenues so that fair compensation could be paid to outstanding researchers.

Micro-Teaching

Micro-teaching is a training concept that can be applied at various pre-service and in-service stages in the professional development of college teachers. Micro-teaching lessens the complexities of normal classroom teaching: class size, scope of content, time. It focuses on training for the accomplishment of specific tasks – practice of specific instructional skill. Immediately after teaching a micro-lesson the teacher engages in a critique of his performance. To give him a maximum insight into his performance several sources of feedback are at his disposal. With the guidance of a supervisor or colleague, he analyses aspects of his performance in the light of his goals. A video tape will show the teacher how he performed and how he can improve. All this feedback can be immediately translated into practice when the teacher retouches shortly after the critique conference.

Micro-teaching is a success because it 'works'. This technique has been field-tested and refined. Now there is plenty of research evidence, consistent and promising, to show micro-teaching does benefit to the teachers–pre-service and in-service.

Priorities in Higher Learning

Now the question is that what are the modifications required to make higher education more effective and relevant to the needs of our society. The most important defect has been the lack of harmony between the content of education and the socio-economic condition of our country. We have to think ahead and the future needs of our society have also to be taken into consideration. The priorities of action have also to be enlisted without any conflict between objectivity and political commitments.

Our programme of immediate action for higher education should be to:
- Consolidate the existing facilities, contain the numbers, and improve the quality.
- Maintain peace and keep up the sanctity needed in the 'Temple of Learning'
- Remove frustration from among the youth and inculcate a sense of discipline and bring home to them the importance of certain values in life.
- Motivate faculty and staff, get adequate support and ensure necessary participation and co-operation from the community.

- Restructure the curriculum and make it more relevant to the needs of society and relate it to agriculture and industries.
- Facilitate smooth working to give effect to the main functions of higher education teaching, research and extension.
- Provide necessary personnel well-equipped to appreciate the problems that confront the community.
- Moreover, explosion of numbers in the field of higher education has been a headache for long. Attempts should not be made to start too many new arts and science colleges. Higher education is to be extended only to those who have the correct aptitude to take up higher studies and who are likely to be benefited by it.
- The classroom climate and campus culture in our educational institutions should be such as to facilitate apt functioning of higher education.
- Members of faculty and also other staff in the universities and colleges have to be fully conscious of their duties and responsibilities. Teachers do not exert influence on students any more.
- All the activities of the teachers at least inside the campus of the educational institution should be such as to generate higher teacher effectiveness through an interaction between the teacher and the students.
- Teaching, research and extension are the three important functions of higher education. Teaching was considered the most important function of higher education in our country for long and still continues to be so. Teaching is complete when learning has taken place. In order to achieve this, there should be complete understanding between the teacher and the taught.
- Curriculum has to be made more relevant to the needs of the society.

Community Services

Priority has to be given to projects that have direct relevance to the problems of a community. In addition to teaching and research a third function has come to the fore under the label of community services such as NSS and NCC with the desired effect.

Students who come out of the educational institutions should not only be able to get employment but be able to face life without flinching and appreciate the problems that confront the society.

A university is a part of the society it seeks to serve. It cannot shut itself away from the realities of the world around it. It is time for our academic community to take a more positive role in grappling with the problems of contemporary life. The teachers and students with university education must share their knowledge, expertise and experience with their less fortunate brethren. After all, knowledge is something that can and must be shared. It does not improvise the giver; it only enriches him.

Development of Personality

Our objective is all-round development. This development need not necessarily be confined to economic development only. Economic development by itself will not take us forward. We have therefore, to lay adequate emphasis on the development of personality and it is this role that makes education very crucial. For this, much depends on what is taught, how it is taught and how the students absorb that knowledge. Attention to these aspects makes education relevant and meaningful. Unless our educational programmes are related to our economic and social environment, we will not be able to impart relevance to our programmes.

Examination

One important aspect which causes concern is that too much emphasis is being placed on examinations. One could even say that education at present is examination oriented. Though it may not be easy to dispense with the examination altogether, it is necessary to consider development of tools that can test the ability of students objectively.

At any rate, there is need to discourage mugging, cheating, mass-copying and variety of other malpractices which are eating up the vitals of our educational system. Examinations should be such as to encourage the students to learn substantially rather than cram.

Service to the Nation and Community

We should think seriously of re-organising the courses offered by our universities and prepare programmes which could offer opportunities to students to develop their creative abilities. Participation of students in community activities, developmental projects or such activities that develop their personalities like sports, games, music and so on should get the recognition. Equally important is the promotion of our great values, traditions and ideals of secularism, democracy, socialism and national integration. Such an effort in education would indeed make education a meaningful investment. It is only then that our universities can become institutions of service to the society and the nation.

Enriches Personality

Education for a person is like an ornament which enriches his personality. If an educated person does not utilise the education he has obtained, his position becomes like that of a scentless and fruitless flower. Everybody, therefore, should make use of their education for the cause of the betterment of the society and the progress of the country.

Living as a Dynamic Entity

An institution is not merely the buildings or their classrooms. It is a body of people, with teachers and the students, who make the institution a living and dynamic entity. It is the interaction between the teachers and the students that shapes ideals and transmits them. Learning is a process that never ends. One learns all through life, the sources of knowledge are everywhere: Nature itself provides unlimited sources of knowledge. The primary objective of any educational system, therefore, should be stimulating a learning process in which everyone is learning all the time.

Skills to meet the challenges

The primary task of a university is to equip young men and women with the skills to meet the challenges of life. The foremost of these challenges is the amazing pace of changes which the technological revolutions of the present age have brought in its wake. Knowledge has grown with such a tremendous speed that adjustments and innovations that were previously achieved through the efforts of many generations have now to be coalesced into the strivings of one generation only or even less.

Correct Solutions

With this, the growth of knowledge is also changing the physical, intellectual and moral facets of the universe. The old values are getting new meanings. The university consisting of students and teachers has a formidable role to play in interpreting these changes. Therefore, the success of a university and its greatness in the ultimate analysis will not depend on the size of its buildings or the strength of its staff or students, but on its power to give correct solutions and fresh explanations to the developments in the society and the world in which it operates.

Life-long Learning

It is no longer possible to attain a particular degree of knowledge and expertise at a certain stage which would be sufficient and relevant for all time to come. Fast changes in the conception and technology of things make it imperative on all of us to go on learning continuously if we do not want to be branded as obsolete. This emphasis on life-long learning cannot but leave its impact on the teacher and the taught relationship which has become more informal. It has also proved that the teachers have to learn as much and perhaps more than the students in their charge if they have to maintain their hold over the latter and command respect and admiration. This is applicable to all careers in society but more particularly in the case of university professors.

Churning Out Balanced Citizens

The university has a formidable responsibility of bringing out balanced citizens who are capable of crisis-management and self-discipline. It is one of the foremost functions of a university to develop in the young minds a spirit of enquiry and desire to gain knowledge about different ideologies and view points and at the same time develop their capabilities to look at them dispassionately with academic discipline. It is only then that they would be able to be constructive in their outlook. The value of self-discipline in life and thought has to be conveyed to them in formative stages to enable them to battle with life later.

Madras University

The University of Madras was incorporated by an Act of the Legislative Council of India, dated 5th September 1857, along with Calcutta and Bombay and was organised on the model of London University of the day. The activities of the University were confined to the conduct of examinations for candidates who have been trained in Liberal Arts, Mathematics and Philosophy in the affiliated colleges of the University.

Research in Medicinal Plants

The Madras University has taken up the task of developing a seed bank of 23 bio-endangered varieties of herbal medicinal plants. These plants have been authenticated for their medicinal properties. There is a need to maintain the bio-efficiency of these plants and perpetuate their life. The seeds of the endangered herbs will be bio-typed and provided to researchers, traditional medical practitioners and anyone else who would need them.

The university is more than a glorified extension of a school whose sole aim is to turn out human products stamped with degrees. No less important than teaching is doing research. Unless the teaching faculty is involved with research as well, the system will become stale and sterile.

University Departments

Altogether there were 68 teaching and research departments functioning in the University of Madras at the end of the Twentieth Century. The number of Academic Staff was 263 with 208 professors 46 Readers and 9 Lecturers and 1080 Administrative Staff.

The 68 departments of the University are located in the four campuses namely Chepauk, Marina, Guindy and Taramani. These departments were grouped under 11 schools during 1984-85. At present these departments function under 18 schools.

Indian Universities

Rights and Responsibilities

Universities as centres of learning can be termed as homes of intellectuals. They produce students of caliber. Universities provide strong institutions and provide infrastructure for better education and better learning. Higher education can also create awareness about people's rights and responsibilities.

Brotherhood

The happiest period of one's life is the time spent at a university. The debates and discussions broaden your mind. A feeling of brotherhood emerges from living together. You must strive to reach the pinnacles of excellence in your chosen career.

Shortcomings of the Indian Universities

- Objectives of the universities are not clearly defined and spelt out in most of the Acts. Infrastructure facilities are inadequate to fulfill the objectives.
- Composition of the major university authorities. For e.g., Senate, Executive Council and the Academic Council are not appropriate to their roles.
- Excessive controlling role is played by the State Departments of Education. By and large, all authority in a State is vested in the Director of Higher Education and Education secretary. Financial autonomy does not seem to be a possible prerequisite.
- Lack of proper state level body to facilitate, promote and co-ordinate with higher education authorities in the states as also with the UGC.

- Lack of provision in the acts of the Universities for granting autonomous status to colleges, Departments, institutions or campuses of colleges.
- Lack of adequate authority to the Vice-Chancellor to discharge his responsibility as the Principal Executive and Academic Officer.
- Lack of or inadequate dencentralisation of powers to Directors of institutes, Deans of faculties and Heads of departments.
- Absence of adequate and effective machinery for planning and development, academic monitoring accreditation of institutions and recognition of individual merit.
- Inadequate and generally ineffective technical and administrative services.
- Poor financial arrangements and over dependence on government, leading to infringement of autonomy and also resulting in inefficiency.
- Lack of effective, independent judicial machinery with proper status and powers for resolving internal disputes in the university.
- Failure to provide adequately for balancing the needs of various interests and groups involved in University functioning, viz., the academic community and the lay representatives, the University and colleges, the teachers, the students, the non-teaching staff, etc., and to provide for proper interaction between them in the larger interest of the University itself.
- Universities have programmes of teaching, research and extension; teaching programmes in many cases have not much relevance to social and national needs. Rigidities of Boards of studies do not allow introduction of new multi-faculty or inter-faculty courses as also redesigning of courses. Extension hardly finds a place in the Acts of Universities. There is hardly any collaboration between different departments and the universities collaborate only in marginal manner with industry, research and other academic institutions.

Problems in the system of Higher Education

- Inadequacy of infrastructure for providing physical facilities and academic inputs.
- Financial and resource problems.
- Problems of Curriculum Development and need for more flexibility in offering courses to students.
- Recruitment and training of teachers and human resources management problems.
- Evaluation and appraisal problems.
- Inadequate community relations.
- Need for establishing proper relations with other research institutions and industry.
- Problems of providing co-curricular facilities.
- Problems of organising, promoting, monitoring and evaluating research.
- Problems of time management.
- Problems of adapting to new challenges like distance education, non-formal education, continuing education open learning and newer educational technologies/techniques.
- Problems of looking after the interest of special groups like weaker sections, women, etc.
- Institutional and academic autonomy and accountability.

Senate

The Senate is a larger body representing diverse groups from academics and other social groups, mostly elected. In some universities the non-academic groups in the senate include local bodies, non-teaching staff, representatives of trade unions, women's bodies, commerce and industry, progressive farmers (in Agricultural Universities) registered graduates, co-operative societies and college managements in addition to MPs MLAs, MLCs and Government nominees, student representatives, Alumni, etc.

Syndicate

The syndicate (or Executive Council as it is called in some universities), being the executive body, is a small body, usually consisting of not more than 20 members. The representatives are elected / nominated from amongst the principals, teachers, senators, Academic Council, etc., besides, some ex-officio members and Government nominees. The entire syndicate consists of only ex-officio and nominated members in some universities. While in most universities the university faculty members are represented in the syndicate, in the University of Madras, Madurai Kamaraj University and a few other universities, no teacher in the university is eligible to be elected/ nominated to the syndicate.

Academic Council

The Academic Council comprises the representatives of faculties, principals, university, Heads of Departments/Deans, Senate, etc. Most of the members are ex-officio/nominated; there is very limited elected representation in the Academic council. In some universities, the Academic Council is too large. In most of the Universities there is provision of members getting in by election; students are generally not given any representation, but in some universities, the students are given representation.

Overlapping Functions

The authorities of the University system (Senate, Syndicate and Academic Council) do not have mutually exclusive powers and functions. Most of the decisions taken by one authority are to be approved by or remitted to for information or ratification by other authorities. Though the syndicate is the apex executive body managing the administration of the university, it has to seek the policy approval and budget sanction from senate. The Academic Council is primarily concerned with the academic curricula, syllabi and regulations. However, it does not have the ultimate authority over them as most of these are provided under ordinances, which have to be approved by the Syndicate and not disapproved by the visitor/Chancellor.

State Council for Higher Education

Autonomy of a University is inconceivable without a clear understanding of working relationship with the State. It is necessary to provide an agency which would minimise the possibility of direct interference through the Government, political and other channels in the functioning of the universities. Such an agency will also be useful for keeping constant vigilance on the functioning of the universities. The UGC has suggested certain roles and functions for such a Council including the following:
- To monitor the progress of implementation of development programmes.
- To advise the State Governments in determining the blocks maintenance grants and to lay down the basis for such grants.
- To examine the statutes and ordinances of various universities in the State and suggest modifications wherever required.
- To advise the State Governments regarding the statutes proposed by the universities in a state.
- To perform any other functions necessary for furtherance of higher education in the State.

Powers of the Senate

- To review, from time to time, the broad policies and programmes of the university and to suggest measures for the improvement and development of the University.
- To advise the chancellor in respect of any matter which may be referred to it for advice and
- To exercise such other powers and such other functions as may be prescribed in the statutes.

The statutes of Bharathidasan University (1983) as given under, are more specific about the role of the Senate. The senate shall:-
- Consider the Annual Report of the University
- Consider the audited annual accounts of the University
- Consider the ordinances made by the Syndicate

- Consider the regulations made by the Standing committee on Academic Affairs
- Consider the reports on affiliated colleges presented by the Syndicate at the end of every three years.

It may be noted here that the Senate is to consider and discuss; its approval has not been made mandatory.

Powers of Syndicate

The executive decision making and implementation are vested with the syndicate. The syndicate, in actual practice, wields enormous powers, more often than contemplated in the Acts/Statutes. The proceedings in the Senate and the Academic Council are regulated by the Syndicate as a result of some statutory provisions. On many occasions, the senate or the Academic Council is constrained to ratify what has already been decided upon and even implemented by the syndicate. The concentration of powers, administrative, financial and to a considerable extent academic also in the syndicate naturally leads to evolution of vested interests among its members.

Finance Committee

It is a statutory committee in many universities. The Finance Committee, with the Vice-Chancellor, as Chairman and Registrar (Finance) as the Member-Secretary shall consist of two or three syndicate members, two Deans, the Finance Secretary and Education Secretary of the Central/State Government concerned or their nominees not below the rank of a Joint Secretary as its members. This Statutory Body should have the following responsibilities
- To prepare the budget after ascertaining the requirements of the various Departments of the University.
- To monitor the utilisation of funds and make budget revisions and (re-appropriation) after an interim assessment.
- To explore the possibilities of and resort to augmenting further resources for campus Developing and other needs.
- To productively invest and manage the university assets and resources.

- To prepare the Annual Financial Report and Audited statements and be answerable to the Executive Council on all financial matters.

Pro-Chancellor

The office of the Pro-Chancellor is a decorative post. Ordinarily, Pro-Chancellor is next to the Chancellor and a number of University Acts provide that in the absence of the Chancellor, the Pro-Chancellor may perform such functions as may be assigned to him by the Chancellor. More than 20 Universities have Pro-Chancellors. In the Central University of Delhi the Chief Justice of India is ex-officio Pro-Chancellor of the University. The Ministers of Education/Higher Education are the Pro-Chancellor in the State Universities.

Functions of the University

- Teaching through faculty divisions and schools of Excellence
- Research and Extension
- Continuing Education
- Curriculum development
- Evaluation
- Affiliation, approval, accreditation
- Awards and recognition
- Funding and Finance
- Human Resources Development
- Public Relations and Communications
- Student Welfare and Co-curricular activities
- Publications and Library Development
- Maintenance of Hostel's Staff Relations
- Grievances Settlement and Municipal Function

Dean

The title of Dean is given to the head of a Faculty. In an affiliating university the Dean of a Faculty may not have ordinarily much work to perform day to day, but this is different in a unitary or federal university. In the latter case the Deans have to coordinate the work of the different departments included in the Faculty, e.g. preparation of class time-table. In addition to this, it would be necessary for them to exercise certain administrative functions. The Deans could provide valuable assistance to the Vice-Chancellor in dealing with organisational problems and in matters of general discipline in the university. In an affiliating University they could also assist the Vice-Chancellor in exercising some general supervision of the work of the affiliated colleges. The Dean of course should be a full time teacher of the University.

Registrar

The office of the Registrar is also an important one. The Registrar represents the permanent part of the university executive. Vice-Chancellors hold office for a limited period in the best circumstances. The Registrar is therefore the custodian of the traditions of the university, its efficiency and integrity. It is also necessary that his entire loyalty should be to the University. The Registrar must exercise his powers with discretion and understanding. His practices should always be responsive to the academic traditions of the university he serves. The Registrar should be appointed by the Executive Council. The terms and conditions of service should be clearly determined by statutes. It is not likely to do universities much good if officers are borrowed from outside the universities to serve for a limited period, as such an arrangement has all the disadvantages of an interim arrangement.

Finance Officer

Finance Officer should be a whole time salaried Officer appointed by the Executive Council specially charged with the responsibility of looking after the finances of the university. It would be his duty to attend to proper investment of the university's funds; watch the expenditure, and to deal generally with matters connected with the finances of the university. He should not operate as a brake or as an instrument for delaying progress. This, however, should not be understood to mean that the importance of keeping correct accounts and following the budgetary laws is underestimated.

Formulation of University Guidelines for Model Act

The principles necessary to promote efficiency, economy and responsiveness of the University administration listed below needs to be incorporated in the legal framework of the University Act.
- Autonomy of the University system, coupled with provision for its responsibility and accountability to the society.
- Clear and unambiguous enunciation of the powers and responsibilities of the University.
- Clear-cut, well-defined division and separation of powers among the University authorities/bodies.
- Broadening the role perspective of the university, with effective linkages with other social sub-systems.
- De-politicisation of the campus and ensuring healthy academic environment.
- Decentralisation of decision making, by specific division of powers and responsibilities among officers.
- De-bureaucratisation of the administrative machinery by infusing academic thinking into the university administration; adequate flexibility in decision-making and execution guided by academic rationale, without being technically bogged down to set rules and regulation.

University Research Board

The University Research Board will function under the chairmanship of the Vice-Chancellor and may include Deans of Faculties, representatives of social groups, National Laboratories, R&D organisations, industry, etc., and of Government. One of the Deans should be the Secretary of the Research Board by rotation for one year. The functions of the Board will broadly be the following:
- To identify the "thrust areas" for research, so as to make effective contribution to the society.
- To arrange internal and external funds for research activities.
- To allocate adequate funds for individual research projects.
- To monitor the progress of research projects.

- To disseminate research information for public use.
- To prescribe general guidelines for the Faculties/Departments
  - research schemes/projects
  - multidisciplinary research programmes
  - award of research fellowships
  - foreign fellowships
  - to promote and foster
  - to co-ordinate research work in universities and research laboratories
  - the number of students to be attached with each category of teacher, i.e. Professor, Reader and Lecturer.

Faculty Research Board

It will function under the chairmanship of the Dean of the Faculty and will include Heads of Departments, Professors (20% of the strength), Readers (10% of the strength) and Lecturers (5% of the strength) by rotation according to seniority for one year. The functions of the Faculty Research Board would be:
- To identify the 'thrust areas' for research at the faculty level.
- To co-ordinate interdisciplinary research at the faculty level.
- To monitor the progress of Faculty research projects.
- To disseminate relevant information.

Departmental Research Committee

This committee will function under the Chairmanship of the Head of the Department and would include all the professors, 33% of Readers and 10% of the Lecturers by rotation according to seniority for one year. The functions of the committee would be:
- To take all measures for strengthening and consolidation of research activities in the department;
- To identify the 'thrust areas' for research at department level;
- To select students for registration as doctoral students and allot supervisor for them;
- To arrange for presentation of Ph.D. research synopses by candidates before the department committee;

- To arrange for viva-voce examinations for award of doctoral degrees;
- To channelise and monitor all departmental research projects; and
- To arrange funds for research through contract, consultancy, etc.

Towards New Educational Management

University-Government Relationship

The Governments should normally perform the role of a partner in the promotion of higher education and not that of exercising control.

The Universities should have complete autonomy in administrative and academic matters. They should also have financial autonomy as per guidelines formulated by the UGC/State Councils of Higher Education and agreed upon by the Universities and the Governments.

The statutes making powers should rest with the universities. However, the statutes would need the assent of the Visitor/Chancellor, if any of their provisions are at variance with the Act Statutes, or if they involve sizeable recurring additional financial commitment not acceptable to the funding agency.

The powers of affiliation/de-affiliation of colleges should rest with the University. The Governments' approval for grant purposes should follow, once affiliation is given by the University and not vice versa. The University should, however, seek the opinion of the Government before granting affiliation.

The provisions of University legislations, which inhibit the Universities, in the exercise of their academic judgement on matters like affiliation, appointment of key functionaries like Registrar, Finance Officer, etc., should be withdrawn.

The Appointment of all executive officers like Registrar, Finance Officer, etc., should vest with the University and not with the Chancellor/State Government.

Powers of University

The following matters should particularly be included in the powers:
- To provide for interdisciplinary courses of study and research and allow for adequate flexibility in the curricular mix as opted by the students and the user agency.
- To organise and undertake extra-mutual studies, training and extension services including adult and continuing educations, NCC, NSS, etc.
- To make provision for research and advisory services and for that purpose to enter into appropriate arrangements with other institutions or bodies or industry, as the university may deem necessary.
- To provide for and maintain common resource centres to be jointly utilised by a group of colleges in the region, in terms of library, laboratories, computer services, etc.
- To designate a college or an institution or a Department or a campus as autonomous and encourage innovations in curricular designing, methods of teaching evaluation.
- To provide for instruction through "Distance Learning" and "Open Approach" and for mobility of students from the formal to non-formal (Open Learning) streams and vice versa.
- To evolve an operational scheme of enforcing the accountability of teachers and non-teachers to the university system. To prescribe minimum work load for teachers in accordance with the UGC norms.
- To establish a grievance redresser machinery to look into the grievance/discontentment among the staff and students and seek to remedy them.
- To generate resources by frugal and productive utilisation of the university resources; and to explore new avenues of revenue-raising research and development activities such as consultancy based research projects and training programmes for outside agencies.
- To provide joint appointments in more than one department in a University as also between University Research Laboratories, University Industry, etc.

- To make special provisions for enabling benefits of University education available to classes and communities that are socially and educationally backward, or economically weaker sections and women population specially from rural and backward segments.
- To provide establishment on the University Campus of Inter-University centres research laboratories, autonomous institutes set up by the UGC/Central Government/State Government/Industry/Any other organisation which may be used by a group of Universities /Colleges, etc.
- To establish autonomous sub-campuses for serving a group of colleges.
- To prescribe code of Ethics for the teachers, code of conduct for other staff and code of discipline for the students.
- To regulate and enforce discipline among the employees and students and to take such disciplinary measures in this regard as may be deemed fit by the University.

University Committees and Other Bodies

The Finance Committee, Planning and Monitoring Board, Board of Research, Board of Examination, Board of Evaluation, Admission and Academic Calendar Committee, Grievance Redressal Committee, Collegiate Council and Staff/Student Welfare Committees, etc., are essential in every university system as statutory bodies/committees. They should, however, be under the overall control of the relevant authorities. More than one committee could be put under one Pro-Vice Chancellor/Dean/Director to avoid proliferation of officers. The committees should also consist of only nominated members selected on the basis of seniority or rotational or any other academic criteria with a tenure that is shorter than that of authorities.

Criteria for Assessing Performance of Universities

Criteria need to be developed for the assessment of University performance. They may essentially include:
- Alumni Performance, faculty members' achievements and student achievement.

- The internal working, indicating the number of actual working days, work-load of teachers, observance of academic calendar, proper and timely conduct of examinations and declaration of examination results and state of discipline, etc.
- Contribution of the University to scholarship, new knowledge, fund-raising, public relations, social work and economic development, etc.
- The performance should finally be rated by unbiased knowledgeable individuals and on the basis of points scored by different universities may be classified into identifiable categories.

Colleges and Their Governance

Every college should formulate its mission and goals in terms of academic, social and other objectives and channel its personnel and other resources accordingly towards optimum realisation of their objectives.

Each college should aim at having management structures as envisaged for the autonomous colleges in the guidelines of the UGC. These could be, wherever necessary, modified by the Universities in consultations with the State Government in the case of Government colleges and SCHE in other cases.

The principal is the key person in the college being its academic and administrative head. His appointment should be based on a rigorous search and selection process. It will be most desirable for a college to categorise and manage its campus activities into:
- academic affairs,
- student affairs, and
- business affairs, and assign each to a competent member of the faculty who could be designated as Dean (or Vice-Principal or Director or Co-ordinator) holding office for a term of three years. The Officer in-charge of each major area of management should be assisted by a small committee consisting of 2 or 3 teachers/hostel wardens, etc., as the case may be. Student should be associated with the committee for student affairs.

Each college should have a planning and monitoring cell to facilitate academic planning and monitoring. Administrative machinery should be available in all colleges for redressal of grievances and resolving internal disputes.

Every affiliating University should establish an office of Dean of colleges with the backup of a Collegiate Council. The council should also be made responsible for the maintenance of standards of teaching in the colleges. The UGC/SCHE should have a standing advisory Committee for continuous monitoring of the functioning of the autonomous colleges with a view to ensure maintenance of standards.

New Colleges should be set up only after a joint survey by the affiliating university, the UGC/SCHE. It would be desirable to have separate colleges for science/Professional subjects by bifurcating large multi-faculty colleges.

Affiliation of colleges should vest only with a University and should be given on academic grounds alone and no extraneous considerations should be allowed to come into play. The UGC guidelines should in this respect be taken into account in determining terms and conditions of affiliation.

A reasonably uniform and sound system of grant-in-aid for affiliated colleges all over the Country should be evolved from time to time by the UGC for the guidance of the State Governments.

Powers of University Academic Council

The Academic council shall be vested with exclusive power of statute making in respect of:
- Designing and prescribing new courses of study and research;
- Prescription of qualification for teaching posts;
- Academic norms of recognition/approval of other institutions;
- All matters pertaining to admission of students (eligibility, recognition and exemption etc); and
- Such other academic matters that are required to be prescribed by the statutes.

All other residual matters such as, conditions of affiliations and monitoring of their fulfillment of such conditions by the affiliated colleges, institutes, centres; conditions of linkages with National Laboratories, industry and such other centres; conditions regarding the approval of Autonomous Colleges and overseeing the working of the autonomy from time to time; issues which are dual in nature, bearing both administrative and academic aspects, shall be decided by the Board of Management, after consideration of the recommendations made by the Academic Council; but the final authority shall be vested with the Board of Management.

*****

Vice-Chancellor

Vice-Chancellor is the academic and administrative head of the university. The appointment of the right person as Vice-Chancellor is therefore crucial. It decides the fate of the University. He stays on the job for three or five years and he is crucial to the working of the institution and the lives of those who work in the institution.

It is essential that the Vice-Chancellor of a University must have a clear and clean moral personality, which will inspire the confidence and respect of teachers, students, the administrative staff and the public.

The second qualification is that he must have a strong independent character. Enormous pressures from all sides — the students, teachers, the administrative staff, the UGC and the Government are exerted on the Vice-Chancellor and he must be capable of standing up to them. He must be strict in adhering to principles, but must be flexible on details. The Vice-Chancellor must instill the conviction that justice and right will prevail, not strength of numbers and pressure. He must be a person gifted with an objective judgement, free from linguistic, communal and regional bias. This objectivity and freedom from irrational prejudice must be a habit with the person. The record of the person must clearly bear out that he is free from parochial prejudices.

Discussion and Consensus

Universities cannot survive unless they are democratic. Their normal procedure is discussion and consensus with the Vice-Chancellor providing the necessary leadership, an unobtrusive leadership. No man is fit to be a Vice-Chancellor unless he is a convinced democrat who appreciates that truth is many-sided and no one has a monopoly of right or wrong either, for that matter. He must not rule through cliques, cabals, coteries and kitchen cabinets. He must inspire the faith in the people around him that everyone will be treated equally and equitably.

Appointment of Vice-Chancellors

Appointment of Vice-Chancellors should be governed by the overall consideration of academic merit, administrative experience and expertise or such other relevant distinction uninfluenced by political pulls and back door pressure.

The next qualification follows as a corollary. Since differences of opinion are natural and inevitable, people should not be penalised for expressing their views freely and frankly, especially if they occupy subordinate positions in the hierarchy. The Vice-Chancellor must resist the temptation to use his powers of patronage and discipline arbitrarily. He must avoid toadies and sycophants.

Deep Commitment

What is required of a Vice-Chancellor is that he should have a deep commitment to the life of the mind, the moral and social purposes of a modern Indian University. He must understand and know how to respond to the social and economic problems of the country and how to bring into being academic programmes that make young men and women fit to tackle those problems. It shows that the Vice-Chancellor must be a man of some intellectual distinction, not necessarily an outstanding academic himself. He must be a man of culture and humanist. Considering the necessary and urgent role of science and technology in the development of the country, he must be, if not a scientist or technologist himself, at least someone who understands that

Swift Decision

The Vice-Chancellor need not be an outstanding administrator himself. But he should know the art of management of people and resources. He must be capable of swift decision and decisive action. He must be a shrewd judge of the strength and limitations of the people working with him and getting the best out of them. He must know how to reward sincere and intelligent work – often no more is required than a kind word or gesture – and discourage malingering and inefficiency, often no more is required than a glance in the direction of the culprit.

Dealing with Students

The most important relationships that a Vice-Chancellor has to maintain are of course with the students, the teachers and with the government. If the Vice-Chancellor possesses the qualities indicated above, these relationships will, for most part, strengthen themselves. But certain qualities need to be emphasised. The Vice-Chancellor should not be afraid of students; nor they should be treated with suspicion and dislike. In dealing with the students, one requires patience, temperate speech, sincerity of tone and purpose, friendliness which does not descent to backslapping and a genuine desire to encourage their good ideas.

Dealing with Teachers

The qualities needed to deal with teachers are not fundamentally different. In the first place, a Vice-Chancellor must never forget that they are his colleagues and they carry the daily burden of fulfilling the aim and objectives of a University. They must be encouraged to live as members of a self-governing community who in spite of differences of outlook, training and temperament share the common ideals of a modern Indian University. The one major complaint of most teachers against a Vice-Chancellor is that he is guilty of favoritism. There may be no justified basis for this feeling. Every teacher should have the conviction that if he is a worthy member of the university Community, his interests are safe in the hands of Vice-Chancellor.

Dealing with Government

With the government, the Vice-Chancellor's relationship is more problematic. It calls for neither confrontation nor subservience. This relationship requires a co-operative outlook, independence of judgement, persuasiveness of speech and argument. The government has enormous resources and enormous powers. To deal with them is not easy, and a Vice-Chancellor needs to have enormous patience, tact and strength of mind.

*****

2
Conceptualising Higher Education

Vision For Education In India

Broad-based Education

India's system of higher education needs radical changes. The problem of quantity is well known - the supply of good colleges is simply not keeping up with rapidly growing demand. But importantly, the absence of even minimum standards in the quality of education being imparted is becoming increasingly apparent.

An undergraduate education cannot be tailored only to getting a job after graduation. There is intrinsic merit in a broad-based liberal education. Our society also needs intellectuals, thinkers and citizens who are aware. The challenge is to find the right balance between a vocationally oriented curriculum and a more broad-based education.

India's educational system is inherited from the British, but with one crucial difference.

In the UK students spend 13 years at school and then three in an undergraduate degree. In the US, they spend 12 years at school and four years as undergraduates. So, in the two major English speaking countries of the world, students complete 16 years of education at the end of an undergraduate degree. That is enough to enter the job market and get a good opportunity to work. In India, students complete 15 not 16 years of education by the time they finish college. That puts them at a disadvantage when applying for further studies abroad. But it may also put them at a disadvantage in the local job market. Employers recruit a limited number of fresh graduates from colleges - usually only students from top-ranked colleges get this privilege.

Institution - Organisations

The Universities and Colleges have to be envisioned with one clear objective: to create an institution not an organisation. What distinguishes an institution from an organisation is that an institution is an edifice built on the foundation of a better thought-out, deeper value system. An institution resonates and impacts deeply on the thought-processes of a society, whereas an organisation is merely an efficient way of being. This core belief will certainly bring the Colleges/University to the top rankings, accreditations and awards from leading media and international academic organisations.

World Class Faculty

The finest resource for the College/University is its world-class faculty, hand-picked carefully from among the finest academicians across the world including India. These finest hand-picked, world-class faculty bring not only their immense academic weight to campus, they also bring in their deep knowledge of the finest pedagogies, education processes and methodologies, experience in research and an easy familiarity with entire ethos of end-to-end industry integration into education.

International Teaching

The University/College needs to have holistic combination of international teaching pedagogies to ensure all-round excellence. The advantage of having a world-class faculty is that the institution can have access to tried and proven pedagogies in use at the world's finest Universities.

Academic Tie-ups

It is necessary for University/College to develop strategic international partnerships with reputed Universities and institutions of higher learning across the globe. These tie-ups add muscle to syllabus enhancement processes add to teaching pedagogies and infrastructure on the ground as well as access to new global education processes. They also provide faculty, students and researches at both institutions with opportunities for International Collaboration and active involvement in multidisciplinary projects at a global level.

Market-Ready Excellence

Placement is the concluding component of an end-to-end education system. The institution needs to work towards enabling students to be completely market-ready through industry led syllabi and continual industry interface. When industry is involved with the gestation and development of talent completely suited to its needs, placement of students is usually a foregone conclusion, even before the end a student body's academic education. Corporate and society have ample productive and remunerative space for students who are problem solvers and thinkers.

High-Caliber Student Peer Group

Universities/Colleges need to have vision to create and perpetuate a thinking ecosystem where outstanding students could enlarge their thinking and imagination in a world-class learning environment to enable them to emerge as intellectually, socially and spiritually evolved global leaders. The students from India and abroad need to be carefully chosen to ensure exceptional student intake in all respects. The institution needs to bring the finest students faculty and learning environment together, to create a thinking ecosystem that emerges as a leading centre of knowledge generation and dissemination. It is essential for the institutions to develop and nurture world-class professionals and leaders, by imbuing them with the Thinking Quotient. The Thinking Quotient is about learning how to learn for life. This is what will attract excellence and generate excellence for society as a whole.

Freedom for Courses and Timing

Colleges should be allowed to conduct their own courses and give degrees. Students need freedom to choose their courses and timings. If a person wants to leave college with a limited number of credits, he or she could do so by taking a certificate. Similarly, one could stay on longer, take some more credits and get a diploma. If one got a maximum number of credits with core skills, he or she should be able to get a degree.

- Primary education should be made compulsory and free, and secondary education compulsory.
- Regulation for continuous teacher training and quality upgradation should be made.
- Government should leave postgraduate higher and professional education to the private sector.
- Government should also keep the economy free from controls to foster new opportunities that will create a market for graduates from the education system.
- Foreign direct investment in education should be allowed, to begin with, limited to science and technology and management areas, subject to major holding by local participants.
- Any form of political activity on campuses of universities and educational institutions should be banned.
- A system for periodical rating of all educational institutions by independent agencies should be instituted.
- A common national system for educational content at the school level, after providing for regional and local variations should be introduced.
- Research should be encouraged right from undergraduate level in all fields.
- A common system for admissions to professional courses based on nationally standardised tests should be instituted. Concurrently, the system of migration certificates should be abolished and students be allowed to move from one institution to another based on a system of transfer of professional credits.

- The vast resources in information and communication technology should be leveraged to bring about smart schools that integrate computers, networks and content.
- Learning through practices and experiences should be emphasised and the teacher's role should transform to one of a facilitator.
- Trained teachers should serve for a specified period in rural areas as part of their development.
- Value education and physical education at pre-primary and primary level and vocational education at the secondary level must be stressed.
- Schools of learning should be encouraged to constantly upgrade content and facilities to make them more market oriented.
- Government should support disciplines that have no market orientation but have social impact; selectively support centres of higher learning, provide financial guarantees for student loans, and ensure uniformity in content and quality.

Society and Education

Anyone can help the education sector. Only the education sector needs to be open to it.

- Production engineers can teach housekeeping and maintenance techniques to teachers and students. All Government institutions/offices without a single exemption are dirty, unsafe and sick. They can be benefited.
- Medical professionals can conduct specialised health camps and offer disease prevention tips for a healthy life.
- Scientists and R&D professionals can provide opportunities for 'live projects' and tap innovative thinking.
- Entrepreneurs can come and share their highs and lows in business to refine the business ambitions of the students.
- Behavioural scientists can help students and teachers to become more effective and efficient by conducting personality and other need based programmes.
- Any professional who has the aptitude and willingness to share can help this process. There is a dearth of talent. What is required is human will.

Rights, Responsibilities and Professional Ethics for University and College Teachers

Higher education should strive for academic excellence and progress of arts and science education; research and extension should be conducted in conformity with the national needs and priorities and ensure that the best talent makes befitting contributions to international endeavour on societal needs.

Rights

Teachers should enjoy full civil and political rights. They have a right to adequate emoluments, social position, just conditions of service, professional independence and adequate social insurance. The divergence between employment prospects and financial gains of teachers in modern technical/science vocations and those in the arts/economics/legal/ linguistics/ social service sectors needs to be corrected.

Responsibilities

Every teacher should see that there is no incompatibility between his precept and practice.
Teachers should:
- seek to make professional growth continuously through study and research,
- express their opinion freely and frankly at professional meetings, seminars, conferences, etc.,
- perform their duties (teaching and tutorial, practical and seminar work) conscientiously and with dedication,
- cooperate with and assist the college and university in carrying out functions such as processing applications for admission, advising and counselling students and conducting university and college examinations including supervision invigilation and evaluation, and
- participate in extension, co-curricular and extra-curricular activities, including community services, to interact with the society and exchange ideas.

Relationship with Students

- Respect the right of the students to express his or her opinion.
- Deal justly and impartially with students regardless of their religion, caste, political, economic, social and physical characteristics.
- Recognise the differences in aptitude and capabilities among students and strive to meet their individual needs
- Inculcate among students a scientific outlook and respect for physical labour and the ideals of democracy, patriotism and peace.
- Be affectionate towards the students and do not behave in a vindictive manner for any reason
- Make themselves available to students even outside class hours and help and guide them without any thought of remuneration or reward
- Refrain from inciting students against other students, colleagues or the administration.

Ties with Colleagues

- Treat other members of the profession in the same manner as they themselves wish to be treated.
- Speak respectfully of other teachers and render assistance for professional betterment.
- Refrain from lodging unsubstantiated allegations against colleagues to higher authorities.
- Refrain from allowing considerations of caste, creed, religion, race or sex in their professional endeavours.

Teachers should also:
- refrain from undertaking any other employment and commitment including private tuitions and coaching classes, and other business activities which are likely to interfere with their professional responsibilities,
- adhere to the conditions of the contract and
- refrain from taking leave except on unavoidable grounds and as far as practicable with prior intimation, keeping in view their responsibilities for compliance and completion of the academic schedule.

Backbone of Economy

The intelligentsia and echelons of higher education have a unique role to play in furnishing a variety of increasingly sophisticated and ever-changing manpower that agriculture, industry, administration and services need. A self-reliant and endogenous trait of an economy can be ensured only when competent people are available to forecast, plan and operationalise research and development in the world. Our R&D institutions and universities are therefore the backbone of our economy and a reliable catalyst for the fulfillment of our national aspirations and goals.

Adequate Fund

Taking a clue from the experience of developed countries, higher education in India should be adequately funded so as to make it world competitive and of highest quality and at the same time relevant to the individual society. In this context, it is desirable that springing up of new universities and colleges is brought under judicious control.

Special Consideration on Backward Areas

The new universities and colleges should be set up only when the need for them is established through feasibility studies. Socially and economically backward areas should be given special consideration.

Selective Higher Education

The universities are being flooded with students without any objectives or aim as neither the students nor the administrators have a clear idea of who is in need of higher education. The university education should be selective in the sense that it is for only those having aptitude and talent.

Common Syllabus

Common syllabus for all universities could be framed up to a point where certain parameters are met but extending it to the postgraduate level is not advisable as it would curtail independent ideas among students and faculty.

Decentralisation of Administration

Educational management within the Government is to be viewed afresh in a new decentralised perspective. All major resource institutions and standard setting agencies at the Central, State or District level may redefine their respective roles so as to strengthen institutional capabilities at the local levels all along the line, rather than building themselves up into remote control agencies. Academics are to be involved intimately with educational administration at all levels.

- Education is to be built up as a people's movement wherein the Government, Central and State may play a supportive and facilitative role.
- The UGC should establish regional offices and delegate substantially funding and monitoring powers to these centres and also delegate some of its responsibilities to the State Council for High Education.
- Donations given to higher educational institutions must be made eligible for 100% tax exemption.
- The existing Acts framed for the State Universities have become outdated in many respects and need to be amended suitably to reflect more recent developments and changed situations.
- Another crucial reform that is needed is that those who are involved with decision-making in Central and State Education Ministries should primarily be persons with some expertise and commitment to the cause of education and not non-professional bureaucrats.
- The Government of India may think in terms of reviving the All-India Specialised Service cadre in the case of Education – the Indian Education Service.

*****

Mobilisation of Resources

Mobilisation of resources includes increasing the tuition fees and reducing government subsidy, introducing a differential fee structure depending on the courses and levels, students' family income, and also the likely benefits from a given kind of education. Other suggestions included students' loan scholarships to cover at least 10% of the enrolment, educational chess, getting community contributions, making the users pay for the cost of education of the trained manpower employed by them, and getting tax exemption for donations to universities and colleges from the tax authorities.

All questions of generation of resources must cater to the unmet needs of universities.

Economy Measures in Resourcing

The possible economy measures in this context are:
- Introducing a culture of sharing of facilities such as library, laboratories and equipments between departments within each institution and also among the neighbouring ones.
- Making functions like Convocation and others simple in order to cut down expenses.
- Introducing the shift system in the colleges with adequate infrastructure in order to make optimal use of available facilities.
- Integrating the distance mode of learning with the regular classes.

Cost-effective Education (Faculty)

As regards the cost of education, a serious study should be organised to determine staffing pattern, work norms, working days and accountability for engagement of classes to ensure that cost per student for turning out a graduate or a postgraduate or an engineer or a doctor is within limits and not exorbitant due to definite norms for opening or locating a discipline or a faculty to avoid under utilisation. There are also instances where there is faculty but no students and as such there is gross wastage of resources.

Conceptualising Higher Education

There is great disparity between the work norms of university and college teachers. This must be revised upwards to make it more rational. These are dubious ways of inflation periods and work load and these should also be curbed drastically. Nobody can deny the urgent need to ensure engagement of classes and accountability of teachers towards students.

Cost-effectiveness in Non-Teaching Staff

Administrative and non-teaching cost of university and college systems has also been growing very fast. There is a need to off-load certain routine and repetitive tasks like cleaning, gardening, security, etc., on contract basis to avoid cost of permanent staff and this saves on permanent and increasing liabilities. In many places, costs of examination, rechecking of mark sheets, etc., which can and should be recovered in full are also not recovered and there is a deficit on that account too. Fees for specified job or a service must be on cost or cost plus basis and there is no justification for deficit on this account.

Cost-effective Utilisation

Effective management of resources available with the university or a college is essential. There are instances of duplication or triplication of instruments or books or libraries without proper utilisation thus adding to the cost. The resources available should be pooled and multiple user systems should be introduced. Computers, laboratories, libraries and buildings are all capital intensive and they should be used efficiently and fully. The equipments so far not in use should be either put to use or transferred to where they can be used. There should be a system of Annual Maintenance contract for the equipments to avoid damage or wastage of costly equipments.

Cost-effective Technology

Introduction of advanced Education Technology can save on cost and at the same time improve the quality of education. With the advent of VCR and Audio Tapes, Telecast and conferencing facilities speeches and class lectures of eminent professors can be recorded and multiplied and supplied to the universities and colleges. A library of such tapes can be built in every college, department or university and with Projector, VCR or Audio-player facilities students should be encouraged to view or hear the talks of such eminent personalities. The cost of such tape libraries will not be very high and looking to the quality and efficiency it is justifiable. Specialised lectures such as UGC telecasts on different subjects by expert and versatile teachers/ professors should be made use of fully, to overcome mediocrity.

Foreign Students Funds

Financing of higher education should not be restricted to fees and grants alone but community sources, industries and other philanthropic grants should also be tapped. Attracting foreign students for specialised courses at suitably high fees should allow the university to mobilise resources and even foreign exchange to import costly equipment, if needed. The university must sell its programmes and thus earn from them. It should not wholly or substantially depend on grants and that is essential if it wants to maintain its autonomy and status. Students passing out of higher educational institutions like IITs, Medical and Research centres, who wish to skip a prescribed minimum period of pre-service in India and seek lucrative jobs abroad, should be under contractual obligation at the time of initial admission, to reimburse when they start earning abroad, the huge amounts that Government spends for their education.

*****

Future View of Higher Education in India

Global University Marketplace

Throughout the history, most training and educational institutions have served only their local geographic regions, and their financial support has usually come from local or national public funds. Now all that is changing, as evidenced by two signs: The first is the development of global training and education markets. A student routinely travels thousands of miles for an MBA course. Also, satellite links are commonly used to join student and tutor across half the world. The second sign is the decreasing role of public funds, as governments push public organisations to seek other sources of funding. Training and education are becoming market oriented and are on the way to becoming market driven. Companies such as Motorola, Xerox, IBM, Procter & Gamble, G.E., and others are educating their executives and workers informally.

Compete with Quality

Once competition enters the higher education market, each provider must find ways to distinguish the service it offers from that of its competitors. A competitive advantage must be identified. Some will seek that edge through providing special courses or facilities, others by providing flexible programs, and yet others by reducing price while adding value. Most, however, will have no option but to compete on the basis of quality.

Selecting a College

What is the difference between college A and college B, between college A and neighbourhood college C, or between college A and the local tutorial college D? Are not they essentially doing the same job? So why should a prospective student or his parent choose college A over the other two? After all on graduation, he is going to get his degree from the same university! So what is the advantage in going to college A?

To attract the best and the brightest high schoolers, a traditional college must have excellent facilities for academic and non-academic growth competent faculty, resources for career development, and must offer unlimited opportunities for experimenting new and creative ideas, and so on. The choice of a college/university by a prospective student or his parent(s) must be driven not by convenience of a short distance to the college from home, but by the quality of the programmes it offers, the prestige of its faculty, the quality of its facilities, and the availability of diverse resources.

Credit Based Semester System - Advantages

A credit-based semester system is ideal since it offers maximum flexibility in terms of course offerings, course selection faculty and student schedules, and optimum use of existing facilities. For example, multi-section courses can be offered at different times of the day spread over a week, so students can select those sections convenient to them and taught by competent professors. Further courses can be offered throughout the day, say from 8 am to 5 pm to meet the needs of a variety of majors, adding the much needed flexibility.

By-products of Credit-Based System

One of the greatest by-products of such a system is that not all students, faculty and support staff need be on the road along with other travellers at the same time, a process that invariably overloads our limited transportation system. Besides, faculty schedules can be adjusted to yield large blocks of badly needed time to devote for research and advanced studying.

A scheduling reform that will free up space and virtually eliminate overcrowding in college cafeterias and dining halls in hostels is another advantage of the system. It has added bonus that the support staff will not be burdened excessively during the traditional lunch hour.

Orientation Programme in Colleges

Colleges and universities must organise orientation programmes to make the transition from school to college a smooth and pleasant experience and not a shocking and painful one. We cannot take it for granted that everything will be fine. To graduate top quality students, our academic institutions must become user-friendly and responsive to student needs. Whatever system we adopt for colleges and universities it must be a natural extension of the one in schools: only then will it be meaningful and successful.

Value of Flexible System

The new system must be flexible enough for students to switch to different majors or minors depending on interests or market fluctuations. There should be provisions for students to develop valid, individualised minors that must be approved by the major department in advance. Students should be free to select a variety of courses known as free electives outside their major and minor to gain knowledge in related disciplines, to acquire additional skills and even to have a taste of an unrelated field.

If a student is not ready to declare a major at the time of admission or would like to try another major within one year, he should have that option. He then must realise that he might not graduate with his classmates. Nonetheless, majoring in a subject he likes is better than majoring in something he is no longer interested in.

Customer Delight

While all providers undoubtedly like to think of themselves as supplying a quality service, any provider who complacently assumes that quality will somehow materialise and will rapidly be overtaken by those who listen to the market. Only those providers who consciously strive to meet the demands of their markets will survive. What does striving mean? What it does not mean is expecting to be rewarded for hard work. The market rewards results, not effort. Tom Peters would call this customer delight.

Mission

ISO 9000 starts with a clear sense of what the university is to achieve in its mission. Deming calls this Constancy of Purpose. It is a timeless, qualitative statement, such as:
- To be the best provider of qualification courses in our area.
- To maintain the highest possible level of repeat business in our area.
- To have a reputation for excellence among parents in our area.

Basic Problems of Higher Education

The problems of higher education are many, and important among them are the inadequate budget allocation and control of finance in higher education, lack of academic freedom, want of co-ordination between educational institutions, the government and industrial organisations, lethargy in co-ordinating the curriculum to the needs of the society at large, lack of discipline and accountability among teachers. The roles of National Assessment and Accreditation, the UGC and the State Council of Higher Education have not been effective to the extent needed.

Nation Building

We have to redesign our higher education system to facilitate not only quantitative expansion but also qualitative improvement which would result in the production of skilled manpower and professional who could play a pivotal role in the nation-building process. The higher institutions have to be managed by people who have clarity, courage, conviction, competence and compassion.

Policy Makers

Higher education system can be made more productive and responsive to the needs of the national development if it is managed on the basis of sound principles and strategies. The policy makers should be endowed with the requisite professional knowledge, managerial skills and appropriate vision. The policy makers should also be endowed with scientific problem-solving capabilities. This would pave the way for the development of higher education institutions as a knowledge industry.

Achieving National Goals

The management techniques should include the scientific and systematic strategies which aim at undertaking the task of solving higher educational management problems and achieving certain targets in accordance with the changing environment. Higher education is expected to help to achieve the broad national goals of excellence, justice, equity, efficiency and competitiveness.

Role of University Grants Commission

The UGC must remain formally committed to using its leadership and network of resources to support the colleges and universities through a new framework with concerted outreach initiatives to achieve quality-oriented higher education in India. Its concern should be institutionalised and schemes should be implemented effectively through proper management. The UGC has to enforce academic and financial discipline and foster competition to stimulate quality in the management of colleges and universities regardless of ownership. Its performance indicator such as proper admissions, faculty and relevance of course, teaching base, appropriate examination procedures, results, placement, etc., should be taken into account for primitive grants resources and other supplementary. A sound regulatory mechanism is needed to supervise all these aspects of higher education in India. New subjects have to be offered in place of those which are deemed irrelevant and de-emphasised.

Assessment and Accreditation

The National Assessment and Accreditation Council (NAAC) should develop scientific parameters, namely infrastructure development, human resources development, maintenance of higher academic standard, quality of academic discipline, reformation of examination system, contribution of the institution for socio-economic uplift and participation in national and international research and development activities and so on which could be the basis for evaluating the academic excellence and contributions of educational institutions and issuing gradation certificate. There is a need to formulate a transparent assessment and accreditation system covering the entire gamut of higher education programmes in India which pave the way for qualitative higher education and optional utilisation of resources to increase production and productivity.

Pre-plantation accreditation and post-accreditation after utility of the programme is required in order to improve professional excellence. The UGC should make it mandatory for all colleges and universities to submit a status report and obtain accreditation certificate from NAAC. Besides this, the universities and colleges which fail to live up to the expectations of NAAC and UGC in terms of maintaining better academic standard should not be given any kind of financial, technical and administrative support. The NAAC should pay particular attention to the preparation, training and upgrading the staff both academically and administratively.

Curriculum Development

The courses should be devised in such a way as to incorporate the specific needs of the national economy as well as global economy. The interaction between university and industry is highly essential in order to make higher education need-based. The course curriculum should also incorporate international finance, international marketing, export management, technology transfer, inter-cultural communication and integration. The planning and designing of curriculum should be done at the university level of integrating regional development needs and national interest.

Teacher Training, Development and Participation

Regular in-service training of teachers would deepen their specialised knowledge, improve their professional competence and motivate them to contribute positively for the development of student community who are future builders of the nation. The staff development programmes should be designed in consultation with administrators, researchers and students.

Evaluation of Teaching

We have to develop appropriate standards of assessing the educators in terms of prosperity, utility, feasibility and competence. The teaching behaviours have to be evaluated through a proper monitoring system. The evaluation of university teaching should become a core sector of higher education since the area of teacher evaluation is relatively uncultivated. The students rating should be free from bias.

Multi-disciplinary

There must be a shift from micro-specialisation to interdisciplinary and multidisciplinary fields at the university level. The professionals need to involve themselves in teaching, research, development, extension, consultancy and publication activities. Imbalances are observed with respect to contribution of teachers in these areas. The major issue before teacher education system is to prepare teachers who would be serving the country as catalysts of development. Participatory learning environment has to be created on a regular basis to the teachers.

Active Role of Faculty

Teachers should be actively involved in deciding crucial matters such as admission, course curriculum, teacher training, institution-building and examination and so on. The faculty development programmes shall have to be in response to the changing demands of curriculum as well as of the society. The teaching faculty requires the regular benefit of training in order to enrich professional excellence and accountability. The university teachers should be aware of acts, statutes, ordinances, rules, regulations and all other aspects of higher education management. This would enable them to understand the academic environment fully and play an active role in reforming the higher education.

Teachers and Teacher Education in 21st Century

The teacher's educational institutions are expected to equip potential teachers with the latest methods, techniques and strategies for imparting instruction including the use of media devices and educational hardware. The curriculum should make all possible efforts to increase further teacher's awareness of global interdependence and transitions. Professionalism in the 21st century expects teachers to be keen researchers, intense practitioners and active catalysts of development of students' personality with emphasis on tolerance, self-reliance and understanding. Teachers must be fully equipped with intellectual and practical abilities to understand their role and responsibilities in the 21st century, which shall be knowledge-oriented, technology-oriented, and interaction-oriented to suit competitive society.

Performance Appraisal

The performance appraisal is an essential and inescapable managerial activity. Appraisal is necessary for all important decisions relating to teachers such as placement, training, promotion, remuneration and rewards. Scientific assessment encourages accountability among the teachers. In the absence of effective appraisal system, the assessed remains ignorant of their professional status and hence cannot make efforts to improve professional competence as well as accountability.

Inter-cultural Relationship and Harmony

The 21st century shall be characterised by the emergence of a global village based on multi-culturalism. The citizens of tomorrow should be trained to be more tolerant and understanding towards various cultures free from any ethnic and cultural prejudice. Therefore, the system of higher education shall have to be re-oriented to check the invasion of cultural imperialism and enable future citizens to maintain intercultural relations and harmony. The teachers should be motivated to think above narrow nationalism and to accept universalism as a way of life. The teachers will have to develop the competencies to enable the learners equip themselves with better skills, techniques and strategies and learn to live in harmony. The teachers should also be able to develop and impart cross-cultural understanding and develop a global perspective towards promoting a better understanding of human relationship and their environment.

Academic Staff Colleges

The Academic Staff Colleges in India are established to enrich the human resources in the higher education field. These institutions aim at improving the professional competence of teachers. These institutions require staff, hostel facility and financial resources. New types of teacher development programmes are required to update their knowledge on the subject, to introduce them to new techniques and technologies and to enrich their personality. There must be learner-centered, experience-centered, economic-centered, profession-centered and community-centered training programmes. The teachers must learn how to harness the new resources, technologies and experience in their field of teaching and help the society to make full use of their talent and experience. The UGC should empower these colleges in all respects and provide moral and material support.

Management Information Systems

A computerised management information system could also provide authentic database for systematic development of higher education system. The conflict between availability and market demand should be properly understood and that manpower resource development should be in-tune with the country's socio-economic development process and needs. India's enormous manpower resources can become an asset in this century when it is properly trained and education oriented.

Research Support

Research and development at the university level should be in-tune with long-term goals of national development. Action taken on research programmes at the grass roots level would really facilitate distributive educational justice and decentralised economic development. University research should form a significant component of budgetary allocation of government. The governments at the State and Centre should also develop the practice of utilising higher educational institutions for socio-economic uplift of the nation.

Targets

We should set the targets for our students in such a way that they not only get good marks in public examinations but also acquire the knowledge and capability to become responsible members of society. The targets for teachers should be set in such a manner that they not only train the students sincerely but also build the educational institutions through academic excellence, professional competence and personal integrity. The target for researchers should be set in such a way that they not only acquire qualifications but also contribute towards the upliftment of the society through need-based, socially relevant and development-oriented research programmes. We should set the targets for our administrators in such a way that they not only manage the institutions on sound principles and practices but also become catalysts of national development.

Foreign vs Indian Universities

Indian universities are mostly engaged more in teaching as if they are schools. They are largely teaching and examining bodies without research base and hence they are not effective to cope with the challenges. Universities abroad have opened continuing education departments, patent and technology licensing departments whereas many Indian Universities do not have these departments, and technology pack and incubators are conspicuously absent. Indian Universities almost had no connection with industry and industries have almost no confidence in universities. The industrial progress in India is not propelled by our universities; but by foreign collaborators. Consequently what is taught in universities is not wanted and what is wanted is not taught.

Globalising Indian Universities

Globalisation of Indian universities is a pressing need of the time. Redefining their scope, missions and visions in the light of the worldwide changes, ought to be carried out forthwith. Restructuring the organisations, methods, systems and procedures, revising the university acts, granting of autonomous colleges should become the priority items on their agenda. Research in universities is the most cost-efficient and cost-effective model for employment and income generation. Research should therefore become the most focused university activity. Outdated universities are costlier than the cost of their modernisation. They should be revamped forthwith. The speed and direction of change in universities in the coming years matters most to the well-being of the people. It is hoped that with the given will and spirit of leaders in academia, industry and politics, we will be able to achieve the desired goal in India.

Need for Globalising Indian Universities

Indian universities by world standards are far behind their counterparts in developed countries, whereas, universities in developed countries like the USA, Germany and the UK are primarily research universities and research output oriented, specially need based is their main contribution and education is their byproduct. It is because of this philosophy that the education in universities of the US is observed to be innovative and creative in nature. Without research, education remains stale and outdated. Universities in developed countries have become life magnets which attract not only scholars but also industry, entrepreneurs and venture capital funding companies from across the globe.

They are globalising their operations to meet the world needs both of education and of technology. By virtue of strong research bases they are a source of latest knowledge in education and a source of new ideas, enabling companies to win spin-off of companies from universities, which is a common phenomenon, so also spin off of technologies.

"Learning is wealth of wealth
It is the crown of all wealth" (Kural 411)

*****

Higher Education Stakeholders

Stakeholders: Definition and Classification

A stakeholder is a person or a group that has an interest in the activities of an institution or organisation. In the context of higher education, stakeholders are those groups that have inter-alia an interest in the quality and provision of standard outcomes. The stakeholders in higher education can be broadly classified as students, parents, faculty, administrators of universities and institutions, private investors, political executives, government (Central and State), civic society and NGOs.

Priorities of Stakeholders

Students

Students are concerned about the value of instruction provided by the colleges and universities. They are interested in attaining the skills appropriate to international requirements, look for immediate employment and would support initiative.

Parents

Parents are concerned about better employment opportunities for children to overcome global challenges and would welcome the proposal. The constraint may be for those who are not in a position to meet the cost of study and this may provide an opportunity to the government to subsidise the cost to a certain extent.

Faculty

Faculty members must strive to prepare globally knowledgeable and intellectually competent graduates. This would lead to the establishment of infrastructure of international standards thereby providing opportunity for promoting research and development.

The major resistance may, however, come from teachers unions since there will be continuous monitoring of teachers' performance. Hence, there is a need to involve them in discussions from the beginning.

Administrators of colleges and universities

They should be made to understand the critical aspects of identifying, defining, managing and delivering superior values to all stakeholders of the institution. Resistance may come from universities for fear of losing autonomy. However, it provides opportunity to upgrade the infrastructure for which provisions can be made besides adequate time frame.

Private investors

Provide a conducive climate for investments and promote better business model. The major problem may arise in rural areas in procuring quality manpower. High fees structure may affect intake capacity and this may lead to viability issues. Another relevant modification required in law is to allow the educational institutions to function as for-profit organisations. The industry can benefit a lot by targeted training to the students which can be permitted under the flexible education norms.

Government

Achieves enrolment and retention targets, enable to overcome budgetary constraints through promotion of private-public partnerships and meet the equity and gender concerns through widened base in access. Can regulate grants to private Higher education institutes. Higher budgetary allocation can be considered for those universities and colleges located in rural areas.

Civil society and NGOs

Increased retention rates and quality manpower leads to sustainable development of the society. Promotes peace and development.

*****

Opportunities in Higher Education

- Quality education in basic science and other disciplines.
- Infusion of Technology and innovative approaches.
- Reducing isolation in education and learners.
- Learner-centered models and tools.
- Encouraging study in regional languages to meet the needs of local people without compromising quality.
- Meeting the needs of education in crisis-situations and disasters.
- To keep channels of non-formal and lifelong learning and training for disabled persons/physically challenged.
- Interactive usage of Radio, TV and other broadcasting tools.
- Promotion of online learning.
- Access to latest books and journals through digital linkages.
- High training models for education administrators.
- Enabling learning to take place parallel to work and social obligations.
- Promote infrastructure improvements and all-round development of faculty leading to enhancement of confidence and capability of educational institutions.

Strategies for Empowerment

- Systematic approach by higher educational institutions to identify employment skills, knowledge and competencies.
- Preparation of curriculum to suit the market needs to prepare society for entrepreneurship and employment skills.
- Linkage of vocational education with employment market.
- Designing curriculum at the certificate or Diploma level using DACUM approach.
- Curriculum to focus towards gainful employment and not for the sake of knowledge alone.
- Identify a variety of matching skill-based courses at regional level through assessment study in industrial, commercial and service sectors.
- Integration of communication skills and computer knowledge in the courses.

- The courses prepared should be interdisciplinary and aim at work and active life besides facilitating conversion from one profession to another.
- The content designed must integrate theoretical, practical, field, technological knowledge in the curriculum.
- Hands-on experience should be part of the course work. Industrial exposure and linkage with industry are essential.
- Promoting life-long education and this means that business, industrial and agricultural firms should have extensive educational functions in their agenda.
- Courses aim at self-employability rather than seeking employment.
- Aims at reducing mismatch between the demand and supply to market needs.
- Courses having socio-economic relevance and interdisciplinary nature as against the academic interest need to be introduced.
- Internship should be integrated in the technical/vocational courses designed. Guidance and career counselling need to be provided for selecting appropriate technical and vocational courses.
- The courses, besides, having internship should have a linkage or roots in the community providing holistic experience.
- Need to develop matching skills with the employment opportunities available in the local community to avoid migration to the cities.
- Promote only job-oriented, work-related, skill-based, competency-based and life-coping education.
- Courses should aim at small business development for the sake of alleviation of poverty, economic regeneration and human resources development.
- The outreach programmes and their delivery to be entrusted not only with higher educational institutions but also with community based organisations.

- Universities and Government must recognise the identified courses as an alternative education system to solve the acute problem of unemployment.
- Close linkage with local industries and vocational institution is essential for not only designing curriculum but also for practical exposure.

Outreach Programme Results

Enhances a variety of skills and community participation at large.
- Helping to build right attitude towards work and life.
- Making an individual competent in a chosen area to become employable/self-employable.
- Gearing up rural economy including the agriculture and allied fields towards industrialisation.
- Increasing the productivity and GDP of the nation.

Expansion of Higher Education Since Independence

Year	Universities	Colleges	Students
1947	20	500	100000
2000	236	11000	8 million
2005	320	16000	8.8 million
2007	400	18000	11.03 million
2014	693	35500	29 million

The higher education system has witnessed a 13-fold increase in the number of universities, a 25-fold increase in the number of colleges and a 30-fold increase in the enrolment of students since Independence. With about 400 universities, more than 18, 000 colleges and 11 million students as against 32 universities, 695 colleges and 0.174 million students during 1950-51, India has developed one of the largest higher education system in the world.

Broadening the Aims of Higher Education

The institutions of higher education generally admit the students for pursuing academic career and confine their programmes to the traditional function of propagation of knowledge and skills. But the need of the present day is to broaden the functions of the institutions for professional and vocational courses for improving employable skills in the area of their choice and allow entry to those students who do not wish to pursue their academic career. The aims of higher education should be:
- Generating new knowledge (Research).
- Propagation of knowledge (Classroom teaching learning).
- Output of knowledge (Evaluation in terms of productivity).
- Application of knowledge to life (service to society).

Rethinking the Role of Universities

Universities are the international institution, which are the life blood of higher education. Colleges are the veins that carry life blood to the whole body of the nation. There is a need to redefine the role of universities in providing quality education and also be vigilant enough to check the quality of teaching, research and technology in their affiliated colleges. There should be regular interaction between the faculty of universities and colleges. It must also be ensured that the colleges also raise the international standards meeting the demands of modern society and economy embedded with national culture and circumstances. All these institutions must play their specific role keeping in view the local, regional, national, international, discipline specific and inter- as well as intra-disciplinarian perspectives.

Universalisation of Higher Education

India has one of the largest systems of higher education in the world. Despite the rapid and massive growth in higher education, India has only about 17% of its relevant age-group enrolled for higher education as against 50-85% in developed countries. In the present day of globalisation, illiterate individuals are misfits in the main stream. Survival in the 21st century will depend upon spread and quality of higher education. Therefore, the first and foremost task should be to expand higher education and cover as many individuals from the eligible group as possible. The accessibility must shift from elite to masses without diluting academic standards. India has to attain a gross enrolment rate of at least 1.5% by 2015. The focus would have to be on new universities but some clusters of affiliated colleges could also become universities. But care should be taken to enroll students on the basis of merit and those who intend to undertake intensive and extensive research.

Infrastructure Facilities

If we are to achieve the goal of universalisation of higher education, the existing network of colleges and universities will not be able to cope with the influx. To increase the gross enrolment ratio to at least 25% means more than doubling the scale of higher education within the next few years. The solution of the problem lies in that we must create virtual infrastructure, i.e. online education with open and flexible system. Many foreign universities are providing online education but our system of higher education still remains around student-teacher contact. No doubt student-teacher contact is important, but if we do not have enough infrastructure and required faculty, we must also adopt the organisational structure of online education. The electronic network should be used for sharing academic resources and modernisation and technological up gradation should be a regular feature.

Explosion of Knowledge

Knowledge is expanding at a very fast rate. It is doubling itself in less than five years. New fields and sub-fields of study requiring new professional skills are being generated every day. This explosion has made systems of yesterday redundant. The fast changes in the domain of knowledge have outdated the concept of outdatedness. It has been replaced by the term 'upto moment'. And what is not 'upto the moment' is ignorance. Therefore universities and colleges, the seats of higher education must have the criteria of being 'upto moment'-ness and create a new learning environment. Knowledge must be discovered, conserved, transmitted and applied in everyday life. Every student in higher education must have the access to the same world of knowledge as students in any other country in the world.

Revolutions in Communication and Information Technology

The tools and technologies of information and communication are a must in the modern society and these have provided unanticipated opportunities that have enabled multifaceted growth and development. These advances have brought a paradigm shift in the higher education system. Therefore, everyone must be well-versed in these advances as these skills are needed in every field. Multinational companies pay higher for these skills. Moreover, it takes much longer to transmit the latest knowledge and research findings to reach the books as compared to the Internet. It can happen only when each and every student has access to the computer and Internet and the teachers should also be well trained to help them; otherwise we will miss to fulfill the promises of information age. Efforts need to be made for the establishment and extensive use of these technologies in every institution so that the students become well-versed in these areas.

Quality Maintenance

India's progress in quantity is quite impressive. Every year India is producing 2.5 million graduates and this figure is just after US and China. But quality is an aspect which often gets overlooked amidst quantitative aspects and in terms of quality India is far behind the developed countries. No doubt, quantitative growth is vital from the angle of widening of access. But quantity must not dilute the academic standards, otherwise there is no use of quantity. Quality may be in terms of inputs such as students, teachers, infrastructure and the process of education and output in terms of students and their competency acquired. Quantum of knowledge transmitted to students must have its effectiveness and applicability. Quality is the main issue today and it must not be diluted. Everyone is in the pursuit of excellence. The teacher in higher education must aim at bringing out the best out of the students. Evaluation by students as well as by peers should be encouraged. The stakeholders of higher education must be accountable to the consumers of higher education. In today's age of information, only knowledge based work would bring us on par with the rest of the world. Various accreditation bodies should assess the institutions fairly and inform them where they stand in the global perspective.

Networking of Institutions and Teachers

There is a need for networking of institutions and teachers for collaborative teaching. It will enable the sharing of the best human and material resources and cutting the costs, ensure homogeneity in standards of instruction and ensure quality. Digital presentations of excellent teachers must be used by the institutions all over the country. If the teachers continue to work in isolation and curriculum concerns are tackled by each institution individually, without drawing on the benefits of each others' experience, it may become a race in which the goal post is receding at a pace faster than the speed of approach and reaching the target will remain elusive.

Disparity Among the Learners

There exist vast disparities among the learners coming from different institutions located in villages, towns and cities and from different strata. The students coming from resource-starved institutions can never be at par with the learners coming from privileged and elite institutions. The efforts are needed to bridge the gap by providing best expertise and learning facilities to everyone irrespective of their background. Communication technologies, Internet network and multimedia centres can make it possible to bridge the gap.

Employment Opportunities

In today's competitive world, many of our higher education courses are not job-oriented. This is bewildering for the students when they find themselves that there is not any job for them. Higher education sector has failed to map out the future demand patterns for various skills and it has not kept pace with industry's growth. There is lack of opportunities in the public sector and private sectors in the field to provide jobs. The private sector employs only those who possess skills and competencies which can keep pace and constant updating with the global competitors. Educational institutions should have their products laced with multifarious skills, oral as well as written and practical with excellent research skills. Employers want their employees to be comfortable with multiple cultures and diverse languages, with strong oral communication skills. Therefore, higher education must be tailor-made according to the needs of the private sector and other job-opportunities.

Coping with the Problems of Globalisation

Everything is under the influence of Globalisation, higher education is no exception. There is an increasingly free flow of ideas, increased mobility of students, teachers and professionals, goods services and capital which is leading to the integration of economies and societies. We cannot isolate our students from the rest of the systems of education of the world. Globalisation is also posing various threats to our educational system which is a challenge to us.

Setting up of Foreign Institutions

In the higher education a large number of foreign institutions are in the fray and the degrees awarded by foreign universities are favoured. Multinational companies prefer their certification as compared to degrees awarded by our universities. They are attracting better and more affluent students who can pay higher tuition fee, thus eating our enrolment through digital and e-learning. Affluent class students can afford to join these institutions, while poor students opt for public institutions which cannot provide good environment due to financial crunch. These are giving a tough time to the public education system as these are being deprived of the revenue to support the public system of education and subsidised segments are relegated to the periphery. This is a big challenge to our education system because it is leading to re-establishment of elitism in education.

Role of Universities in Educating Society

Since ages, universities have been inseparable elements from the growth of any society and an indispensable mechanism to give strength and support to any society.
Universities are essential to:
- Build a shared vision;
- strengthen and focus on research and development;
- build networks to foster the generation and spread new ideas;
- build banks of case studies and models and examples of practices;
- link education reforms to broader community oriented strategies; and
- foster a range of industry partnerships

Universities today need to act as providers and play the role of nation builders. This calls for public universities acting as private businesses to generate profit in terms of education. As pointed out earlier education is directly linked with the economic output for any state, country or society.

Outreach Higher Education Programmes

Our society is divided into various sections based on culture, economic status, time, costs and geographical distances. It is education that serves to bridge the gaps. Hence, the concept of borderless education takes its prominence. Universities have to foster the concept of partnerships with the private institutions spread geographically to reach the people. This stands true especially in the case of developing countries.

The Outreach programmes open new avenues to cross sectoral links, i.e. it cuts across culture, economic classes, distances and time but aptly articulating the need of the corporate social responsibility and ethical code of conduct. These programmes create new modes of provision for the development in subject areas, mode of delivering and distribution, different learning and teaching patterns.

> *"Education is a liberating force and in our age, it is also a democratising force, cutting across the barriers of caste and class smoothening out inequalities imposed by birth and other circumstances."*
>
> **- Indira Gandhi**

Higher Education Measures to be Initiated

- To offer new courses and course combinations for meeting varying learning needs of students.
- To recruit high caliber teachers and provide better infrastructure with best appraisals.
- Courses in competition with professional education are to be introduced.
- Research work needs to be carried out for knowing the required pattern of education.
- The regulations of education needs to be vested with only one association.
- Unhealthy competition among the institutions is to be avoided.
- Students centered faculties are to be appointed in proportion to the number of students.
- The burden of large number of subjects is to be avoided and a chance is to be provided to the students to learn the subjects of their own interest instead of offering a list of elective subjects.
- There must be involvement of students, teachers, industrialists and other interested parties while designing the education policies by the state or centre.

Measures to Increase the Enrolment in Higher Education

- Increasing the number of universities depending upon the need.
- Enhancing the quality of higher education to be commensurate with needs of the competitive world.
- Providing the modern and updated infrastructure.
- Regular appointments for vacant positions on merit basis.
- The system of affiliation of college needs to be reconsidered.
- Free higher education for the meritorious students of economically weaker sections.
- There is a clear need to establish an independent Regulatory Authority for higher education.
- Financing sources are to be identified and developed.

Classifying the Students in Class

Some students are knowledge seekers and some are seeking knowledge for the purpose of career. There is a need to separate the students and to afford more knowledge to the knowledge seekers and required carrier-oriented knowledge to the latter. The object of this classification is to help the students and the teacher to know the expectations of the teaching and learning, which in turn will be helpful to measure the task of performance. If we still follow the old system of general interest method of teaching the needs of the students will remain unsatisfied and they will not be able to cope up with the practical work place needs, where they have to progress after the education.

Relevance of Quality Management in Higher Education

The competitiveness of Indian Industry is going to be the key factor of India's wealth. Industry is the only sector besides agriculture in society, generating something. That can be transformed from goals and services, into the wealth that the society needs. There is a strong link between quality education and training systems and a country's level of industrial productivity and competitiveness. Industrial competitiveness depends on a firm's products, technologies, markets and the simultaneous ability to maintain or expand its real income. For an enterprise to remain effective, it must be innovating, learning and adapting, otherwise it would decline.

Productivity, the yardstick of the economy for the past 300 years, is still a necessary condition for competitive success, but it is no longer a sufficient condition. The new competitive standards are quality, variety, customisation, convenience and timeliness. Each of these success factors depends on human competence.

Efficient Educational System

The Education System has begun to realise the importance of Quality, and more specifically, of Total Quality Management, that has gained popularity and Universal acceptance all over the world. Professional & Higher Educational Institutions are under pressure to become more efficient and effective. There is a need to identify and apply the relevant concepts of Total Quality Management to each and every aspect of academic life, that is, to the teaching, learning process, library and administrative activities.

Quality Issues of Higher Education

- Creating relevance of curriculum
- Managements' responsiveness
- Motivating the faculty
- Improving institutional academic climate
- Effective curriculum implementation strategies
- Attitudinal change for achieving excellence
- Linkage with industry and other institutions
- Self-learning and self-paced learning
- Students taking initiative in learning
- Effective evaluation system

On the above basis, action plan can be prepared for each activity at management level, teacher's level and at the level of students. Quality management techniques will give long-lasting solutions to all the problems and challenges faced by the higher education system.

Globalisation of Higher Education

It has removed the physical restrictions imposed by national boundaries. Globalisation brought in its wake the IT revolution as well, which has removed the restrictions imposed by time and distance. Think globally and act locally is the watchword for success in any economic endeavour today. Almost all fields of human endeavour, be it Politics, Economics, Commerce, Science, Education, Health and so on, have acquired global perspectives. The paradigm shift from "Self Reliance" to added "Global co-operation for all-round development of all" has changed the direction and speed of human effort which has influenced these fields tremendously.

Survive and Prosper

The impact of Globalisation as in other fields has been very much felt in the field of higher education. Again the philosophy of global competition and global co-operation has joined hands for primarily economic aims. University leaders all over the world come to believe more and more in the principle that to survive and prosper in a rapidly changing world, they must embrace the marketplace and become customer-focused business enterprises.

Knowledge Driven World

Many eminent academicians believe that Globalisation of higher education would immensely enhance the chances of the students for self-development, help the faculty to enhance and refine their skills and also help the community. Further, the most glorious prospect seems to be the partnership between Universities and local/National/International business houses. As such, higher education stands to benefit from this broadened outlook-in terms of quality, variety and effectiveness to industry/usefulness to individuals and society. As we move towards a 'Knowledge Driven world' the broader the horizons of perception, the better. For one thing, youngsters cannot restrict their job markets to local boundaries. If they have to move out, they should get an education that is comparable with that which is given in more developed parts of the world.

Interactive Learning

Globalisation of learning and teaching is often misunderstood as moving towards total electronic delivery of education. It need not be so. Higher education in its modern approach may bring more and more students of arts, science, commerce and management studies into direct contact with leaders of big, medium or huge international corporations of international repute. The global education has the potential to become more and more a process of interactive learning. As on date, our Universities are still the powerful masters of higher education and they have much to offer to the students worldwide.

Placement in Privatisation

Higher education is no longer a matter of charity. It is a high quality service and a reasonable price is always to be paid; but then, when such a price is paid, is it not true that the students expect 100% placements. Sure, liberalisation makes it easier to develop liaisons with reputed organisations and secure decent placements for the students of higher education in every field.

Market Survival

When private providers of higher education are encouraged these providers always enter the market with the dreams of super profit. No one can deny it. But when a large number of them come to play, the very proliferation and competition would force them to offer reasonable terms to the students, just for the sake of survival in the market. Then an equilibrium will be reached and the prices stabilised. In the case of quality, respective governments in states and the centre can definitely suggest and permit formulation of a single body consisting of eminent scholars, academicians, industrialists, business leaders, social reformers and thinkers to tackle this problem and suggest measures.

Utilisation of Capacity (Resources)

The vast resources that we have created in our higher education system both physical and intellectual, remain grossly underutilised. Effectively, the system works for about 150 to 180 days in a year, and that too for 6 to 8 hours a day. For the rest of the time in a year, the entire resources are idle. And that means less than one-third capacity utilisation. There is immense potential to use these resources for national development in a variety of ways. These physical facilities and personnel can be put into use for extending education to a much larger proportion of our youth. The participation of the relevant age group in higher education in India is one of the lowest in the world, even among the developing nations. While, the unused capacity is also in a bad state. By and large, the teaching community has not done justice either to their profession or to themselves. The lack of any concern for productivity and accountability in the profession is the cause.

Urgent Reforms

Before we can find a level ground in the 21st century for competitiveness based on knowledge, we must carry out the following reforms:
- Granting deemed university status to as many good institutions as Possible.
- Granting autonomy to all good colleges.
- Introduction of semester system and continuous internal evaluation.
- Promotion of modularity and credit system.
- Revision of the existing pattern of holidays and vacation.
- Establishment of a State Council for Higher Education under the chairmanship of an academic.
- Introduction of a high degree of professionalism in policy formulation, planning and management of higher education.
- Conscious promotion of academic leadership.

Vision 2020

It is necessary to visualise the developments that could take place in higher education, in future. Considering the rapid rate at which changes take place and the progress made in science and technology, and its impact on the content and conduct of education, it may not be possible to look far into the future. It may be desirable to aim at a period of 20 years. We already have VISION 2020 documents for many sectors though education explicitly is not yet one of them.

Class of Manpower

Whenever we consider the possible developments in education, we are often tempted to produce an impressive and all-embracing document, irrespective of the availability, or otherwise of the institutional machinery, political will and resources for implementation. We do not also take into account the preparedness of the society to absorb and benefit by such developments. While higher education has a universal component, and employment opportunities are global, we prepare manpower not fully apt to meet either our needs or needs of people who complain that opportunities do not exist in India that match their expertise. The most important requirement that education and training must satisfy is to be able to substantially improve national productivity, starting with and improving upon, whatever level of technology and management practices we may have. We need to produce designers or planners who could do the job with whatever data are available, or could be gathered, and not those who declare that they could make a beginning only if all the data to suit their theory are made available. It must be clearly understood that in every country the education system prepares manpower for its economy primarily. If we decide to prepare consciously a class of manpower, necessarily limited in number, for international market, or if the manpower we produce for our need has an international demand, it is a different issue.

Agriculture and Industry

There are two branches in technology that march forward incredibly fast, and they are: information technology and communication technology. There is a distinct possibility that there will soon be a congruence of these two. The impact of the possible future developments in information technology and communication technology may have to be assessed. We must remember, at the same time, that however fascinating, they by themselves, will not do the job of a plough on the field or a machine tool in the workshop. The two major sectors of the economy, agriculture and industry may continue to play their role. The farmer, the worker and their modern tools may gain in productivity, nevertheless they only have to produce. Access to knowledge will improve, dissemination of knowledge will be enormously facilitated, creation of new knowledge could be accelerated to the extent that one may command input to one's research work from many sources at an incredibly fast rate, but a creative mind has to be there, it can be neither replaced nor produced by any of these technologies. The limitations on the ability of a society with a high level of illiteracy as at present, to avail itself of these developments must also be borne in mind. The rays of several developments could be seen on the horizon; some of these may evolve on their own, and some may have to be brought about by appropriate intervention and initiative. These are:

- Networking of institutions
- Interaction with the environment
- Emergence of distance teaching and learning
- Globalisation of education
- Virtual universities
- Education market
- Private enterprises in education
- Private universities
- Continuing education
- Education and social justice
- Research and innovation

Functions of Universities

We are concerned essentially with academic accountability. Here again, accountability can be both at macro and micro levels. The macro accountability is that of the University system to the society as a whole in terms of fulfilling the expectations and meeting the needs of the society as set forth in the functions of the University at the time of its establishment and modified from time to time. The micro level accountability is that of every component or the authority of the University in order that the sum total of their contributions will meet the macro level accountability. While we realise the importance of the macro accountability which ultimately is what matters, the discussion relevant to the seminar falls within micro accountability and that too, with emphasis on the academics. There were times when academics and accountability were considered unrelated and mutually exclusive; today, the situation has radically changed; the change of borders on a revolution. It is now explicitly stated and clearly understood that, besides the three classical functions associated with the University, namely, preservation of knowledge, communication of knowledge, and evolution of new knowledge, the universities have to play a part in and contribute to development. In other words, the academics besides scholarly pursuits, have to get involved in developmental functions also. Three components of developments are:

- Political development
- Social development
- Economic development

The university system has to create new knowledge and generate qualified manpower to meet the developmental needs of the society in all spheres of activity. The academics are expected to perform such functions and discharge such responsibilities as may devolve on them in helping the system fulfill the tasks assigned to it by the society. The expectations are clear and the accountability is unambiguous.

In this context, one can understand what 'accountability' means; no explanation is needed: however, for the sake of providing a basis for discussion, we may take 'accountability ' in the case of academics to mean ensuring satisfactory performance with regard to teaching, research and related functions expected of them in the institutional environment. The other two aspects are: moral and contractual.

- Moral accountability is based upon a sense of responsibility-a realisation that one is responsible to one's clients, i.e. students and parents in this case, to colleagues and to oneself.

- Contractual accountability requires that one is responsible to one's employer in terms of fulfillment of the terms of one's employment.

Knowledge as Resource

The 20th century has seen many breakthroughs; changes bordering on mini-revolutions in some countries and major ones in some others. The most important of them all is the emergence of knowledge as a resource.

In the early stages, in the agricultural economy, knowledge was perceived as an embellishment, an ornament and not an economic force. In the industrial economy, it became a tool for economic development. In the era of high technology, which we see today, knowledge has become a resource. It is a resource that can be renewed and augmented: what is more important, it can create resources that are not available as part of natural resources.

To give one example, the per capita income in the USA rose from $7500 in 1955 to $11,500 in 1980. But the USA did not discover any new natural resource during this period. This prosperity was achieved through: mastery of knowledge in important disciplines, discovery of new knowledge and application of knowledge for economic and social development.

We need higher education and research at a level of excellence to be able to master and utilise knowledge. We need universal education to be able to absorb the advances in knowledge and use the processes, tools and systems created.

Development of Academic Leaders

Education is a specialised field. Planning and development of education requires specialists. 'Specialists' are academics who have a long record of teaching and research in their field of specialisation, and who have through involvement, exposure and experience, developed and demonstrated the ability for perceiving the short and long term needs in Higher education and research and who can advise the Government and guide the nation in the development of education. Such a leadership must develop from a large group, not from a few men and women of rare flush, but a broad base of academics, many of whom have some level of competence in their field. Such a development requires institutions, which provide opportunities for the development and nurturing of the leadership qualities in academics. Leadership qualities may be inborn but leaders are made. Some of the steps that could provide opportunities for the development of academic leadership are:

- Autonomy for colleges in the true sense of the term.
- Reorganisation of the university bodies and enabling the university to function as a body that would keep a close link with the manpower and research needs of the economy, and be continuously responsive to the new demands and challenges.
- Establishment of a State Council for Higher Education in every state.
- Conscious efforts to provide opportunities for academics in all central educational bodies, statutory or otherwise, as well as planning and policy making bodies that may have education as one of the subjects to deal with.

*****

Globalisation and Massification

Universities around the world are increasingly entangled in intersecting local, national and global relations. The unprecedented expansion of higher education has affected many other institutions in the larger society. Globalisation and Massification of higher education being the need of the hour, teaching and learning also needs to be modified accordingly.

The most significant changes that have come to this forefront in the aspect of higher education are:
- character of student aspirations and needs,
- pattern of student compositions,
- new avenues for utilisation of human resource,
- understanding the role of a teacher,
- student--teacher interaction,

- new disciplines of study and continuously evolving content of curricula, and
- the role of changing pedagogies and their implication for quality in higher education.

Revolution

Higher educational institutions in India are poised for a revolution in the coming decade. Several factors contribute to this change:
- the growing demands on higher education and consequently,
- the unprecedented expansion of higher education and diversity of higher educational institutions,
- the changing patterns of student composition, and
- the increased investment by the government as well as private sector.

For changes in higher education to lead to the development of a system which is more responsive to students' needs, institutions need to involve increasing managerial involvement in pedagogy and curriculum design and increasingly student-centered strategies for learning and teaching. The introduction of Learning Technology has acted as a catalyst, accelerating this process of change. A revolution in Information Technology has resulted in visible changes that have left the faculty and students perplexed with sheer volume of information.

International Students Admission

All institutions of higher education should have the freedom to admit international students with a view to promote diversity of students' population on Indian campuses and create partnership for internationalisation of higher education. A nationally coordinated initiative for promotion of Indian higher education should be taken up. Higher education institutions should be encouraged and facilitated to put in place institutional mechanisms and infrastructure and facilities for attracting international students and to enter collaborative arrangements with their counterparts abroad.

Modernisation

The aim and objective of all 'Education' is to maintain, sustain and develop a healthy mind in a healthy body and it is the only sector that sustains possibilities for modernisation. It is useful to distinguish between two levels of modernisation: institutional and attitudinal. The former refers to the modernisation of institutional structure of a society, while the latter concerns itself with the modernisation in the minds of the people.

Culture of High Technology

Needless to say that education has the potential to influence many elements of society. The significance of this distinction lies in the possibility that a society may adopt modern institutional structures without modernising the attitude of its members. The term "modern" here implies the emergence of a culture of high technology, formal organisations, a secularised value system and vigorous psycho-social mobilisation. In keeping with this, streamlining of education with respect to four facets of modernisation, namely technological, instructional, valuational and behavioural, also take place.

As our education system is suffering under the overload of objectives which are ambiguous, multiple and incompatible, the need of the hour is to make the system "purposive". This is the essence of modern education which will address both cultural transmission and social transmission.

Modern education needs restructuring in the context of the present quantitative trends and the new requirements of content. A conservative backward-looking and tradition-bound education system is out-of-date and anachronistic.

Lifelong Education

For too long, education has had "the task of preparing for stereotyped function in stable situations, for one moment in existence for a particular trade or a given job." "Moreover, it prepares for a hierarchical social set-up, oriented, as it is towards building of an "elite". Most of the contents of education are seen to revolve around the past. The educational structure has to be reshaped and refurbished to diversify and widen the field of choice and enable people to follow patterns of life-long education.

Better than Before

Students must be made aware of their status, their wishes, their rights and responsibilities. Teaching must cease to be authoritarian and oracular and seek to foster relationships characterised by mutual understanding, dialogue and good will. We will have to explore new pathways for tomorrow's tasks. In the past we were mainly concerned with doing "more than before" and later on with "better than before". We must now ask ourselves how to do "different than before" for the simple reason that what was before, may neither be relevant nor suitable anymore.

Stimulating Thinking

The role of teachers of today takes on new dimensions of great significance. The teacher–student relationship, which has been the keystone of the arch of traditional education, has to be fundamentally re-evaluated, particularly when it is a dominator-to-dominated relationship. The teacher's duty is not so much to inculcate knowledge as to stimulate thinking.

Merging of Minds

The teaching is to transform by informing, to develop a zest for lifelong learning, to help students become mature, independent learners and architects of an exciting, challenging future. Teaching at its best is a kind of communication, a meeting and merging of minds.

Education does not mean teaching people what they do not know. It means teaching them to behave as they do not behave. Teaching is the training of students into perfect exercise and kingly continence of their bodies and souls. It is a painful, continual, and difficult work to be done by kindness, watching, warning, percept and praise, but above all by example.

What the teacher needs is a psychology of human meaning, a psychology which is interpretive of student's feelings, beliefs, understandings and values, in short, a psychology that is concerned with the question of what goes on inside the learner.

Teacher Leads to the Threshold of Mind

"If the teacher is indeed wise, he does not bid you enter the house of his wisdom but rather leads you to the threshold of your own mind." The education that the teacher imparts should do away with all artificial barriers and assist each student to excel in his work in his own way according to what his skills, understandings, interests and aptitudes permit him.

Profile of a Good Teacher

The ten-faceted profile of a good teacher, in the light of his professional requirements, obligations and commitments:
A good teacher is:
- One who can instruct as well as inspire.
- One who is in incessant pursuit of knowledge and skill.
- One who is not hamstrung by conventions, traditions, obscurant beliefs and stupid superstitions.
- One who tempers his behaviour according to his increasing knowledge.
- One who seeks to explore, adventure forth and create a new vista.
- One who respects, understands and values himself as well as his fellow beings.
- One who helps the student to learn how to learn.
- One who challenges the student to develop his abilities while overcoming his shortcomings.
- One who is warm-hearted and interactive, withholding all sarcasm and ridicule.
- One who becomes humane himself and helps the student to become humane.

Cultivated Citizens

> "The prosperity of a country depends not on the abundance of its revenues, or on the strength of its fortifications, nor on the beauty of its public buildings, but it consists in the number of its cultivated citizens, in its men of education, enlightenment and character."
>
> — **Martin Luther King, Jr.**

Immediate and Ultimate Aims of Education

Education has two-fold objectives – the immediate and the ultimate. The immediate relates to the structure, the curriculum and the methodology which have to be designed and defined in conformity with the climate and contours of societal needs so that youngsters on completion of their educational courses may be able to secure suitable employment and live in decent competence. The ultimate aim in education is the transmutation of the individual into an integrated personality in whom there is a balanced blend of the body, the mind and the spirit.

Quality Products from Universities

Startling social changes and urgent national needs have been exerting tremendous pressures for the restructuring as well as diversification of academic programmes. Universities should seek to cater for a multiplicity of courses and individual needs through diverse routes, such as participation in creative art, job-oriented projects and community related activities. A university should not be a mere manufactory of graduates without due regard to the quality of its products.

Devoted Teacher and Motivated Student

High standard in higher education is possible only through the establishment of the right type of rapport between devoted teacher on one hand and the motivated student on the other. The caliber of the faculty determines the validity, the usefulness and the potency of education. Teaching is not mere instruction or imparting of information. It is the communication of intellectual and moral force which enables the youths to discover their innate talents and grow to their fullest stature. The right kind of teachers are those who induce their students to think, to distinguish and to find out things for themselves, sometimes opening the way, at other times leaving it to them for to open. This is a task that calls for sympathy, emotion, imagination and patience on the part of the teachers.

Disagree Without Being Disagreeable

Students should realise that the precious years spent with on the campus of a university are for preparing them for the challenging tasks of life ahead of them. Undoubtedly the students have the right to express their views without fear or favour so that their creative vigour and vitality are not curbed or stifled. Students must learn to disagree without being or becoming disagreeable. It is highly desirable and even necessary that the student community has an opportunity to play a leading role in the organisation of the university activities.

"A University stands for humanism, tolerance, reason, adventure of ideas and search of truth. It stands for the onward march of the human race towards even higher objectives. If the Universities discharge their duties, adequately, then it is well with the nation and the people."

"Nothing will ruin the country if the people themselves will undertake the task to ensure its safety and nothing can save it if they leave that safety in any hands but of their own."

- Pandit Jawaharlal Nehru

*****

Internationalisation of Indian Higher Education

An unprecedented explosion of scientific and technological knowledge in the current panorama has turned the world into a global village. Change and management of change effectively and efficiently have become the clarion call of the era. In the days of explosion of knowledge, expectation and awareness, the 21st century society is bound to be a knowledge based society. A knowledgeable society is a globally linked borderless one which will impose on institutions the need for international level accreditation and maintenance of standards in the near future (Aaruchami, 2002). It is the intellectual capital, i.e. trained manpower rather than financial and physical capital which gives strength and prosperity to the society. In this context, the world of higher education in the 21st century can truly be a borderless world of knowledge and ideas, which will yield reciprocal benefits for all nations (Periyasamy & Venkatesh 2004)

Major rationale behind the internationalisation of Indian higher education is that:

Internationalisation would lead to an improvement in the quality of education, promote Indian culture abroad, inculcate the cult of international understanding, generate goodwill and social interaction and yield financial harvests.

Partnership and networking are essential for the enrichment of the teaching – learning process and for improved quality in research.

Recommendations

- Urgent action should be taken in the matter of finalisation of Government policies relating to the promotion of Indian education abroad. The proposed committee for the promotion of Indian Education Abroad is constituted at an early date and its functioning activated.
- The UGC Act, 1956, and the Acts of other statutory councils, need to be amended to include a specific provision allowing universities to open off-shore campuses and export Indian education through the distance mode.

- It is also necessary to enact legislation that would regulate the opening of foreign institutions and thereby prevent the gross commercialisation of education. A legislation needs to be framed that would regulate the operation of Indian partners of foreign institutions and allow only genuine academic institutions to participate in turning activities.
- There is a need to simplify, within the existing legal framework, procedures relating to registration, entry-test requirement, issues of 'No Objection Certificate', as also the issue and extension of visa.
- The government should advise Indian Embassies and High Commissions abroad to play a proactive role in providing information regarding the facilities for higher education available in India, and assist in the conduct of fairs, entrance examinations and student recruitment. For this purpose the Embassies and High Commissions could establish counselling and assistance units.
- There is a need to adopt an open-door policy for self-financing students. This would require raising the percentage of international students to be admitted to Indian professional institutions, and also creation of super numeracy seats.
- Urgent steps should be taken to strengthen the data and information base so that prospective international students can obtain information relating to academic programmes available at different universities, eligibility criteria, admission procedures and tuition fees. Apex bodies may be asked to create websites for this purpose and these could be linked to a central education website.
- Government statutory bodies and the UGC should grant greater autonomy and flexibility to universities in dealing with the process of admission of foreign students and in entering collaborative arrangements with foreign institutions especially in the establishment of off-shore campuses and centres.
- The government should set up a single-window clearance mechanism, in the form of Task Force including representatives of different bodies like UGC, AICTE

and MCI for admitting students to different professional programmes. Universities could get their foreign student applicants cleared through this Task Force.
- The government should consider establishing a financing mechanism for international education, such as a possible International Education Development Bank. This institution should provide soft loans to Indian students going abroad, to foreign students coming to India for higher education and to educational institutions wishing to develop infrastructure for international education.
- The government should set up a mechanism for monitoring the standard of education that is imparted by foreign universities. There is also a need to establish a National Equity Framework that would provide for lateral transfer as well as vertical progression, both nationally and internationally. This would facilitate the coming in of students for short durations.

Internationalisation of Higher Education – Suggestions to Academic Institutions

- **Infrastructure**

    Universities and other academic institutions which decide to enroll a large number of international students need to have a good infrastructure in the form of lecture halls, well-equipped laboratories, and adequate library resources, facilities for sports, recreation facilities and above all special living facilities in the form of international houses/hostels. For institutions planning to offer special, short-term courses for groups of students on a regular basis it would be desirable to develop a separate complex with classrooms sectional library and computer unit so that the international students can study in an environment comparable to what he/she has at home.

- **Evaluation**

    The academic institutions must evaluate their strengths in different levels of disciplines in education, and identify areas that would attract students varying in accordance with the requirements of the foreign students.

- **Single Window**
  The procedure for granting admission to international students must be simplified. It is necessary to reserve a certain number of seats for international students, or provide for super numeracy seats. If an admission or entry test is necessary then arrangements for it should be made in the home country (or at least the region) of the prospective student, or online. On arrival at the university campus he should be able to complete formalities through a single-window operation.

- **Cultural Exchange**
  The 'social infrastructure' should be strengthened so as to place the international students at ease. Programmes, such as 'home stay', cultural festivals, celebration of national days of different countries should be organised regularly so as to promote cultural exchange and mutual understanding. Each institution must have an office for International Education and an International Student advisor.

- **Twinning Arrangements**
  International education is a two-way process and it is essential that Indian academic institutions, and especially the universities, should establish partnerships and develop networks with foreign universities in both the developed and the developing countries. The development of international education programmes should be given priority. The faculty should be encouraged to participate in the enrichment of their academic content. International contacts should be nurtured and hopefully these will lead to "twinning" arrangements. Linkage can be 'firmed up' through Memorandum of Understandings (MoUs).

  A recent study conducted by consulting firm Technopark on higher education trends in India shows that the emergence of global knowledge economies has a direct effect on the education scenario here. "With 200,000 students emigrating annually from India for higher education and more than 700 international collaborations of Indian institutes, students and parents are increasingly seeking ways to garner the benefits of global inter-connectedness,." "It's only wise that international tie-ups are encouraged to help develop curriculum, provide affiliation to a reputed brand, assist in transfer of knowledge, placements and student-faculty exchange."

The tie-ups are in the form of student-faculty exchange, twinning programmes, research collaboration and curriculum development. "In the last few years, we have witnessed a growing trend of such tie-ups. The demand for such courses is on the rise because of the emergence of new job opportunities in the areas of analytics, artificial intelligence, sustainability, climate change, fraud examiners and more." India presently has 170 private universities of which 54 have come up only in 2012-13.

Among foreign institutions now accessible are the universities of Virginia Tech, Carnegie Mellon, Raffles, Indiana, Warwick and Lancaster, which offer courses that range from engineering and technological streams to design.

Among the private universities which are offering foreign degrees are Amity University-Amity Business School with 80 tie-ups followed by OP Jindal Global University (65 tie-ups), Galgotia University (12 tie-ups), Ansal University (10 tie-ups), Chandigarh Group of Colleges (5 tie-ups), Ashoka University (4 tie-ups) and GD Goenka World Institute (1 tie-up).

- **Academic Restructuring**
Internationalisation of higher education can be facilitated if the academic structure of the university is similar to that available in the universities abroad. Academic restructuring may be necessary for many universities and this could mean a gamut of reforms including permitting the student to chose freely the courses to be studied, introduction of semester system (with continuous internal evaluation and credit system), allowing transfer of credits, etc. These changes have been advocated for over two decades now and need to be implemented even if there is to be no internationalisation.

- **Curricula of Different Regions**
  Highest priority need to be given by academic institutions to the updating and internationalisation of their curriculum. This implies not only the incorporation of the contents to give an international dimension to the programme on offer, but also it is necessary that, at least at the Master's level, the curricula incorporate information on different regions of the world, especially, Europe, United States, Africa and South east and East Asia.

- **Special English Classes**
  Students coming from the Arab world, CIS countries and countries of South east and East China, more often than not, have an inadequate knowledge and accent of English Language. It is necessary that for students from these countries special English classes be conducted for the first few months of their stay in India. This can be done in a systematic manner if an English Language Cell is created as a part of the International centre.

- **Study in India**
  Indian universities should develop special "Study India" programmes that could be covered in one semester for the benefit of students from developed countries who would like to visit India to learn more about its culture and heritage, natural resources, diversity, language or indigenous technologies and systems.

Internationalisation of Indian Higher Education – Suggestions to the Association of Indian Universities

In order to facilitate the internationalisation of Indian higher education, the AIU should assume the role of a co-ordinator. It should serve as the nodal agency, within the university system, responsible for the co-ordination of activities of universities in the area of international education. For this purpose it should create a Consortium for International Education (CIE) as proposed by AIU.

Recognising the fact that there is a vast scope for attracting students from developed countries to study in India for one semester, the AIU should assist universities to develop "Study India Programmes (SIP)." It could also co-ordinate with the Institute for International Education (IIE), and other similar agencies, to identify programmes and undertake the placement of individual students or group of students.

Implementation of Globalised Education

The Global era has immense implication for education, with at least the following important thrusts:
- Demands on students and teachers to develop global consciousness and global concerns.
- Necessity to arrive at the frontiers of knowledge as rapidly as possible by closing existing gaps and thereafter to keep up pace.
- Emphasis on the development of communication skills, with increasing mastery over information technology.
- Development of a global civilisation and the necessity to share values that can sustain humanity in the global era.
- Challenges to equality and opportunities for delivery.

Aims of Global Education

- To share the international resources and human resources collectively to develop more physical and human resources for sustainability.
- To develop all the human faculties like the physical, vital, mental, moral and spiritual in a gradual fashion as means and as ends.
- To ignore, isolate, exclude and even destroys the divisions of all types and their ideological introduction.
- To treat and understand natural, material and human resources as an indivisible unity and to prepare children to protect his unity.
- To gradually and systematically emerge from the past history of insignificance into a new era of rational living.
- To educate about the limitations of human personality and to awaken autonomy or conscience in them.

- When global unit is at work, while conceiving, designing and implementing global education it covers quantitatively a majority of the people on the globe.
- The planning for education will be done for all the people and not particularly for the people of a nation, region, religion and race. Global education is opposed to all divisions of the present day world.
- Divisions have to gradually disappear to give place to global village and global functioning.
- The ultimate purpose is to create a global humanity who will live in peace with other and in harmony with the planet.

Globalisation of Education and its Impact on Students

Globalisation facilitates students' learning in such a way that local and global resources, supports and networks can be brought in to maximise the opportunities for their developments during the learning process. Participation in international learning programs can help them achieve the related global outlook and experiences beyond education institution learning groups. The networks will become a major driving force to sustain the learning climate and multiply the learning effects through mutual sharing. The aspiring students can learn from world class teachers, experts, peers and learning materials from different parts of world.

Globalisation of Education and its Impact on Teaching

Globalisation has its impact on teaching. Through globalisation, multiple sources of teaching are available. Teaching can become world class. Through participation in international development and research programmes, teachers can achieve global outlook. Their teaching becomes networked teaching. A new professional culture grows and they share professional practice and research.

Curriculum in Globalisation of Education

Even the curriculum acquires a new sheen in globalisation. The curriculum content pools up the world class materials and designs for the learning and teaching processes and maximising the global relevance and exposure to the future developments of individual and the society. The curriculum becomes relevant to globalisation of technology, economy, social development, political development, culture and learning.

Number of Universities

Japan for its 12.7 crore people has 684 universities. USA with 27.6 crore population has 2364 Universities. In UK and Germany there are 104 and 330 Universities whose populations figures are 5.58 and 8.2 crore respectively. However, for 120 crore Indians, we have only 634 Universities. It indicates the acute shortage of universities in India and the need to establish more to provide wider access to higher education.

*****

Higher Education in Rural Areas

Amidst the rapid growth of Indian higher education, there lies the dilapidated and neglected rural higher education. The growth and expansion of higher education in rural areas has been quite slow and sluggish. Even the existing few rural centres of higher education testify to the low status accorded to rural higher education. Lack of infrastructure facilities, paucity of funds and inadequate faculty have plagued these rural knowledge centres. Although these rural knowledge centres are the only hope for the 69% of the rural poor, their status and their scope remain far below the minimum standards. Already in 1986 the National policy on Education recognised this and stated that educational opportunities in India are both inadequate and unequal. Rural higher education scope and expansion is highly conditioned by their total dependence on government funding.

Barriers Faced by Rural Colleges

Rural colleges experience increasing number of barriers at various levels. These barriers are robbing off the competitive edge of the rural students. Some of them are:

Lack of Infrastructure

A large number of rural colleges, unlike city colleges have lack of adequate infrastructure facilities like proper supply of electricity, transport and communication facilities.

Technological Backwardness

In ICT high speed, broadband and digital information infrastructures based on optical fibre cables are essential. It is obvious that rural colleges lack all the above mentioned limitless connectivity. The digital divide has imposed many barriers on the rural students. They are:
- Teaching and learning using ICT
- Curriculum development
- Research and extension
- Carrier Opportunity.

Deprivation of Transnational Tie-ups

Transnational Tie-up is nothing but a natural outcome of globalisation. In the transnational tie-up the language of education goes through a sea change, i.e. marketable, consumer-friendly and client-centred educational programme. This means commercialisation of higher education has to cater to the needs of the global investors. Today students look for transnational tie-ups so that they may have a greater carrier opportunity. The Indian universities and colleges are forced to compete with foreign players who are technologically sophisticated, financially self-sufficient and are motivated on commercial interests. Rural colleges are nowhere in this race and are left in the lurch.

Financial Constraints

In India higher education relies on government funding. The government allocates only less than 3.8% of GDP for higher education. The institutions are forced to generate their own funds by increasing their tuition fee year after year and are forced to start self-financed courses. Here, the performance of

rural colleges has not got much scope for generating internal resources. Starting of self-financing courses is not encouraging in rural areas for these reasons:
1. The students are unable to pay the fee which is high as compared to the regular programme.
2. Institutions are unable to invest.

*****

3

Higher Education: Privatisation Way

Management and Administration of Private Colleges

Structure of Management and Administration of colleges

The managing committee or the Governing body is in overall control of the affairs of a private college. The Principal, with the help of Heads of departments, looks after the day-to-day administration of the college and the college hostels. In some colleges the teachers are also associated in some measures with administration and management.

Effective Management

In the first place, for effective management and administration, a good rapport and an atmosphere of trust between the management, principal, staff and students in their spheres of interaction are a pre-requisite for securing general support for the good functioning of the college. Whenever this is missing in between any two or more sections of the college community, the work and efficiency of the college suffer. As custodians of higher education in private colleges, we are obliged to review seriously this aspect of relationship. These days we talk of participative management. Therefore the managements have to take their staff into confidence and try to get feedback from the students in matters of management and day-to-day administration of the college. To establish healthy practices of management, there should not be any serious frictions in relationship between Management and Principal, between Principal and Staff and between sections of the college community.

Management of Human Resources

The single most important asset of any college is its human resources. Many of our problems on campus can be directly or indirectly traced to lack of adequate skills in the management and administration of our human resources namely the members of managing body, the principal, staff, students and other workers. In management of human resources for effective achievement of the goals and objectives of the college, one has all the time to strive to keep task-orientation and person-orientation in proper balance. Very often we tend or one is forced to lean overmuch on task achievement or on satisfying personal to the determent of one or the other.

In the management of staff and students the demands of the academic tasks on hand and the need of personnel involved in achieving tasks have to be constantly kept in view and balanced judiciously so as to achieve a task without letting the personnel down. Where there is high level of motivation there is a high level of achievement. Motivation depends on morale. As managements we have also to provide facilities for the staff to update their qualifications and professional skills by giving them opportunities for higher education, research, attending refresher and orientation courses and other in-service training periodically. There is also need for orientation at all the levels of management personnel, principal and heads of departments and heads of our college officials in proper managerial, administrative and communicative skills as well as in mature interpersonal relations.

Management of Public Relations

One important area for closer look by managers and administrators of private colleges is the public relations of our colleges. How well do we interact with the community around us which we seek to serve? The secretaries and principals of colleges have a great responsibility in establishing proper public relations with the community, the government agencies, the university, the parents and others concerned, good public relations pay rich dividends for the growth of the college. It may be worthwhile considering the appointment of a suitably qualified person to assist the management and the Principal in each college in this important area.

Management of Time

The proper and judicious management of time is of the essence in effective management and administration in any field. The recent "National Commission on Teachers in higher education" has come out with the finding that colleges in India work only for 145 days in a year on an average, which means lots of institutions work less than that. Can we do something concrete to achieve a better average towards the prescribed 180 days? Secondly, how fully and effectively are even these 145 days used by the staff and students, is a matter for serious evaluation which deserves our immediate attention.

Innovations and Management Changes

These days we talk a lot about innovations of all kinds but it is very difficult to achieve them in practical terms. Innovation implies change and change invites resistance. Most of us do not want change. But where there is no change, there is no growth. Innovation relates to different areas of college life such as restructuring and diversification of existing courses, designing and introducing job and application-oriented courses, new educational technology, semester system, student services autonomy of colleges and so on. Very often we fail in successful implementation of innovations because we have not learnt the technique of management of innovations. Innovation brings in change. Any change to be effectively implemented must carry conviction with those who are involved in and affected by the change. As people, in charge of management and administration, what can we do about overcoming resistance to change and successfully bring about innovations in management techniques, administration, teaching and learning? To give but one instance, let us consider the use of modern teaching aids. Given the modern audio-visual teaching aids such as overhead slide and film projectors, video cassette recorders and players and tape recorders, how many of our teachers are really inclined to use, and are trained in effective use of such aids? To use these aids the teacher has to do a lot of preparation in advance as against merely revising old notes and presenting them to the class. This brings in resistance. We may purposefully discuss ways to overcome such resistance.

Institutional Planning and Evaluation

Any management to be successful calls for evaluation of what is managed. In respect of private colleges, how many of us are involved in institutional self-evaluation in an integrated manner (not merely looking at the percentage of pass in university exams). We have to devise ways of staff evaluation not only during the time of probation of the staff but throughout their career in the college. As for the staff, career development must be contingent upon professional development. How accountable is our staff to the management to the students as well as to themselves? There have to be objective and fair means of evaluation of staff and a credible system of reward and punishment for good and bad work done without giving room for vindictive or arbitrary use of any system of staff evaluation. The staff themselves can be involved in working out a suitable mode of evaluation with the help of external experts. We have also to re-examine our policies, from time to time, of student admissions critically to ensure both quality and equity in the selection of students. In the total evaluation of the institution there is need for machinery like a planning and Evaluation Cell at each college composed of representatives from management, staff and students and the community around as well as external experts. This will help the colleges in assessing the level of attainment of their academic, societal and national goals and objectives. In many cases the buildings of the colleges are used for hardly six hours a day. Ideally, we should be planning the use of our physical resources for at least 10 to 12 hours a day in order to derive the maximum benefit within the existing facilities.

Course of Study

In keeping with the proposals of the New Education policy we have to think in terms of diversification of existing courses to make them socially more relevant and introduction of new job and community oriented courses both at the undergraduate and postgraduate levels. Diversification implies willingness to change, reorientation of staff to handle diversified courses, and additional resources for library books and journals, laboratory equipments, etc. In introducing new courses of study we may do well to survey and study the needs of modern society and design courses in consultation with industries, government, experts, service agencies and others concerned. While deciding on such courses various relevant aspects such as the needs of the community and the country, the demand for the course based on such needs, the availability of books and journals for teaching the course, availability of qualified teachers and financial resources have to be taken into account. This process may take years sometimes before a successful new course of study is designed either by the college or by the university. The efficient management and administration of diversified and new courses of study will be an area of significant contribution by private colleges to national development.

Brain Drain

A large chunk of our professional manpower emigrates towards developed countries. Thus we finance education of these people without any tangible returns to this country. Further, an economically backward country like India provides the cream of professionally trained manpower to developed countries without any quid pro quo in the form of foreign contribution in reverse direction. It would be desirable to legally bind potential emigrants at the time of admission itself, to reimburse full cost of their education in case they decide at any time to migrate to foreign countries, for studies or employment, without serving this country for a minimum initial period, say 5 to 10 years of their service. Suitable endorsements should be made in their passing out documents and passports to indicate their bonds to reimburse costs or return and serve in India immediately after studies/training abroad.

*****

Higher Education: Private Players Demonstrating Excellence

Higher education is vital to a rapidly developing country like India, the governments share in higher education in terms of number of institutes and student enrolment has dwindled over time. Conventional university courses are not able to cater to the immediate demands of the market. Conventional institutions also lack responsiveness to the labour market demands. This academic inflexibility has boosted the rapid development of private initiatives.

Healthy Competition

Establishing of private universities has been a major milestone in the field of higher education in India. The initial mushrooming of private institutions had made us 'suspect' the quality of education offered. However, the last decade has taught the private sector that it cannot compromise quality if it wants to stay afloat the emerging healthy competition between private players and government run institutions and it's the student who stands to gain from it.

Quality can Survive

The private sector is the fastest growing segment in higher education in many countries around the world. During the past few years, more private institutions than public ones have been established in most developing countries and emerging economies of the world. Ten years back, when private institutes started mushrooming in cow sheds with students clamouring for admissions. These private players were only filling the gap between supply and demand, without any government funding. Now, students and guardians are very focused on quality. Only those institutions that give academic quality and good placement can survive in competition.

Decision

Today, government institutes are not even taking 10% of the total students. The number of seats has not increased in proportion to the population. The government realised this, and hence policy decisions were taken at the central and state levels to allow the private sector to come up. Taking into account the capacity crunch in Government institutions and improve the quality of higher education, many state governments and also UGC have accorded deemed university status to many educational institutions that filled the criteria. The private institutions have been known to match the high standards of benchmarks set by institutions such as the IITs for quality standards.

Return on Investment

The public feels private institutions charge high fees compared to government institutions. However, one should realise that private institutions do not receive any grants from the government for the development of their infrastructure. Also, the middle class in India is growing economically and would be more than willing to pay for value education. The private sector has to invest huge funds on infrastructure and faculty to meet the high standards that students expect. It may not be a crime to expect a reasonable return on the investment, but at the same time do no exploitation. What should matter is that quality is not compromised. In fact competition itself sets the standards. To say, that no university chooses its students. It is vice-versa... it's the student who choose the university. So naturally, universities have to pass the litmus test of matching the expectation of students and guardians.

*****

Myths and Facts of Privatisation of Higher Education

The First Myth

There is a huge demand for private higher education, as private education is qualitatively superior to public education.

The facts

The higher quality of private education compared with public higher education is mostly exaggerated. Public higher education provides better facilities, which are significantly related to quality, than private universities and colleges.

- The number of students per teacher in public universities is much less than private universities.
- Private universities are found to employ mostly retired, part-time, and underqualified teachers who are paid less. Hence, teachers in private institutions have less academic prestige.
- The availability of space per student and other facilities are reasonably higher in public universities than in private universities.
- Private universities spend less than half of what public universities spend per student.

All the above facts should indicate that quality differences are more in favour of public universities than private.

Private universities may sometimes show better results in final examinations, as essentially they admit only best prepared students.

Even if the quality of output is taken into consideration, that is, internal efficiency, measured in terms of academic achievement success rates, dropout rates, failure rates, etc., private education does not compare favourably with public educations.

The Second Myth

It is widely believed that graduates from private universities receive higher rewards on the labour market in the form of lower unemployment rates, better paid jobs and consequently higher earnings.

The facts

The empirical evidence does not support these assumptions. Unemployment rates among graduates from private universities are much higher than those from public universities. Estimated rates of return, a summary of statistics of the external or labour market efficiency of education, show that public higher education pays better than private higher education.

The Third Myth

Private institutions provide considerable relief from financial burden to the government as they are self-financing.

The facts

It is not true; most of the private higher education institutions receive the subsidies from the state's budget allocation for higher education. In U.P., 77% of the budget allocation on higher education goes as aid to private colleges. In most of the developed countries major portion of scholarship money goes to students in private universities. The details lead to conclude that most private institutions are not totally run on private finance.

The Fourth Myth

Private sector responds to the economic needs of the individual and society and provides relevant type of education "The major advantage of private universities has been in responding more quickly or efficiently to market demand."

The facts

The private higher education institutions offer mainly low capital intense disciplines of study. Only a few private universities are involved in research activities, but they are also involved in providing cheap commercial and vocational training as in the case of "Parallel" Colleges in Kerala state. Private universities do not provide higher education in law, medicine, pure sciences, engineering and so on. A negligible proportion of private institutions offer courses in medicine and pure science. However, when the potential for economic profit is high, the private sector entered into professional fields and opened engineering and medical colleges in India. On the whole, research and broad educational needs of the economy are barely served by the private sector. Private institutions tend to provide more personal and fewer social benefits to students and country.

The Fifth Myth

It is generally believed that private enterprises have genuine philanthropic motives in opening private colleges and universities, which are by definition part of the 'non-profit sector'. They also make huge investments in higher education.

The facts

Private institutions are largely funded either from students' tuition fees and charges or from public subsidies. Very few private institutions make any investments from their own resources. These institutions are operated in a kind of seller's market, recovering the full costs plus profits from some source or other. Private Colleges that receive little public support in India expect huge donations and capitation fees and charge abnormally high fees, ten to twenty times higher than those charged by Government Colleges. While universities and colleges are, by definition, non-profit institutions, these private institutions do not merely cover their costs, they also make huge and 'quick profit', which is not necessarily reinvested in education. Educational considerations hardly figure in this context and lend commercialisation.

The Sixth Myth

It is generally noted that private education is elite and caters to the needs of the wealthy. Education in private institutions is costly and presumably of high quality affordable largely by the elite, while education in public institutions is generally compelled to choose quantity rather than quality.

The facts

Private universities generally serve a privileged clientele. Fees in private universities are very high compared with public universities, only the relatively well to do opt for private higher education. The access to public higher education is restricted, students from the upper and professional classes are forced to go to private universities. However, public universities continue to be the first choice for many due to educational and financial reasons.

The Seventh Myth

Most public higher educational institutions are politicised. Only private institutions are apolitical institutions.

The facts

Basically the inadequacy of public policies results in the growth of private institutions. Public policies favoured leftist political activism in public universities. Private universities have grown to counter these forces. But private institutions are not free from political forces. Private education has been found to strengthen a given political ideology and to help in reproduction of class structure. In several countries, state support to private universities is based on political and ideological factors, which can be called 'political economic' factors. In India, more than half the private engineering colleges are owned by politicians, and used for political purposes. Motives of profit, influence and political power explain the growth of private colleges.

The Eighth Myth

Privatisation of higher education improves income distribution, as public funding of higher education, with all its 'perverse effects' is generally found to be regressive.

The facts

From the studies it has been found that the private education system contained forces that contribute to disparities, and that the state sector was not adequate enough to counteract these forces. As a result, the whole education system was found to be a contributing factor towards accentuating income inequalities.

Pros and Cons of Privatisation

The growth of privatisation is largely due to the failure of public universities, while private universities have certainly made positive contributions. Each private university has its own identity, tradition, culture, etc. In contrast public universities hardly offer only diversity or individual choice.

In this sense, privatisation increases the possibilities for individual choice in type and quality of higher education. But the stress upon individualism—upon individual preference at the expense of social responsibility and cohesiveness must be a matter of concern.

- Private higher education eases the impending financial burden by the public authorities.
- In most cases, resources for the private institutions come from students, not from private sector.
- Private institutions supply manpower to the private as well as to the public sector of the economy.
- Private universities reduce the number of students going to foreign universities.
- The goals and strategies of private sector in higher education are on the whole highly injurious to the public interest.
- The private sector has turned the 'non-profit sector' into a high profit making sector.
- Profits are not allowed in educational enterprises but private educational enterprises have resorted to illegal activities in education.
- Private institutions provide market-oriented vocational training in the name of higher education.
- Private universities ignore broader higher education by concentrating on profit yielding, cheap, career-related commercial studies.
- Private universities totally ignore research, which is essential for sustained development of higher education.

Higher Education: Privatisation Way

- Private institutions create irreparable socio-economic inequities between the poor and rich income groups by charging high fees.
- Access to higher education by lower income groups is negatively affected by the rapid growth of privatisation.
- Private education is in no way not economically efficient, qualitatively superior and socially equitable.
- Growth of privatisation in higher education would create more problems than solutions.

*****

Important Private Universities in India

Manipal University, Karnataka State

The Manipal University, which started with a medical college in 1953 now has 24 colleges with an enrolment of over 80,000 in a range of disciplines at all levels. Manipal, a small town in coastal Karnataka, has now become an education hub that attracts students from across the country, and even from overseas. From its initial narrow focus on engineering and medicine, programmes in humanities and social sciences are on offer now. The university is spending Rs. 400 crore to upgrade its facilities in Manipal and other centres. Other than India, it has presence in Nepal, Malaysia, Dubai and the Caribbean. It has massive expansion plans, both in India and abroad. Four more campuses with an initial investment of around Rs.100-130 crore for each campus are planned in India. Overseas expansion plans are to enter Oman, Indonesia and Vietnam.

Amity University

The Amity University, which started just a decade ago, has two universities and 700 institutions that cater to 50,000 students in 130 different courses, from sciences to humanities to media. It has spent around Rs. 1000 crore so far and plans to invest around Rs.2000 crore in the next five years and increase the student intake to 500,000 in the next five years. It claims it has been consistently growing at 50% for the last five years and plans to accelerate its growth to 100% in terms of student intake and revenues, which the university management is confident to achieve in the current Indian scenario.

Birla Institute of Technology and Science (BITS), Pilani

The Birla Institute of Technology and Science (BITS), Pilani, started in early 1900s as a small school and blossomed into a set of colleges for higher education, ranging from the humanities to engineering until 1964, when all these colleges were amalgamated into a reputed private deemed university. By setting up campuses at Goa and Hyderabad in India and at Dubai abroad, BITS, Pilani, is now a multi-campus university with about 8000 students and 12,000 students enrolled in off-campus work integrated programmes. In recent years it has even set up a virtual university. Its main source of funding both to meet recurrent costs and capital costs for expansion – come largely from the tuition fees that are not steep and yet 22% students at BITS receive scholarships.

SRM/VIT-Reversing Brain Drain

The newly recognised private and deemed universities have been taking measures to introduce innovative courses and have designed their curriculums according to the needs of the market. They also have tie-ups with foreign educational institutions so that faculty and students can have better exposure to the cutting edge in research and developments in their fields. Globalisation of Indian higher education has achieved something amazing by reversing the brain drain Indian student's rank among the best in the world. Their PCM (Personal Criteria Management) skills are considered the best the world-over. It's only the weak processes that don't allow them the opportunities to excel and reach their optimum. Indians have been occupying top positions in foreign universities.

Chain of Private Institutions

An interesting development in the country's new private higher education sector is the emergence of institutions tied together in a chain with common for profit ownership (though often legally cloaked as non-profit). Their operations are put together under one brand name. This is not only a marketing ploy, but also a strategy that declares their product is working and can now be offered, through institutional cloning, to populations that cannot reach the initial places. Though the multiple sites may have some autonomy, but only some, as the core idea is a rather standard package for scale and growing demand, they are able to generate huge surpluses from their operations, most of which is ploughed back in expansion and consolidation.

Internationalism (International Standards)

Many students could well be taking the most defining decision of their life about which university or college to join? A cursory glance around would suggest that the students are spoilt for choices. After all, every university/college these days claims to provide quality education that meets international standards. In fact, there are hundreds of them around and students generally have a tough time picking up the right one. But what exactly do these universities /colleges mean when they say 'world class' or use the word 'international'? A little investigation would tell us what they actually mean is that either the courses they offer are aligned to international standards or they have facilities that are comparable to some of the best in the world. But as anyone can tell us, 'internationalism' goes much beyond that, and only that university which is committed to the all round development of the students can understand this.

Institutional Diversity (Private Higher Education)

Not only has private share increased over the years but its complexion is very different now. Initially, private colleges in narrow specialisations affiliated to public universities dominated the private higher education landscape. These were not very different from their public counterparts except for finance and administration. Now, there is a large variety of private institutions. It does not entirely comprise small affiliated colleges now, there are many big players with large operations and massive expansion plans. Many of them are making huge investments in modern and expensive infrastructure and facilities. Some of these institutions have fully air-conditioned buildings, Wi-fi enabled campuses and classrooms with smart-boards.

Private Tuitions and Coaching Centres

A large and growing non-formal sector comprising private tuition and coaching centres have spawned on the fringes of the formal system of higher education in recent years. Traditionally, poorly paid teachers used to supplement their meager stipends by teaching a gathering of 10-15 students in makeshift classrooms after school hours. Essentially private tuition was given to weak students for remedial purposes.

Cost Sharing in Higher Education

The shifting of the financial burden of higher education attendance from the general tax payers to the students and their parents, 'Cost Sharing' as Johnstone (2005) calls it can take different forms. Seven types of cost sharing arrangements are seen worldwide. These are:
- Introduction of tuition fees (in China in 1997, in Britain in 1998, in Austria in 2001, and most recently in Germany in 2005.)
- Introduction of a dual tuition track with high level of fees for less meritorious students with capacity to pay (practised in Russia, most of Eastern and Central Europe, India, Uganda)
- Sharp rise in tuition fees (public universities in the United States increased their state fees by an average of 10%) in 2001-02. Several institutions in India like IITs and IIMs have increased their fees sharply in recent years.
- Imposition of user charges (happening in China, several African countries like Ethiopia, Mali and Guinea and the Nordic countries)

- Diminution of student grants or scholarships (done in Britain, Russia and most of the Eastern and Central countries)
- Increase in the effective cost, recovery of student loans through various measures.
- Encouragement of tuition-dependent private higher education sector. This has happened in Japan, Korea, Philippines, Indonesia, Brazil and some other countries in Latin America. This has increased the participation of parents and students in cost-sharing and even in profit-making institutions.

Students' Financial Aid

As the tuition and fee levels rise, either driven by policy or on their own (as in India) due to resource crunch faced by public institutions and the emergence of the private sector, higher education becomes beyond the reach of a large section of the population. Equity in access to higher education has become centre to debate on funding higher education. Equity in access is the ability of the brightest students to study at the most intellectually demanding universities, unrelated to their socio-economic background. To ensure this, higher education has to be free at the point of use. Thus an increase in fee levels is usually accompanied with the introduction of suitable grants and loan programmes that are designed to be, as closely as possible, both need-based and generally available to the academically prepared students without regard to the wealth or credit worthiness of their parents or their individual career and earning prospects. There can be variety of grants and loan options designed to address this problem.

Tax Benefit/Incentive

Apart from grants and loans, many countries find tax cuts rather than tax increase as a good solution. The people who would benefit the most from this are the middle class families who are overburdened with education costs. It would cost the Government revenue in the short term, but a college educated worker has significantly more taxable income than he or she would have otherwise. Taxing the moneyed individuals' spent on education is not the Government's best source of tax revenue. In India there are tax incentives for spending on higher education. However, their impact is limited due to the low proportion of people covered under the tax net.

It is unfortunate that in the present age of trade and commerce, money has entered the field of education as well. In these times, it may be impossible to divorce education from money and materialism.

- Dr. Rajendra Prasad

Higher Education and Economic Growth

Higher education for the public benefits ranging from growth to political coherence and social order. Among them, the evolution of the economic purposes of education is seen as the single most important educational development of the 20th century. Developments – first marked by the way of industrialisation in one country after another and then with the emergence of knowledge of economies – endowed with education explicitly with an economic value by forging both direct and indirect, backward and forward linkages between education and economy. The economists found that often 50% or less of the growth in gross domestic product could be attributed to the stock in capital and the amount of labour. The residual factors were responsible for most growth. These factors are closely linked to the way knowledge is used in better way or more productive use of inputs. Technological progress or advances and human capital, the various forms of education and training that make workers more productive were two main components of residual factors. (Harbingers, 1998).

Investment in Educational Training

Education and training enhances the skills and capacities of people and therefore their productivity, and the employers award such people with higher earnings. People therefore invest in education and training by making rationale estimates on returns of education. This has been the central idea of the human capital theory that dominated the discourse in the economics of education since 1960s. Recognition of human capital as an agent of growth transformed not only development of economics but also led to a new field in the economics of education. Since then, the productivity enhancing effect of education and its differential impacts on income in accordance with differences in educational attainments of workers attracted attention of policy-makers and analysts; this, particularly higher education, usually connects formal education to the world of workers.

Higher Education and Labour Market

Demand for higher education could either be private demand from the students and their parents or demand from labour markets for specific skills and very often the two are unrelated. Higher education, which was viewed primarily as social experience earlier is now seen as a way to get ahead in life. This culture of aspiration is continuously pushing up the private demand for higher education. The policy makers are required to respond to this rising demand. Exalting the public benefits of higher education, policy usually has an expansionist bias resulting in over-education, leading to unemployment and under-employment of graduates a phenomenon common throughout the world in varying degrees.

Formal Higher Education

Since the link between fields of study and occupational areas are relatively loose in most countries and the process of transition from higher education to employment has become more complex and protracted, it has its own dynamics of raising and dashing hopes (Gibbon, 1998). The formal higher education does not necessarily equip students with skills required in the job markets. This creates a problem of unemployment on the one hand and skill shortage on the other.

Multi-level Co-ordination

Public policy is required to find a link between supply of skilled people by the education system and the demand for skilled manpower from the labour market and to ensure provision of adequate number of places in the higher education system to meet students demand. This requires co-ordination at two levels between the demand for qualified manpower and places in higher education system on the one hand, and places in higher education and students' demand on the other. Ideally, the two should relate to each other. Poor labour market outcome of graduates should dampen the demand for places in a higher education system. In reality this does not happen, because the feedback mechanism and co-ordination system is often weak. Co-ordination is required for different types of education, at different points in time and at different locations. Given the enormity and complexity of the task, this multilevel co-ordination is not easy to achieve. Central planning would not be very useful.

Dynamics of Co-operation

The nature of work has changed and is continually changing with technical changes. With increasing integration of the job markets, the national content is no more relevant. These aspects need elaboration in order to understand the dynamics of co-ordination between higher education and labour market. In this complex scenario, market forces usually do a better job than central planning in matching the skills of the graduates with their own preferences and the demands of the labour market, though some planning may be desirable.

Manpower Forecasting

Manpower forecasting in India is very weak and based on the assumptions of the past. Disjointed efforts to provide long-term forecasts and post-mortems are of little use. Assessment of skills required within the country, its supply and the dynamics have to be considered keeping the future in mind. Dissemination of such information would enable the higher education and training systems to create new facilities or adopt the existing ones to bridge the demand-supply gap. A system is required to take charge, create and motivate the entire supply chain of skills required dynamically and ahead of the curve.

Universities and Colleges

India has nearly 18,600 universities and colleges in the formal system of higher education. This number is more than four times that of higher education institutions both in the US and Europe. Higher education in China, having the highest enrolment in the world (nearly 23 million), is organised in only about 2500 institutions. Whereas the average enrolment in higher education institution in India is only 500-600 students, a higher education institution in the US and Europe would have 3000-4000 students and in China this would be about 8000-9000. A smaller size of higher education institution has implication on governance and regulation of the systems. Of the 18600 higher education institutions, nearly 400 are university-level institutions and the remaining are affiliated colleges.

Academics and Standards

Universities are self-regulatory bodies that determine and maintain their own standards. However, there is a need to put in place a mechanism for comparability of academic standards across universities to enable transfer of students from one university to another. Academic degrees awarded by the universities send signals to the job markets to facilitate the selection process. Such signals should be easy to interpret. As a result, harmonisation of academic standards across universities becomes necessary. The UGC has the primary responsibility to co-ordinate and determine academic standards across the university system. The UGC discharges this responsibility through its various rules and regulations.

Regulation for Award of First Degree

The UGC Regulation of 1985 on the minimum standards of instruction for grant of first degree through formal education lay down working days, working hours, attendance requirements, supplementation of lectures by tutorials and/or problem-solving sessions, term papers, nature of evaluations, work load of teachers and several other matters. There are similar regulations for non-formal distance mode of education. All universities and colleges in the country are expected to follow the UGC regulations on minimum standards across various disciplines. Many professional types of council also have similar standards. This results in overlap and confusion.

Comparability of Qualification

The UGC with the approval of the Central Government specifies the titles of degrees that can be awarded by the universities. Standard nomenclatures of degrees become necessary for the purpose of comparability of qualifications across institutions and also to ensure that degrees send out unambiguous signals in the job-markets. In many countries an independent body of experts discharges this important role. Countries like Australia, New Zealand and South Africa have independent National Qualification Authorities (NQAs) that lay down a National Qualification Framework (NQF). Various academic titles with their duration, content and learning outcomes are specified under the NQF by the NQA.

Regulating Private Higher Education in South Korea

Private higher education in South Korea grew in an environment marked with very tight regulations until 1995. South Korea not only had strict guidelines regarding how to establish and operate a higher education institution, it also controlled the number of students in each department for each school, as well as students selection methods. In most cases, student quotas and school licenses were rationed to those institutions that could demonstrate to the government their capabilities of providing quality education.

Naturally, their strict regulations created substantial rent-seeking activities, while leaving little room for individual educational initiatives among institutions. Recognising various problems from heavy regulations, in 1995 the government started to loosen conditions. Among other things private universities were allowed to regulate the number of incoming students as well as the distribution of students within the institutions. The rules to establish a new institution were liberalised. The government also gave some small incentive grants to reward performance. In short, the government introduced competition among universities and colleges by making them more autonomous and more competitive.

Regulating Admissions

With 37 school boards and 634 universities with varied academic standards, developing a common yardstick to determine inter se merit is not easy. Hence, entrance tests for admissions become inevitable. The issue is only whether these should be held by individual university/college or conducted jointly for an academic programme having similar eligibility criterion. Ideally, each university should be allowed to decide on the criterion for admission and conduct entrance exams if required. Considering the short time for conduct of such exams and mental and financial burdens due to multiplicity of these exams, common exams are always preferred. Many All India and State Level Common Exams are now being conducted.

However, many universities would like to retain control of these exams. The main reason for retaining control is financial. Both public and private universities generate huge surplus from this activity and would not like to forgo that. Some private universities also manipulate entrance tests and maximise their earnings. A huge coaching industry (according to some estimates with an annual turnover of Rs.100 billion) thrives on this.

There is a need for streamlining the entire process of common entrance tests. The practice of universities and examining bodies making huge sum of money through this mode from parents is unethical. There is a need to put in place a system of common entrance exams for professional programmes. These common entrance exams could be held at the All India Level, where admissions are from the All India body of students and at State Levels, where admissions are from the State level body students. Admissions through these common exams should be insisted upon unless there are valid reasons for a university not to participate in that for reasons of uniqueness of their programmes. On a long term, a National Testing Services (NTS), independent of the school boards, could be set up. Such exam could be conducted several times a year on the pattern of the Scholastic Aptitude Test (SAT) and the Graduate Record Examination (GRE) in the United States.

Unethical Practices in Admission Process

A majority of private institutions could be accused of collecting exorbitant capitation fees and other institutional fees, not brought into regular accounts, manipulation of entrance results and admission processes to maximise illicit payments and disregarding admission norms in favour of those willing to pay more. In these circumstances, exempting from common entrance exams of any private institutions or category of private institutions on account of their minority status (or any other status) or in the name of safeguarding their autonomy could lead to exploitation of students and parents.

The fact that private providers are looking for loopholes to escape the common exam system is evident from the recent experiences. Many deemed universities opted out of common exam for entrance to undergraduate programmes in engineering as soon as the government gave them this option. Ostensibly, they opted for their own tests to safeguard their academic autonomy, in reality, however, it is different. Now they are conducting their own exams; some of them are making huge sums of money through entrance exams. They have unreasonable refund policies that create dilemma for parents. Some of them even manipulate the result of entrance exams conducted by them to collect illicit payments.

New Regulatory Environment

As noted in the NKC, a meaningful reform of the higher education system, with a long term perspective is both complex and difficult. Yet, it is imperative and necessary to overhaul the entire regulatory structure governing higher education. An ideal regulatory system should be based on addressing the minimum set of regulatory concerns. These concerns could be those arising from possibility of market failure or need for market co-ordination or to address the issues of public health and public safety. The system should ensure fair play, transparency and accountability. It should be non-intrusive and student friendly. The new regulatory environment needs to provide adequate space for innovation and experimentation and facilitate growth of the private sector in a healthy atmosphere. The problem of information asymmetries in higher education can lead to wrong and costly decisions by students as well as employers. Such information gaps related purely to financial matters such as fee levels, refund policy and so on, can be effectively bridged by enforcing transparency similar to the disclosure norms of listed companies.

Thus, rather than having a regulatory system that is paternalistic there is need for a flexible regulatory environment that adjusts to growing diversity and modulates itself to varying track records of higher education institutions. However, an important element of regulation should be transparency. Compulsory self-disclosure in the form of returns on information by universities and colleges should be mandatory to address the problem of information asymmetry in higher education. Provisions of the Right to Information Act, 2005, could be used for this purpose. This could even be extended to the private for-profit sector. These rules could also define misrepresentation and deceptive practices in advertising, promotion and marketing by higher education institutions.

In the USA, the students 'Right to Know' under the provisions of their Higher Education Act 1965 and Freedom of Information Act requires the disclosure of financial assistance and institutional information to students.

*****

4
Relevance of Foreign Education

Foreign Education

India is self-sufficient in imparting university education in a spectrum of disciplines, ranging from Actuarial Science to Zoo keeping. Then why go abroad for higher education?

The answer to this lies in the fact that even from the US, where universities are a dime a dozen, students travel abroad for education. Even now Rhodes scholarship to study at Oxford is ranked as the most prestigious by the US students. Indian universities also train thousands from foreign lands.

Different Culture and Orientation

Right from the ancient times university education was considered something more than just focusing on the subjects chosen for study. Opportunity to meet students and faculty of other cultures and orientation to a different environment positively contributes to university education. The tradition of travelling to foreign lands for university education dates back to centuries. Universities run by Moors in Spain catered to intellectuals from all over the world. Many years before that, Fa-Hien the Chinese Scholar dared to cross the Himalayas to study at Nalanda.

British Universities

Till Independence, Indians generally looked upto the British universities for foreign education. A few did go to Japan and Germany. Opposition to colonial rule motivated them to seek non-British institutions.

An Ivy League University of the US was within the reach of even mediocre students from India during the early fifties. By the sixties the scenario completely changed. A sudden surge from the Indian and other foreign universities flooded the US universities. Now admission to Harvard or a similar one is a dream for an average Indian student.

Foreign Exchange

After Government policies changed to allow foreign exchange release for under-graduate education abroad, there seems to be a flood of aspirants to go to the UK and Australia. To take advantage of this, many universities are sending solicitation teams to major Indian cities. Admission to Australian universities or the UK could be well within the reach of an average Indian student. The catch is in being able to afford the fees and other expenses, running over Rs. 3 lakhs per year. As a matter of fact, although the expenses are just half of study in former Soviet countries and in East Europe, only a trickle show interest to go there. More than the hurdle of mastering a foreign language, there seems to be a "class problem" to study in non-British universities. The fact remains that many non-English speaking countries run first rate universities.

Obtaining Visas

Obtaining visa to study abroad seems to be a vital problem faced by the aspirants. Most of the Australian universities demand advance tuition fees before processing visas. The UK also demands a strong proof for visas. But for the USA, it is a wild gamble. The countries which are liberal in issuing student visas have sufficient mechanism for checking overstays and illegal employment.

Study in Australia

Australian immigration laws prohibit students to apply for permanent residence while being there. They are supposed to do that after leaving the country. Even the part time 20 hours per week employment does not fetch anything big compared to the burden of huge sums needed from home. All the interest these universities show to recruit Indians amount to be financial in nature, resulting in best talents enriching their schools. Total absence of any form of scholarship is not accidental.

If one is not rich, it is better to forget Australia or the UK option to pursue foreign university education. France and Scandinavian countries offer very good scholarships. But the application process is labyrinthine and there is language problem also.

Community Colleges in the United States and Canada

The United States and Canada have their unique system of community colleges that fulfils certification needs for vocations and skill required in communities. Anyone, regardless of prior academic status or college entrance exam score, is allowed to join a community college. Community colleges are as popular as with students attending high school (who can enroll under concurrent enrolment policy), as with the working adults (who attend classes at night to complete their degree or gain additional skills in their fields). These not only provide a cheaper option than the expensive higher education, but provide pathways for entry to a regular four year college. Research shows the students who begin their higher education with a community college are more likely to transfer to a better quality four year institution. Low fees, focus on vocational skills with easy transfer to regular higher education programmes makes community colleges a preferred option particularly for students with mediocre academic records. In the United States, low-cost community colleges focus on Vocational skills with open admission policy on one side and highly selective and very expensive research universities on the other are a part of an integrated and coherent higher education system. This system provides for a high degree of vertical and horizontal mobility and has a lot of flexibility and variety.

Higher Education in Singapore

The Universities in Singapore offer academic freedom to explore several courses ranging from the principles of quantum mechanics to the history of the Cold War, while majoring in economics at the same time.

Over 16 leading foreign universities have set up centres of excellence in education and research in Singapore. Students can now get degree from the UK, the US, France or Australia by studying in Singapore itself. Singapore is a popular destination for students wanting to pursue finance, management, business administration accountancy, law and economics. There is also a lot of financial help provided for Indians in the form of scholarships and study loans. While Singapore is nowhere near cheap, tuition fees and cost of living are affordable compared to the West. Another key factor that attracts Indian students is Singapore's proximity to India. Also being an Asian country, Indian students adapt easily to the environment. The universities are always ready to pitch in to help make the adjustment easier.

Help Desks in Singapore Universities

Singapore Universities have a network of professional services and advisors to help international students integrate into the university environment and ensure their studies are as productive and stress-free as possible. The International Student Centre in the Student Affair Office is the first point of contact for international students. The centre assists with administrative matters, orientation and the basics of getting essential daily provisions. It also organises social programmes for international students from other countries as well as with local students. Over the duration of the course, students can access professional counsellors free of cost. Most colleges and halls of residence also come up with their own mentors to help guide students and look after their welfare.

Collaborations with Indian Universities

While Singapore Universities are gearing up to sign more collaboration with Indian universities, our country is still looking to expand its presence in the subcontinent. Singapore and India enjoy a strong friendship that is reflected in the many education and research agreements that National University of

Singapore has in place with Indian institutes. Low crime rate and excellent transport system are the added important advantage of studying higher education in Singapore. The National University of Singapore (NUS) is currently ranked at 24th in the world and number one in the 2014 QS University rankings: Asia.) and currently INSEAD Business School was voted as the number four B-school in Asia-Pacific region by QS With over 5000 Indians looking to pursue higher studies in Singapore each year. It is not merely rankings that keep them interested. With over 60 branches, excellent transport facilities and a diverse student community, there is much to attract students. Singapore gives students opportunities to enhance their leadership qualities and prepares them for the real world. Singapore is located close to Malaysia, with Tamil and Chinese influences, students in Singapore are especially fond of its culture diversity. You can eat Canadian beef stew, drink Japanese rice wine and study with a group of Nigerians and party with Brazilians – all in one day. It is like taking a trip around the world and getting a world-class degree at the same time.

*****

Higher Education in the United States of America

Land Mass and Population

The United States of America has four times the land mass of India while its population is about one fourth of the Indian population. In about 400 odd years of its adventurous history, the US has built up a massive and powerful economy both in terms of agriculture and industry. The affluence that flows out of this strong economy is easily reflected in its higher education system of the land. In fact higher education itself has contributed not a little to this affluence of the American economy.

American Higher Education System

The American higher education system is three-tired: 2-year community colleges at the bottom, 4-year liberal arts colleges in the middle layer and the universities at the top. In all these three tiers they have the private and public sectors. Education is cheaper in the public sector while it is much more expensive in the private sector, but unlike in India, there is not much of a difference in terms of quality between the institutions of the private sector and those that are state-run.

Physical Resources

Each university has enormous physical resources such as a well-stocked library with automation and computer facilities which is kept open till midnight, an Excellent Learning Resource Centre, audio and video facilities and comfortable student housing in campus.

All American universities and colleges are autonomous, governed by a system of accreditation. A college or university can only earn and keep its status of accreditation if it has sound finances, sufficient physical facilities, competent faculty and favourable faculty-student ratio and their programmes of study are of nationally comparable standard.

Faculty Evaluation

The American universities and colleges care primarily for quality and intellectual productivity in recruiting and retaining their faculty. The faculties have to go through severe process of evaluation which they accept willingly. The evaluation of a teacher is done first by his/her own students, followed by his colleagues in the department, the Head of the Department, the Dean of the faculty, the Academic Vice-President, the President, and finally by the Board of Governors of the University. As a result, the faculties are highly motivated to work hard and record professional growth in terms of output of their research work, publications and involvement in extension services. Those who do not make the grade eventually leave the institution quietly to join lesser positions.

Part-time Work

Students have to pay high rates of tuition fees for their higher education especially if they join private universities and colleges. Many of them undertake part-time work in order to keep themselves going through their higher education. Where they earn scholarships, they have to maintain a high level of performance in studies in order to retain the scholarship in subsequent years. This leads them to be highly motivated to complete their course with sufficient level of proficiency.

Freedom and Flexibility

Another striking feature of American Higher Education is the enormous freedom and flexibility in course offering. A student can opt for a choice of various courses according to his tastes, needs and ability and does not have to be restricted by a rigid framework of courses as in India. Whenever a particular course of study is found to have outlived its usefulness, it is dropped or modified substantially, a freedom which we do not have in India for fear that such a step will affect the job security of our teachers.

Administrative Structure in US Higher Education

The US universities and colleges have a well-defined administrative structure with the Board of Governors at the top. The President who is the head of the University is supported by four or five Vice-Presidents –one each for administration, academic affairs, student services, finance and so on. The Vice-Presidents are assisted by the Faculty Deans. They, in turn are supported by Heads of Departments within their own departmental faculty. Most universities and colleges have excellent Student Services Centres including a special wing to help foreign students. Many Universities have a very effective student counselling to settle their problems and disputes democratically.

Community Colleges in US

The Community Colleges were originally started to help veterans of the World War throughout the country. Some of them are multi-campus institutions offering as many as 400 to 500 courses of study but they are essentially teaching colleges and do not have any research function. These colleges have functional advisory committees consisting of local citizens who advise them on course offerings and other modes of functioning. Students doing a two-year degree programme in community colleges can have vertical mobility into four-year Liberal Arts Colleges or make the two-year programme a terminal one.

String of Universities

Another noteworthy feature of American higher education system is the string of universities such as the University of Georgia at Athens and the University of Texas which were originally land-grant colleges with a grant of a stretch of land from the local State Government. These land grant colleges have since grown into huge universities and have particularly strong colleges of Agricultures. For instance, the College of Agriculture of the University of Georgia at Athens has established a State-wide network of agricultural services. This college of Agriculture of the Georgia University has contributed a great deal to the growth of agricultural production and marketing in the State of Georgia.

Next to medicine, engineering and management studies, computer courses are gaining in popularity, even as it is in India where we have just about made a beginning.

Admission Policies

The student admission policies in India are severely restrictive because of sheer exuberance of number of applicants, very few students fail to gain admission to universities in the USA if they can measure upto the academic requirements. The State and Federal funding of student aid is another factor enabling students to pursue higher education in the USA without much financial stress. As a result, about 55% of the age-group has access to higher education in the USA, while it is a meager 17% in India.

Foreign Students' Advisers

In the US universities foreign student advisers are appointed to help students from other countries to get admission and also provide after-admission care and guidance. The emphasis laid on international programmes and global studies is a remarkable feature of American higher education.

Student Counselling Services

Special mention must be made of the Student Counselling services provided to students in different areas. This is something conspicuous by its absence in most Indian universities and colleges and is typically American. It helps students a lot in choosing the right courses of study and in coping with their academic personal problems.

Concept of Consortium of Colleges

Another interesting feature is the concept of consortium of colleges. For instance, in Louisville, Kentucky, a consortium of as many as 7 colleges helps them share their resources and facilities for common benefit. Yet another special feature of the American system is the systematic care and concern bestowed on the needs of different ethnic and minority groups in institutions at all levels. Special facility for the disabled is another unique feature in most US universities.

Special Pride

It is interesting to note the special pride that administrators, faculty and students alike take in the unique traditions and ethos of their respective universities and colleges. This is something that contributes a great deal to the growth and development of the institutions in an imperceptible way.

Financial, Physical and Human Resources

The two major advantages of the American higher education system are their enormous financial, physical and human resources on the one hand and their remarkable flexibility in course offerings on the other, both of which the Indian higher education system lacks badly. The high value attached to intellectual merit in the higher education system gives the American nation a clear edge in terms of research output which is directly applied to improving national productivity.

Manpower Supply

American approach to higher education marks out applied research, community and service-oriented studies. The US Federal and State Governments as well as the industrial, scientific, agricultural and service sectors have learnt to look up to American universities and colleges for the supply of their manpower needs and have not been disappointed either in terms of numbers or quality.

Hardly 3% of the American population is engaged in farming but they produce surplus levels of foodgrains with the result that the government has to give incentives to farmers for keeping part of their land uncultivated so as to arrest steep fall in the prices of agricultural produce due to over production.

The Best Education Money can't buy in the USA

Berea College founded 150 years ago to educate the freed slaves and the "poor white mountaineers" accepts only applicants from low-income families and charges no tuition fees. "You can literally come to Berea with nothing but what you can carry, and graduate debt-free."

No-frill Budget

The Berea college with $1.1 billion endowment is the wealthiest institution in U.S.A. But unlike most well-endowed colleges, Berea has no football team, mixed-gender dormitories, hot tubs or indoor mountain-climbing walls. Instead, it has no-frills budget, with food from the college farm, handmade furniture from the college crafts workshops and 10-hour-a-week campus job for every student.

Debate on Tax-exemption

Berea's approach provides an unusual perspective on the growing debate over whether the wealthiest universities are doing enough for the public good to warrant their tax exemption or simply hoarding money to serve a few elite. As many elite universities scramble to recruit more low-income students, Berea's no-tuition model has attracted increasing attention.

*****

Higher Education Under WTO Regime

Effect of WTO on Indian Higher Education

Over the years education has been viewed in India as an activity that leads to a broadening of the mind, inculcation of values and building of character. Higher education is considered to be essential for the cultural social and economic development of a nation. The possible deleterious effects of WTO (World Trade Organization) and GATT (General Agreement on Tariffs and Trade) has decried the fact that higher education is being considered as a commercial product to be bought and sold like any other commodity.

WTO Danger to Indian Universities

When anything becomes a part of WTO regime, and its requirements and regulations, it is subject to complex arrangements. The implications for higher education are many because an entire new set of regulations will become operative and the university will have to be defined in an entirely new way. The overriding goal of WTO and GATT is to guarantee market access to educational products and institutions of all kind. Academic institutions could lose their independence and individuality if they lack quality. In the WTO controlled regime there is real danger of the universities in the developing countries like India being swamped by overseas institutions that intend to earn profit but are not concerned about contributing to national development.

India has the second largest higher education system in the world comprising 693 university level institutions with over 35,500 colleges about 29 million students and over 5 lakhs teachers at the tertiary level. It is very well endowed in terms of both infrastructure and human resources.

The quality of education imparted in the different academic institutions is variable. Yet there are a number of institutions in India, where the standard of education is comparable to the best in the world. Outstanding research is being conducted in key areas. The main reason for the mediocre quality in many institutions is of lack of infrastructure because of inadequate financial support.

Non-formal Stream of Higher Education

A parallel, non-formal stream of higher education exists in India, in the form of training institutes that provide skill-oriented programmes, and these are doing flourishing business even abroad.

Cross-border Supply

The Indian universities have commenced offering degree and diploma programmes through the distance education mode, in countries having an Indian diaspora. Indira Gandhi National Open University has formulated a policy in this regard and is offering programmes in both liberal arts and professional areas. The better-known Indian training institutes globally offer further education programmes, some of advanced level, in professional areas like computer applications. Likewise, some foreign institutions are offering programmes to Indian receivers. However, the foreign open universities have not been able to make much headway, possibly because the Indian Open Universities have been fairly cost-effective.

Education Modes of Trade

The WTO has recognised four modes of trade in education that receive legal protection through GATT.
- **Cross-border supply**
  This is the supply of services across national borders, from territory of one country into the territory of another. Distance education using print media or any other kind of educational material that is sent across national borders, or online education via the Internet, falls in this category.
- **Consumption Abroad**
  This involves the movement of the consumer of a service to another country to get the required service. This is the most common form of consumption with the student going abroad for studies or research.
- **Commercial presence**
  This requires the actual presence of a foreign service provider in another country. In case of education this involves the setting up of programmes, courses or institutions by a member country in another country.
- **Movement of Natural persons**
  This means the presence of an individual from one country to another to provide services. In education it means the presence of a foreign teacher in a host country.

Definitions of Higher Education in India and Abroad

The general perception in India is that higher education is the post-secondary education offered through its universities, colleges and specialised institutions. This restricted understanding is not in consonance with global perceptions that generally include all types of post-secondary education (including that offered by the so-designated training institutes) within the purview of higher education.

International Higher Education — A Lucrative Business

Traditionally, higher education has predominantly been a government supported service. However, paradoxically, after it lost its elitist form and acquired an egalitarian character, government found it difficult to garner adequate finances for it. In most countries governments have started to withdraw from their commitment to higher education. The private interests are taking over, especially in the case of professional education. Today higher education has taken the form of business with commercial interests becoming important, if not paramount. This is true at both the national and international levels. In fact the significance of GATT lies in the growing internationalisation of higher education. The internationalisation of higher education has acquired a 21st century outlook being motivated by profit rather than by government policy. International higher education has become a lucrative business.

The ancient Indian universities, especially Nalanda, Varanasi and Kanji received a number of students from China, Tibet and Korea. For more than a century now Indian students have been going to western countries, mainly the United Kingdom, the United States and Australia for higher education and research.

There are only a few thousand international students in India, mainly from the developing countries of East Africa and South Asia. In contrast there are lakhs of students going abroad for higher education and research. Of this more than 50% go to the United States.

Commercial Presence

No foreign university has set up a campus at the tertiary education level. However, a large number of institutions are offering programmes through franchise, mainly at master's level in the professional areas of engineering and management. An encouraging aspect from the Indian view point is that the deemed universities are now permitted to open institutions/ campuses abroad. A few institutions have taken advantages of this and established campuses mainly in Gulf countries.

Movement of Natural Persons

Faculty members from universities and researchers have been moving to developed countries for temporary periods, or for permanent employment, on individual initiatives. The number is, however, not large. Flow in the opposite direction is still lesser.

Commercial Purpose

The Government is the principle provider of higher education in this country. However, the contribution of the private sector is also significant, especially in professional education. Hence, India cannot take recourse to Article 1-3 of GATT that allows exemption to the service provided by government without commercial purpose and without competition from private service suppliers.

Flexible System

The academic programmes in India are mostly not in consonance with educational system of the Western world. The academic structure is rigid, but the teaching and evaluation methodologies are outdated. Interaction with the academic institutions of the Western countries will require the implementation of a series of academic reform that will make the system flexible. The measures required include the adoption of a credit-based semester system with continuous internal evaluation, a cafeteria-type option to the students for the courses to be offered and facilities of credit transfer. Most of these have been introduced in the professional institutions and for professional programmes. But a majority of conventional universities are far behind, at least in respect of the non-professional programmes.

Issues and Options

India, being a member of WTO, is committed to the progressive Liberalisation of trade in commercial services, including the education services. India has to indentify within the framework of GATT its opportunities in the education sector, and particularly in higher education. It has also to recognise the inherent dangers in opening up the higher education sub-sector and prepare its schedule of commitments with limitations.

The potential of higher education services as an international trade is that in the incoming of the knowledge era, information and the ability to interpret information have assumed significance. It is estimated that for sustained natural development at least 20% of the population in the age group 18-20 years should have the benefit of higher education.

Exporting Education

India has a large higher education system with many institutions that provide good quality education. Therefore, it can benefit both economically and politically by exporting education, especially to the developing countries that have a substantial Indian Diaspora. Non-Resident Indians and persons of Indian origin will benefit from the export of Indian education and will contribute to its development. The disciplines that promise the most are engineering and technology, modern medicine, management, the emerging sciences, the performing arts and areas of study based on ancient knowledge (Ayurveda, Yoga). For the average NRI under-graduate education in liberal arts and sciences would also be welcome. India is one of the undisputed leaders in the field of information and communication technology and could provide training in this area globally. It is in India's interest to endorse the proposal of including Training Services and Educational Testing Services within GATT.

Consequences of GATT

The consequences of GATT from the Indian point of view are the most serious; the academics have led to the 'commoditisation' of education. Education has hitherto been looked upon as a public good with the commitment to the inculcation of values, to social services including community development, and to sustainable development through the creation and dissemination of knowledge. There is a real danger of these ideas becoming a thing of past. In the case of Indian higher education system commoditisation is bound to affect access and equity, funding and quality.

Languishing Public Sector – Dominant Private Sector

Quality higher education provided by reputed international providers will be accessible only to the privileged few who can pay for it. Access to education that can lead to decent employment will probably be limited to those with adequate financial resources. The GATT may lead to inequity and will cause for economic disparity and possibly for social tensions. There is a possibility of the government slowly withdrawing from its commitments to higher education seeing that the alternate mechanism of funding is gaining support from international sources. We may end up with an inefficient and languishing public sector and a dominant private sector. The effects of GATT on the quality of higher education could be both beneficial and detrimental. With quality education being provided by the respected international institutions, the standard of education provided by indigenous institutions should improve because of both interaction and competition. Some unscrupulous international providers offering off-the-shelf degrees on demand but at a cost; graduates of unpredictable quality would become available in the employment market.

Ranking of Colleges

The ranking of the colleges are based on the questionnaires filled in by teachers and students. It should be objective in nature. The National Assessment and Accreditation Council (NAAC) is the authority for placing the rating of colleges in the country. The magazines or newspapers have preconceived notion in assessing and publishing the ranking of the colleges in the country.

- Contouring the Business of Education
  India has the third largest higher education system in the world (after China and the USA) in terms of enrolment and has the largest number of higher education institutions, 693 universities and 35,500 affiliated colleges.
- Total enrolment forms only about 17% of the age group (17-23) out of the total population.

Lowest Rates of Public Expenditure

India also has one of the lowest rates of public expenditure on higher education per student at $406, which compares unfavourably with China ($2728), Brazil ($3986), Indonesia ($666) and Malaysia ($625).

Domestic Regulation

"There is a huge excess demand in India for quality higher education, which is being met by foreign campuses. The WTO service negotiations could be used (to create) a win-win situation for both sides since foreign universities would get a chance to expand their markets and Indian students can have affordable access to world class education," if only a balance could be struck between domestic regulation and providing adequate flexibility to such universities.

Public Private Participation

Available financing model with a mix of public and private participation has to be put in place. Cost recovery through suitable tuition fees and access to loans for students would help in alleviating the financial constraints faced by higher education institutions.

Foreign Education Provider in India – Issues

The issues to be taken into consideration before allowing the foreign education providers in India are:
- What are the areas of potential for expanding education services in India?
- Are we in a position to meet these demands internally?
- Should India allow FEPs in a phased manner after domestic reforms are in a place or not at all?
- What should be the way in which foreign educational institutions can deliver services in India through a joint venture or a wholly owned subsidiary?
- What should be the role of the UGC/AICTE and that of the regulatory body?

- Can much flexibility be given to foreign education providers in the areas of setting fees, admission, hiring of teachers, course and syllabi?
- How can the accreditation mechanism be strengthened?
- Is there a market for Indian educational services abroad?
- What type of educational services can be anticipated for exporting and spreading in the future?
- What are the barriers being faced by the Indian educational institutions in opening campuses abroad?

*****

Top Ten Universities in the World

Harvard University

- Harvard was founded in 1636, even before the US gained Independence.
- The university was named after its first benefactor, John Harvard. Veritas, the Roman goddess of truth, graces the University coat of arms.
- Only nine students attended the first class at the university.
- Top employers include Goldman Sachs, Google and Mckinsey.

University of Oxford

- Oxford is the oldest University in the English-speaking world.
- The university expanded after Henry II banned English students in Paris.
- The coat of arms bears a book which reads 'The Lord is my Light' in Latin.
- Over 140 nationalities are present in the current student body of 22,000. Top employers include NHS UK, United Nations and Credit Suisse.

University of Cambridge

- Cambridge is the seventh oldest university in the world. It was started by a group of Oxfordians.
- The university was formulated to maintain a strong emphasis on math and science subjects.
- Top employers include Bain Capital, Microsoft, Samsung, Yahoo and NASA.

Columbia University

- Columbia is the oldest university of higher learning in New York.
- The university currently has also seven overseas colleges.
- The annual Pulitzer Prize is still administered by the university.
- The university shield has been redesigned over ten times in 60 years.
- Top employers include New York Times, CNN and BBC.

Imperial College of London

- Imperial gained independence from London University only in 2007.
- The College forms a part of London's 'Golden Academic Triangle'.
- As of July 2011, the college had total endowments of over Rs. 6 billion.
- The crest seals 'Scientific knowledge is a safeguard of the empire' in Latin.
- Top employers include Merrill Lynch, Capital One and KPMG.

London School of Economics

- Founded in 1895, the university began issuing degrees only in 1902.
- LSE has produced over 20 Nobel Prize winners till date.
- Today the university has over 90,000 registered alumni members.

- Purple, black and gold are the official colours of the school and its crest.
- Top employers include BCG, Morgan Stanley, Lloyds and City group.

Massachusetts Institute of Technology

- MIT first admitted students in 1865 four years after its founding charter.
- Set up by scientist William Rogers, MIT is the best for technical studies.
- The current campus is 168 acres and employs over 77 Nobel laureates.
- The university seal bears the design of its publishing arm, MIT press.
- Top employers include IBM, General Motors Corporation and Cisco.

Stanford University

- Stanford was founded by tycoon Leland Stanford in memory of his son, who died of typhoid in 1891.
- Stanford has the largest number of award winners, the Noble Prize of the Computer World.
- Top employers include HP, Netflix, LinkedIn, Nokia, Apple and Sun Microsystems.

University of Manchester

- Part of the Russell Group, the university gained its royal charter in 1903.
- With over 39,000 students it is the largest single-site school in UK.
- It is also the only university in the country to have its own museum.
- The official crest bears the design of a serpent and the sun for wisdom.
- Top employers include Ogilvy and Mather, Pepsico and Santander.

Melbourne University

- Founded in 1852, Melbourne is the second oldest Australian University.
- It has over Rs. 65 billion endowments, the largest for any Australian School.
- The university is a member of Australia's 'Group of Eight' lobby.
- The coat of arms depicts victory with the motto: I shall grow freely.
- Top employers include OBS, Net App Australia and Ernst & Young.

Foreign Education Counselling

Foreign education counselling programmes really help make a good selection of a university to apply to. It also helps to access a vast database of students who had already availed the counselling service and were studying in foreign soil to get first hand feedback on various universities. Counsellors do help but it is not worth the hefty fees they charge to the order of rupees forty to fifty thousand. With a little Internet research one can avoid both the services and the bill. Reading up on foreign colleges is not rocket science. All you need to do is to plan ahead and remain focused. This will spare you from having to add a hefty counselling payment to your budget.

Online research is an excellent way to get whatever information you are looking for. All foreign universities have user-friendly websites that provide information about the course content in simple English, fee structures and application requirements. The information on these websites can be completely trusted. And if you are still confused then there are many student forums that will answer your queries for free. What education counsellors tend to do is actually nothing more than Internet research. Whatever may be your query regarding foreign study you may find answers from websites and you can avoid paying a hefty fee.

*****

5

The Need to Revamp Curricular Pattern

Curriculum Reconstruction

Curriculum Development

The curriculum of a country like its constitution reflects the ethos of the nation and its chief concerns and commitments. It prepares individuals of the country to be useful and productive citizens. In such a preparation, it is necessary to take into consideration the knowledge of how learning occurs and what factors facilitate learning, the learning and knowledge of socio-physiological aspects of the learning process that goes into curriculum development.

Curriculum is developed by cross currents of various factors and cross fertilisation of multifarious ideas and philosophies. All these constitute the foundation of curriculum planning. The emerging objectives, the philosophy of education, culture, learning theories and knowledge warrant changes in curriculum. Research studies are undertaken to determine significance and to inhibit unhealthy trends from influencing the curriculum. Curriculum development is known as curriculum reconstruction, curriculum reforms, curriculum renewals and so on.

Implementation Strategies

With a view to ensure the effectiveness of curriculum reconstruction, it is imperative to develop professional support for in-service training of teachers and supervisors, educational technology support for communication efficacy, infrastructure for teaching of work experience and institutional and organisational reform for increasing knowledge and skills.

The strategies for implementing a national curriculum are linked with:
— Reorientation of teachers and other educational personnel.
— Development of professional capability at all levels.
— Phased preparation, production and distribution of textbooks and other instructional materials.

In order to achieve these objectives, it would be necessary to decentralise the technical support system and to standardise the methodology for diffusion of programmes with reasonable flexibility. To ensure success of the process a good number of curricular/learning materials have to be brought out.

*****

Choosing the Right Career

Is it that only doctors and engineers make up the nation? It is a question which all students on the threshold of pursuing his higher studies ought to ask themselves.

As one grows up, he is not questioned as to what his ambition is. He is rather asked – what do you want to become – a doctor or an engineer? Thus in the most impressive years, these two areas of higher studies seem to be the only ones worth pursuing.

There are successful lawyers, teachers, businessmen, industrialists and a host of other professionals but still these two professionals are invested with the 'dubious halo' of 'professional careers'. Almost every student of the XII class considers an 'entry into the two branches of learning' as the be-all and end-all of their efforts.

This view often results in frustration, disappointments and untold mental strain on those who fail to make the grade or can't afford a 'payment seat' to the so called 'prestigious courses'. Often such a thinking is induced by the parents and the society. It is assumed that being an engineer/doctor means a 'cakewalk' in the struggle for existence. This is far from the truth. All engineers and doctors are not successful and there are numerous engineering graduates without a job to suit their taste and even doctors without practice.

Again, a desire to lead a very easy and comfortable life avoiding anything 'risky' or 'under the sun'- seems to point at 'medicine' and 'engineering' as the only source of a 'secure living'. Needless to say, this too is a fantasy and a very false notion. Is the country capable of employing all the engineers and doctors produced in thousands every year? They will have to look for alternative sources of self-employment.

The clamour for medicine and engineering has brought in its wake other serious problems. The bright ones opt only for such courses and consequently the other serious professions like education, agriculture suffer from lack of talent. This can have serious repercussions and shatter the very foundation of the educational system — especially if one has to put up with mediocre talent in the teaching profession. Third grades produce their grades and the process multiplies fast, especially in secondary education.

Career Counselling Centres

Doctors and engineers alone do not make up the nation. There are innumerable professions about which a career counselling centre can enlighten one on the various options available. Ideally, this facility should be available in schools to every student before entering the higher secondary level. This will enable the students to choose subjects that are most suitable to their aptitude and temperament. If the right career is chosen for the right reasons, they are sure to succeed.

Real Term Applications

The quality of higher and technical education has to be in real terms not only to make them relevant to our society as it is and as it is envisaged, but also to cater to the needs of competitive industry, indigenisation of technology and advanced science and technology including research and development therein and their applications.

Identification of some Areas with High Employment Potential

I. **Subjects in Science and Technology**
   Food Science and Quality Control
   Biotechnology
   Biological Techniques and Specimen preparation
   Seed Technology and Seed protection
   Fish and Fisheries
   Still photography and Audio and Video production
   Information Technology
   Aromatic and Medical plants
   Sericultural Management
   Plant Bio-technology
   Fish Production and Management
   Ecology and Environment
   Dairy Science
   Physiotherapy
   Forest Science
   Health/Rural Sanitary Programme
   Rural Health care; Public Health services
   Medical Lab Technology
   Soil Conservation and Water Management

II. **Subjects in Engineering and Technology**
   Computer Applications CAD, CAM etc
   Electronic Equipment Maintenance
   Electrical Equipment Maintenance
   Environment and Water Management
   Soil Conservation and Water Management
   Management of Land, Water and other resources
   Rural Infrastructural Engineering
   Agricultural machinery and Implements
   Post-harvest technology and Agro processing
   Non-Conventional Energy Management

Rural Water Treatment
Irrigation Engineering
Agricultural Mechanisation
Integrated Health
Leather and Animal Based Technology
Micro-level planning.

III. Subjects in Arts, Humanities and Social Sciences
Rural Handicrafts
Early Childhood Care and Education
Food and Nutrition
Rural Sociology
Tribal Development
Women Development
Rural Housing and Sanitation
Performing Arts and Awareness.
Transfer of Technology and Development
Village Crafts
Handlooms and Textiles
Printing
Commercial Arts
Electronic Media and Journalism

IV. Subjects in Commerce, Economics and Management
Principles and practices of Insurance
Computer Applications
Management of Delivery Systems
Micro-level planning
Hospitality Management
Rural Marketing
Agro-industrial Management
Tourism
Rural Cooperatives and Marketing
Rural Financial Services and Banking
Planning and promotion of Agro-based Enterprises
International Law and Word Trade Organisation (WTO)
Empowerment of Rural Women
Management of Micro Enterprises of Rural Women
Planning and Management of Self-Employment projects

Participation in Micro-level planning.
Community level Disaster Mitigation and Preparedness
Social Development and Human Rights
Gender Strategy for Sustainable Livelihood
Social Development in Rural Areas: Strategies and Programmes
Rural Informatics Management
Rural Water Supply and Healthcare Management

V. **Subjects Relevant to Tribal Areas and Arid Zones**
Agro Services
Domestic Animal Farming
Forestry and Wildlife Management
Non-Conventional Energy sources
Dry land Agriculture
Silvipasture
Sericulture
Integrated Development of Rain fed / Irrigated Watershed Areas
Waste land Utilisation and Management
Land Reclamation
Horticulture Techniques
Floriculture, Landscaping and Bee-keeping
Poultry Farming
Plant Protection
Processing of Agro-forest produce.
Mushroom Cultivation
Fish Processing Technology
Sheep and Goat Husbandry

*****

Designing of New Courses

The present system of confining the students to two languages and three subjects on an annual/bi-annual or tri-annual basis must yield a place to a semester and credit system involving many courses from which students can choose according to his or their interest, natural inclination, talents and the market requirements. Today we are compelling the students to take a set of optional subjects. No flexibility is given to the student. In other words, there is no freedom for the student to decide what he or she should pick and choose. We need a system where the students are given more power to determine what they have to study. Similarly, teachers who are proficient in certain subjects must be empowered to introduce new and more socially relevant courses depending on the latest information and social and economic needs.

Related Topics

The present annual system is an exercise in wasting valuable time. Those who want to major in particular subjects must take more course units in that subject, but their study will not be intensive enough if they do not study related topics in the course units offered in other departments.

A physics major must know not only chemistry but mathematics; he should also know something about economics and the mechanics of human body. All knowledge is related, every branch of knowledge is related to every other branch. A student majoring in law should also have knowledge about ethics, cultural history of the society, intellectual heritage and the economics of poverty or affluence.

Everything is Relevant to Everything Else

There will also be faculty advisors in each field of study — the pure and applied sciences, social sciences, arts and humanities. Even an engineering or medical student will have to take certain courses in history, social sciences, humanities and the arts. The basic principle is that everything is relevant to everything else. The interdisciplinary character of knowledge is recognised in this approach.

"The success of our new economic policy will depend greatly on the ability of Indian education to meet the challenges and enable Indian industry to take its policy to the mainstream of the global economy." (Pathak, 1992)

New Strategies

The emerging global economy can be strengthened only by an educated and enlightened population. Private as well as public initiative is required for realising the new objectives of education in the 21st century. But private and government management have to change their objectives of management and devise new strategies to make education universal and socially relevant.

New Educational Management System

Management of educational institutions in India has to be different from that of institutions in developed countries. The number of students going for higher education in the rich, less populated countries does not exceed a few hundred thousands, but we in India have to deal with millions. The total number of university students in India is more than the total population of several European countries. Many millions out of these aspirants for higher education are being turned down as unfit are cruel and unreal. One has to channelise the energies of these young people to productive and constructive activities without throwing cold water on their legitimate ambitions. Non-formal, flexible, self-development channels of higher education have to be provided for them.

Socially Relevant Education

The system of education and contents of education have to be differently conceived and organised so that more people can derive the benefit of socially relevant education without blindly imitating the systems followed in less populated countries. Good aspects of other systems may be adapted to Indian conditions.

Major Obstacles to Excellence in Education

To make education universal and socially relevant and to make it instruments of national development, three obstacles have to be removed — affiliation, inflexibility and centralisation. To achieve excellence in education, de-affiliation, autonomy and de-centralisation are inevitable.

Improve School Education

Higher education could be improved by improving the school education. The rush for higher education has to be streamlined by making high school outputs capable of entering the workforce with confidence and the required qualification. Job generation must be a priority of the government, business and industry must interact with government and educational institutions. College/University education must follow credit and semester systems so that even those who are in the workforce can receive higher education at their own pace at convenient locations and through different modes — regular, part-time institutional coaching, distance education with control classes and mass-mediated instructions.

Excellence and Social Relevance

The present system of affiliation has to cease. Colleges and other institutions of higher learning now affiliated to universities must be made financially, administratively and academically autonomous so that both teachers and the students will be empowered to pursue the path of excellence and social relevance. The whole system of education both at the lower level and at the higher levels must be made vocational and professional wherever possible. The institutions and individuals connected with teaching have to be made accountable to society. No particular stream of higher education is enough for a country of so many millions of aspirants. Drastic problems have to be solved through drastic and unprecedented methods. We must be prepared to approach the new challenges with an open mind instead of falling into conventional grooves and stagnating there.

*****

Some Key Emerging Career Fields

Information-Communication-Entertainment

The proliferation of satellite television channels and the entry of multinational media networks have resulted in a wide spectrum of job openings for directors, producers, engineers, technicians, journalists, script writers, researchers, computer, animators, performing artists, actors, anchorpersons, news readers, script editors, video-film editors, set designers, etc.

The popularity of the FM radio in the metros and the proliferation of radio stations have also made careers in broadcasting attractive. In our global economy Advertising and Public Relations is another expanding sector. A comparatively new field closely connected to advertising is Event Management. This involves conceptualising, planning, organising and finally executing events.

Design

Design has become the cornerstone of every enterprise today. The prospects in the field of design are vast and include product design, textile design, ceramic design, interior design, fashion design, fashion retailing, gem and jewelry design, visual merchandising and communication design. The communication design has three sub-divisions namely graphic design, animation film design and video programming.

Service Sector

With tourism as the fastest growing industry in the world, travel and tourism related business as well as the hotel and catering industry require suitably trained professionals. The recent expansion of the insurance sector has resulted in a demand for many more personnel in this field. Meanwhile, a more organised and quality conscious healthcare sector requires hospital health managers and administrators. This has been identified among top ten careers of the new millennium. What's more, Hospital Management courses are open to non-science graduates as well.

As the "Education for all" movement gains momentum and the world moves from industrial era to the knowledge era there is a great opportunity for professionals in Education and Training. More and more quality schools promoting excellence in the education are being set up. They require committed teachers and principals whose salaries are enviable. Last but not least, IT enabled 'outsourced' services like teleshopping centres, medical transcription, maintenance of data bases, insurance claim processing and records base for multinationals require thousands of English speaking, computer-literate graduates.

Business Management

Future organisations will depend on "entrepreneurial managers" for their profitability. An entrepreneur is an entrepreneur within an organisation. Another emerging trend is business consulting. Business Management encompasses a very wide occupational area.

Law

Globalisation has increased the demand for corporate lawyers. A potential area for specialisation is cyber law. The expansion of internet has created the demand for cyber lawyers. Another emerging and potential area for specialisation is genetic law. All legal systems need trained people who can understand and interpret it.

Apart from practicing as a civil lawyer or criminal lawyer, you can specialise in Business Law, Environmental Law, Patent Law, Tax Law, International Law, Real Estate Law, Labour Law, Cyber Law, Genetics Law, Human Right Law, etc.

NGO Sector

Developmental activities aimed at eradicating poverty are increasingly being undertaken by Non-Governmental Organisations (NGO). Hence, specialisations in Social Work, Anthropology, Human Rights, Gender, Development Economics and HRD have good job prospects in the social sector. Social work as a career requires specialised skills in optimising a community's development with people's participation and in catering to the most vulnerable sections in society such as elderly people, physical or mental handicaps and children at risk. Other areas of specialisation are labour welfare, industrial relations, family welfare, counselling services etc.

Social workers are also involved in conducting research studies, data evaluation, project formulation, training activities as well as programmes of awareness raising, gender sensitisation, etc.

Science and Technology

Information and Communication systems are broadening the scope, accelerating the pace and increasing the synergy of scientific discovery and technical applications. It has also led to great improvements in medicine and engineering. Hardware and software are developing at an unprecedented pace. The biotechnology frontier, especially developments in the field of genetics have already achieved significant breakthroughs in agriculture and human healthcare. Biotechnology could eventually eliminate food shortages improve health and life expectancy. Bioinformatics — the convergence of telematics and micro-genetics will be the basis for a major jump in evaluation. The biotechnology sector will be the driving force of the markets. Herein lies a vast career opportunity.

Some other key areas of growth are:
- Robotics
- Nanotechnology
- Neuroscience
- Cognitive Science
- Space Research
- Environmental Science
- Agriculture
- E-governance
- Self-employment and entrepreneurship

Finally, what is important is to rise above all stereotypes and select a career that brings out your creative best. This will result in job satisfaction and career growth.

IIM-Bangalore Selection Criteria

IIM-Bangalore is the first B-school to go to the public with the details of their admission procedure. So, the aspiring managers can be able to chart out the marks that they will require to score at various stages to make it to the elite institution.

The Score

CAT	– 20
Class X Marks	– 15
Class XII Marks	– 10
Bachelor's degree	– 15
Work experience	– 5
G.D. Score	– 5
GDSC Score	– 5
Personal Interview	– 20

Besides, little did many know that the Bangalore Campus also scored students on their verbal English skills during the group discussions.

The marks are set aside for language under the head — GD Summary Content (GDSC). This component is in addition to the usual Group Discussion and Personal Interview (PI). Including English here obviously highlights the need to create orally smart managers as much as to reiterate the importance of English to rural students and to policy makers.

IIM-B has developed admission process based on academic performance (School, High School and graduate), CAT score, GD/PI and prior work experience. The selection criteria and weightage given several parameters are based on data from previous cycles as well as inputs from the IIM-B faculty and various stakeholders.

Entry into the B-school involves a two-phase selection process. The first phase applies to all eligible candidates who appear for CAT to determine those qualifying candidates who will be called for GDPI. During the GDPI, two faculty members will evaluate each qualifying student on his/her performance in the group discussion, the summary of group discussion and a personal interview. For those with work experience, each interviewer will evaluate the quality and relevance of job experience. These scores in addition to the pre-GDPI selection parameters will be used cumulatively in the second and final phase of selection.

IIT-JEE Entrance Examination

For the 5500 odd seats across nine institutions of IIT-JEE, around 300000 students are pitted for admission, most of these students are considered India's crème de la crème, but one mark short and you are out of the race. In IIT-JEE, that is the margin between success and failure. So what can you do to make it to the finishing line? Simple, plan and strategise.

Syllabus for IIT Entrance Test and coaching

The syllabus is the same as prescribed in the NCERT curriculum (Class XI and XII). So don't move on to your resource book until you have covered the entire NCERT syllabus quite thoroughly. And take extra coaching and take the mock tests that all coaching institutes conduct. While choosing an institute don't be swayed by the institute's proclaimed "success List". There is a lot of overlap and some lists are fabricated.

Other than IIT

Besides the IITs, JEE is also an entrance examination for IT - BHU and ISM-Dhanbad as also the Indian Institute of Science Education and Research at Kolkata, Pune and Kohali and the Indian Institute of Space Science and Technology. But if you don't get admission into any of these, try institutes which accept the IIT-JEE ranks.

You can also appear for the AIEEE and Delhi College of Engineering and Nethaji Subhas Institute of Technology's entrance test. The level of these tests is simpler than IIT-JEE.

Practising for IIT Entrance

The time is ideal for joining a test series programme at any of the reputed coaching institutes, preferably one where the maximum number of students are appearing. This will help in building a proper examination temperament. Practising quality problems are more important than trying to solve a huge pile of simpler problems. Try to maximise your performance at the mock tests. This means keeping tight tabs on your step-by-step progress. Also time your work. Try to set a study routine which aligns with the examination schedule. Since the IIT-JEE mains start at 8.00 AM and end at 5.30 PM your study routine (call it biorhythm) should be so synchronised that you are most alert during this time of the day.

Final Ranking

Don't ignore chemistry, thinking it's the easiest of the three subjects. It can make a world of difference to your final ranking and you should not insist on benchmarking your performance with fellow students. Instead, try to master the fundamentals, practise and acquaint yourself thoroughly with your grey areas. That should more than suffice. In a nut shell, in an exam like the IIT-JEE, use your grey cells to superimpose your grey areas and you will win the game.

*****

Teacher Training For Higher Education

The new National policy on Education envisages the proper training of teachers as one of the vital requirements to impart necessary dynamism to the higher education system. In view of the need for a well-conceived and designed policy and planning for higher education staff development, there are some basic parameters. The entire system can be dovetailed into a three-tier programme. There should be one for staff development in higher education, to cater to the requirements of the central universities and institutions, regional centres for state universities, as well as colleges and institutions in the respective regions. Further, there must be another staff college at the national level to train the trainers working at the national and regional training centers.

National Staff Development Centre

The national staff development centre, can function in the different related areas of training and staff development, teaching and academic problems in higher education, management and administrative problems in the institutions of higher learning including regional centres for staff development.

In higher education, the centre can offer its own programmes as well as respond to requests for advice and assistance on the problems affecting institutional behaviour and performance. Its own programme will include organisation of pre-service training, refresher courses for serving teachers, orientation programmes, seminars, workshops, symposia and summer institutes. Besides providing consultation in training and management development programmes have to ensure effectiveness of teaching in higher education vis-à-vis the working world outside higher education.

The regional centres will act similarly in their respective zones. The training institute at the national level will impart updated training and guidance.

Training Curricula

Training curricula at the national centre, the regional centres and the master trainer centre should invariably include courses on teaching methodologies, educational psychology, research and reference methodologies, case studies, seminars and symposia, group discussions, interdisciplinary approach, interaction with the public, production and use of modern teaching aides and the like. These centres should also act as catalysts to improve the existing system to accord teachers a proper economic and social status, opportunities for professional and career development, motivation, initiatives for innovation and creative work, proper orientation in concept, techniques and value system to fulfill their role, responsibilities and obligations. Last but not least, with the tremendous increase in budgetary provision for education, the staff development centres must be adequately funded and staffed.

Co-ordination with Industries

A leading industrialist states, "In India we are now reaching a sort of plateau where Indian industries having acquired a certain degree of maturity, finds itself handicapped that it has not built up a sufficient support mechanism to take it forward on its own." This support mechanism should come from our technical institutions. For that there should be proper collaboration between industry and engineering colleges. The executives can be sent to engineering colleges as teachers in exchange for some of the teachers. It is better if all professional colleges are declared residential institutions with provision for the staff to stay in the campus.

Orientation Programme for Teachers

A teacher is the pivot of the entire educational system and he is the main catalytic agent for introducing desirable changes in the teaching-learning process. Explosion of knowledge in all fields or subjects areas has posed a great problem to teachers of nearly every discipline. The use of modern media, methods and materials constituting educational technology can help teachers not only to improve their teaching skills, but also to upgrade their knowledge in the respective fields. Teachers have to be provided with systematic and well-organised orientation programmes with different objectives and approaches.

The objectives of Academic Staff Orientation Courses are to enable lecturers to:-

- Understand the significance of education in general, and higher education in particular, in the Global Indian Context.
- Understand the linkages between education and economic and socio-cultural development with particular reference to the Indian Polity where secularism and egalitarianism are the basic tenets of society.
- Understand the role of a college/university teacher in the national goal of achieving a secular egalitarian society.
- Acquire and improve basic skill of teaching at the college/university level.
- Be aware of the development in his subject.
- Understand the organisation and management of a college/university and to perceive the role of a teacher in the total system.
- Utilise opportunities for the development of personality initiative and creativity.

The Orientation and Refresher Courses should provide for teaching methodologies, pedagogy, educational psychology, etc., and latest developments in various disciplines. The refresher courses should be organised for serving teachers at least once in 5 years. The Orientation Programme will work as an induction course for the new entrants to cater to the needs of acquiring adequate teaching skills, developing interests and attitudes towards their own provision.

Instruction in Design Practice

The role of the instructor in design course is essentially advisory and consultative by nature. The instructor should be free to discuss the various ideas and questions presented by the students. The discussion is more effective in smaller groups (e.g. a design team of three students); so that all the students can participate. The students should also be made aware through the discussions that even the smallest details can be a design problem by itself with more than one possible solution. As far as possible the students must be encouraged to arrive at decisions about these details by themselves. Standard solutions should not be imposed on them straight away.

Teacher Training and New Communication Technology

To obviate the difficulties experienced by the teacher in a class and to render the instrumental process all the more effective, the latest communication technology may be availed of, which is not possible if the teacher is not trained in the media. The radio and television may be excluded from our purview since they are not part of classroom set-up nor can be included effectively in its scenario. But the video and audio cassettes can be made use of to reinforce the traditional mode of teaching and even refashion it. The teacher has to learn the basic grammar of video production since it is he who has to transform the purely linguistic mode of expression into what is live and visual. Moreover, he has to work in close collaboration with the producer in order that a realised educational image overwhelms everything else, for which the teacher has to utilise the findings of education technology.

Teacher–Student Contacts (Conference Method)

The reward of the conference method is undoubtedly tremendous. With this new method, there is a marked increase in the effectiveness of our teaching. First of all, simply in terms of quality one can give much more fieldwork per minute orally than has to write it all out. The teacher can observe if the student assimilates his/her comments examining the facial expression of the student.

Another plus point in this method makes the evaluation work more effective, efficient and productive, for it sets a higher level of concentration. When the student is right in front, the teacher's mind cannot wander.

Thirdly, this conference method demystifies for the students the evaluation process. Under achievers can no longer shrug of their poor performance by making the teacher a scapegoat, since the teacher skillfully shares the ongoing evaluation process with them.

College Days - The Formative Period of Students

It is that phase when students have lasting influences that shape their development. They discover who they are and what they will become. When a student looks at the way his teachers are functioning, he is bound to follow suit. A change should thus come about so that the student models his future on good lines. And this will have to come from the teaching community who should not hesitate to put in hard work. Constructive teaching is helpful in building up the character of the students. Syllabic lessons are not the only thing that a teacher should concentrate on. Let us request the teaching community to do something different from others. They should strive for better world.

Indian Languages as Media of Higher Education

The Union and State Governments together have taken initiative to change the medium of higher education from English to Indian languages. It was expected that such a change would provide (i) students from rural and backward areas, who are supposed to be not so good in English, to get an opportunity for higher education and (ii) would strengthen the growth of Indian languages. It was also felt that a change in the medium of instruction would not be possible so long as relevant books and other materials in the new medium were not available. The Union government took initiative in 1961 to fix standard for and undertake the preparation of technical terminology in Indian languages through the Commission for Scientific and Technical Terminology.

University Level Books

The government also encouraged agencies like the UGC, the National Book Trust and the Council for Scientific and Industrial Research (CSIR), Indian Council for Agricultural Research (ICAR), etc., to prepare university level books in science and humanities by translation and commissioning original writing in Indian languages.

It is argued in pro-change circles that such education can be easily given in any Indian languages if technical terms involved here could be suitably rendered and translated in that language.

Attitudes are changed not as easily by mere propaganda as by results. If we can produce better, both content and print wise, cheaper and more books and related material in our languages keeping priority areas in view with as little translation as necessary, we may find more teachers and students using more of these languages than they do now.

The methodologies that have succeeded in countries like Japan, China, Russia and Europe in the matter of adopting vernacular languages for technical education are worth examining.

Information Technology for Teaching and Learning

Information technology made up of computer communication technology has been affecting every walk of our life. The effect of this technology on education, in particular teaching and learning methods are:
- It is widening the age range of participants in formal education. This is due to the need for re-education and re-training as the information is increasing at a rapid rate.

- Need for stimulating real life experience can easily be achieved by computer communication technology.
- Teaching and learning aspects can no longer be institutionalised in a four-walled structure. There is a continuously diminishing boundary for education and entertainment, education and work, and even education and business.
- Education may be progressively distanced from the formal educational structures now used and new options, approaches, entities and structures may be opened up.
- Institutions of higher education have long assigned part of their function to the production of such educational tools. For e.g., textbooks, course of outlines, audio-visual materials, etc. This may be broadened to include a more deliberate allocation of facilities and time to provide content packages required for incorporation within the enlarged media spectrum for education.

Mass Education Media

A global transformation of human affairs is beginning, one in which human information handling are being simplified much as muscular power was in the past. The emergence of interactive video-computer systems, cheap microprocessor programmes for a specific institutional procedure and increasing interest in distance education schemes presage a radical shift to home and job based education. Thus one can see that information technology can be utilised to enrich for individual learners as well as mass education media. One of the major means of education is the video-cassette recorder during the course of a conference. Video-conferencing provides a kind of vibrant, real life, fully projected natural context of participants. It can be direct line telecast and it can also be a recorded cassette. It is the most effective form of simulating a kind of conference learning.

Computer Assisted Learning (CAL)

Recent developments in computer-assisted learning (CAL) make it possible to provide the student with greater control over the learning process. It helps the learner to pace and time his/her learning to his own comprehension, at his/her terminal. Computer-based learning systems increase educational flexibility eliminates duplication of effort, cuts down on overheads and increase learner motivation. Such systems enable teachers to write the contents of their programmes and to define in advance the interaction to take place. This has been made possible by the development of authored languages-software which allows the teacher to programme the system to meet the needs of individual learner (or group of learners) without the need for any programming expertise on the teacher's part.

Interactive video is a combination of two technologies i.e., optical video disc system and microcomputers. The essence of interactive video is that it is a simple system and one need not have the problem of learning about computer techniques.

Television as an Educational Medium

Television as an educational medium allows for distance-independent mass delivering of tailor-made programmes. TV also supplements the development of cognitive skills. In a sense, TV helps avoiding teacher-duplication. Yet, it remains interpersonal though mediated through the TV. In addition, recorded TV programmes invest ability for interaction and feedback facilities. Cable TV is a fast growing medium which has tremendous potential. It increases the number of broadcasting channels potentially available to educators. It also helps intensive- target specific audience oriented telecasting. The talk-back TV contains one-way telecasting fitted with the telephone-hook ups for audience to converse with the telecasters. Show-scan TV is a technique which uses inexpensive audio-channels to transmit visual information.

Tele conferencing is an interactive personal contact mediated by telecommunication system. It has been identified in the following four modes:
- Computer conferencing
- Audio teleconferencing
- Audio graphics and
- Video teleconferencing

Computer-Conferencing

Computer-conferencing is a kind of voiceless transaction. It is based on the display of interaction on the screen. Audio-teleconferencing is a voice only communication linked by telephone lines. Audiographics use the ordinary telephone line to transmit information other than speech. This allows the voice element to be enriched with written, printed or graphic materials.

Interaction between Learner and Teacher

Information technology has extended interactive facilities between a learner and his teacher. It has enabled the simulation of a classroom environment to be free from space and time. It is a very valuable aid for a learner to augment his adaptability to his own learning capabilities and choice. One can learn a technique, a language, or a theory at any time of his choice, at his own speed and mood. Thus education becomes open and compatible.

Faculty Vacancies

The number of technical institutions in India, imparting education and research skills in engineering and technology has risen to 1475 with an annual intake of nearly 5,00,000 in 2006 as per AICTE. The approved intake for 2011-12 at the undergraduate level as per AICTE is 10.66 lakhs. Based on the established AICTE norms of student teacher ratio 1:15 and the cadre ratio 1:2:6 for professors, readers and lecturers. The total shortage of teaching staff is over 40,000 and the shortage in the different cadres is professors—4531, readers—9,063 and lecturers—27,187. The shortage of PhDs exceeds 30,000 while the short fall at the master's level is over 24,000. This is the picture of India as a whole.

Shortage of Teachers in Engineering Colleges

In many engineering colleges all over India the dearth of teaching staff is a burning problem. This is creating an unstable position which could lead to a rapid collapse in supply of really qualified engineers. It is obvious that teaching advanced technical subjects to a mass at the college level, is a most difficult job. It requires high concentration and hard work. But teachers with good experience require little preparation and this makes them lazy and they neglect upgradation and refresher courses; unless they are involved in some research or commercial activities.

The status of teachers in engineering colleges during the fifties and sixties was far better. Their pay was comparatively good. Hence, it was possible at that time to attract the best talent for this profession. During that initial period, the lecturers got promoted to higher cadres in short duration. Due to tough competition, the right recruitment norms were formulated to maintain the standard of selection.

Salary and Promotion

In these days, the public sector companies and commercial organisations have increased the salaries of their executives. But the increase in salaries of teaching community especially in the engineering colleges has been nominal. The monthly earnings of persons holding similar degrees and experience are not comparable at all. Added to this, is the tragedy of very limited promotion opportunities in the teaching profession. Those who take up the teaching posts now are therefore often not best teachers and they also wait for the earliest opportunity to quit. The primary factor that governs job satisfaction is money. Hence, special consideration has to be given while fixing the pay scales of teaching staff in engineering faculties. These scales should compensate all other perks that engineers are able to get in companies. The existing pattern of promotion requires a complete change. Already the 13/15 year automatic promotion scheme has been implemented in some engineering colleges. This can be standardised throughout India and by creating more cadres it is possible to give raise for every three or four years of service in a lower cadre.

Importance to Qualification

Nowadays the engineering faculties are maintained by inducing temporary and lesser qualified personal. This again can be standardised as permanent posts with firm regulations for their eligibility. Facilities should be extended to them to complete their post-graduation, either part-time or by research. The wage pattern of teachers should strictly depend on their qualification. Moreover, for every additional qualification and paper publication extra increments should be given to encourage their work. The heads of the institution and departments should have administrative qualification.

*****

Remodeling Classroom Instruction

Every well-meaning educator would agree that the main aim of classroom instruction is to enable the students to learn at their own pace — the pace suitable to one's potential and maturity. But, on the contrary, the same standards are fixed for all students irrespective of their capacities, interests and paces of learning. Consequently many students fail to reach a level of achievement they are capable of. The main method of teaching in our country is the lecture method, which has many drawbacks. The lecture method is teacher-centered and teacher-based instructional model and many students are unable to proceed at the pace of the teacher and start lacking in studies. Moreover, in a lecturing situation, hardly any questions are asked by the students and it gives a facile impression of learning that is taking place. According to Skinner, "Frequently so much new material is hurled at the students within a brief time that assimilation and mastery becomes difficult. As a consequence, what was unknown in the beginning becomes a mass of confusion."

Remodeling (Splitting text into small units)

The implementation of self-paced instruction does not entail huge new expenditures, nor does it need new text and technology. It just requires to reorganise the subject matter into small units. The student is allowed to interact with the study unit at his own rate of learning, seek the individual guidance when needed and demonstrate his mastery over the unit by taking a readiness test. The student is not allowed to go on to the next unit until he has consolidated his present unit. Moreover, the failure on the readiness test is not counted against the student; rather he is given the remedial and corrective instruction to overcome his learning deficiencies.

To implement the self-paced instruction, the teacher must select a standard text book and split it into small units and prepare a cyclostyled commentary on every unit, listing the specific objectives and a set of self-testing exercises for each unit. The self-pace instruction is carried out in the following steps.
- Specification of behavioural objectives
- Presentation of learning sequence in the study unit
- Interaction with the study unit, fast learners and teacher
- Administration of readiness test

If the test is passed, the student goes on to the next unit. If the test is not passed, the student is given the individual remedial guidance by the fast learners and the teacher, and is followed by a retest.

Thus, the self-paced instruction is helpful in the initial detection and correction of subject deficiencies. Also it serves the purpose of preventing more serious problems in learning. The self-paced instruction makes learning a process of active seeking rather than passive absorbing.

*****

Quality Improvement in Teaching

Introduction

Improving quality of teaching is (or should be) an important goal of any professor in an educational institution. Total Quality Management (TQM), which is a widely accepted concept in business organisations, could be used as a means to achieve this goal. TQM is a management philosophy that solicits participation and commitment from all levels of employees to improve quality of goods and services that customers of the organisation needs. TQM is not a onetime activity; rather, it endeavors to continuously improve quality. "Employee participation and commitment" and "customer focus" form the foundation of the TQM concept. Based on this foundation are built the key themes of TQM which include the quality of "design", the quality of "output" and the quality of "process" to meet customer needs. In this chapter, we will discuss design, output and process as they relate to the goal of "teaching" in higher education.

Educational System

An educational system is similar to any other operating system consisting of a set of input resources which go through a transformation process to produce a set of outputs. However, the following important characteristics of an educational system distinguish it from any other systems:
- There are inadequacies in the current measurement system of inputs and outputs.
- The interrelationships among different activities in the transformation process are not clearly understood.
- Incentives and reward structures are not clearly defined.
- The decision making process is diffused and limits managerial control.
- There are no industry standards and norms.

Briefly, the outputs, input resources and the transformation process of an educational institution include the following:

Outputs
The outputs are the educated people, research findings and service to the community.

Input Resources
The resources of an educational institution include, but are not limited to students, faculty, staff, administrators and other

personnel, financial support, library, computing and laboratory facilities, recreational facilities, student housing, buildings and other physical facilities.

Transformation Process

The transformation process in an educational institution consists of activities performed to disseminate knowledge, to conduct research and to provide community service. The transformation process also specifies the "interactions" among the input resources.

Sub-systems

The educational system could be viewed as consisting of several administrative and academic subsystems. These include admissions, registration and records, financial aid, purchasing, teaching and research, etc.

TQM in Teaching

Teaching as a subsystem, within the larger system of higher education, consists of its own sets of input resources, outputs and the process. To put it in the context of TQM, we have to identify "customers" of teaching and the "quality" of teaching desired by these customers. Once this is done, an appropriate transformation process could be designed.

Customers and Their Expectations

Students are generally considered to be the customers of "teaching." The expectations of students from teachers include more knowledge in their chosen field of study, good grades, and acquisition of diplomas and degrees. However, there are several other customers of "teaching" who include the employers of graduating students, graduate schools, professors, and the society at large. From the view point of these customers, students could be viewed as "input" to the educational system. The expectations of these customers from an educational system are as follows:

Employers

Employers want our universities to produce well-qualified and trained graduates who could work efficiently and effectively in the jobs for which they have been hired.

Graduate Schools

Graduate schools require that students who are admitted into their programs possess enough knowledge, skills and preparation to take up higher studies.

Professors

A professor teaching a particular class requires that students have acquired appropriate background in the requisite courses.

Society

Society wants our universities to produce educated and responsible citizens. The quality of teaching would change with a change in the mix of input resources. A different teacher, a different mix of students, a different classroom and the availability of computers would make a difference in the quality of output. Here, we are not establishing quality objectives of any individual course or a program of study or passing judgement on different approaches for teaching. Rather, the objective is to propose that the systems approach is one of the effective ways to analyse and improve the quality of teaching.

House of Quality

The metaphor used here to present the basic concepts and principles associated with total quality is the House of Quality. As in a well-built house, the major components of the House of Quality are:
- the roof, or superstructure, consisting of the social, technical, and management systems
- the four pillars of customer satisfaction, continuous improvement, speaking with facts, and respect for people
- the foundation of four managerial levels-strategy, process, project, and task management; and
- the four cornerstones of mission, vision, values, and goals and objectives.

As in building any house, the plans must be developed first, usually by experienced individuals working together as a team. Once the plans are approved, construction (implementation) can begin.

Pillars of Quality

Total quality management in any organisation is supported by four driving forces, or pillars, that move the organisation towards the full application of quality services. The four pillars of the House of Quality are customer service, continuous improvement, processes and facts, and respect for people. All are distinct, but equal in potential strength. All the four must be addressed; minimising any one weakens the others. By not addressing one, the entire House of Quality will fall.

Serving the Customer (The First Pillar)

The very notion of having customers is alien to most campuses. Considering students as customers is perceived by many in the faculty as relegating themselves to the position of being employees. The traditional role of faculty is threatened when defining the academic role within the framework of its impact upon the end user. Within this framework, the student (the customer) is seen as a partner in developing and delivering quality education (the product or service). To many a faculty, this is anathema to the historic, traditional academic role as the purveyor of knowledge.

Mission and Vision (Second Pillar)

Continuous improvement is both a commitment (continuous quality improvement or CQI) and a process (continuous process improvement or CPI). The Japanese word for this second pillar is Kaizen and is, according to Imai, the single most important concept in Japanese management. The commitment to quality is initiated with a statement of dedication to a shared mission and vision and the empowerment of all participants to incrementally move towards the vision. The process of improvement is accomplished through the initiation of small, short-term projects and tasks throughout the organisation which collectively are driven towards achievement of the long-term vision and mission. Both are necessary; one cannot be done without the other.

Plan, Do, Check and Act (PDCA)

Continuous improvement is dependent on two elements: learning the appropriate processes, tools, and skills and practising these new found skills on small achievable projects. The process for continuous improvement, first advanced many years ago by Shewhart and implemented by Deming, is Plan, Do, Check, and Act (PDCA), a never-ending cycle of improvement that occurs in all phases of the organisation (e.g., admissions, registration, student affairs, academic programming, maintenance, etc.). While no rigid rules are required to carry out the process, the general framework of each step can be described.

Respect for People (Fourth Pillar)

For whom does one works? No one works just for the customers and the college or university (in that order, preferably). In the end, each individual works for himself or herself, trying to create a meaningful and satisfying life in the best way possible. The output of colleges and universities is not only teaching, service, and research. It also encompasses the quality of life of everyone who works in, or is affected by, the college or university. Fortunately, quality of output goes hand-in-hand with quality of work. The only way total quality will be attained is through total commitment and participation.

Value-added Resource

Every employee must be fully developed and involved. The result will be an empowered individual—a value-added resource, with loyalty to the program, the team, and the entire college or university. Respect for people often boils down to such simple things as:
- Creating a sense of purpose in the workplace so that people are motivated to do their best.

- Keeping people informed and involved, and showing them how they are a part of the bigger picture.
- Educating and developing people so that each individual is the best that he or she can be at what they do.
- Helping people communicate well so that they can perform their jobs with peak effectiveness.
- Delegating responsibility and authority downward so that people are not just doing what they are told, but are taking the initiative and try to make things work better.

It is not enough just to go through the motions. These behaviours work well when they are part of a genuine attitude of respect and caring for other people. Managers who do not have this attitude of respect and caring cannot pretend for very long that they do.

Deming Principle 8
Drive out fear, so that everyone can work effectively for the college or university. Create an environment in which people are encouraged to speak freely.

Deming Principle 9
Break down barriers between departments and programs and between faculty, administration, staff, and students. Those involved in teaching, research (faculty and institutional), student services, food service, accounting, academic affairs, etc., must work as a team (work teams and cross teams). Develop strategies for increasing the cooperation among groups and individuals.

Second, there is a difference between leadership and management (often still referred to as administration in higher education). Bart Giamatti, former president of Yale and former baseball commissioner, made it clear that he believes that this distinction applies to universities.

Management has the capacity to handle multiple problems, neutralise various constituencies, motivate personnel; in a college or a university it means hitting, as well, the actual budget at break-even. Leadership, on the other hand, is essentially a moral act, not—as in most management—an essentially protective act. It is the assertion of a vision, not simply the exercise of style; the moral courage to assert a vision of the institution for the future and the intellectual energy to persuade the community or the culture of the wisdom and validity of the vision. It is to make the vision practical and compelling.

Bennis summarised the differences between the management and the leadership:

Manager	Leader
Administers	Innovates
Is a copy	Is an original
Maintains	Develops
Focuses on systems and structure	Focuses on people
Relies on control	Inspires trust
Has short-range view	Has long-range perspective
Asks how and when	Asks what and why
Has an eye on bottom line	Has an eye on the horizon
Imitates	Originates
Accepts status quo	Challenges status quo
Classic good soldier	Own person
Does things right	Does the right thing

Both management and leadership are necessary to produce an effective, efficient organisation. Most managers have at least some leadership skills, and most leaders have some management skills. The focus in this chapter is on leadership, because it takes leadership to introduce the principles of quality and sustain the practice of quality management in an organisation.

Help students to achieve their full potential
- Improvement recognition for teaching, academic advising, and student–faculty interaction.
- Improve students' experiences in living groups, orientation, peer relationships, academic learning/assistance centers.

Expand research and artistic creativity
- Recruit and support faculty, staff, and students of high research, artistic capability.
- Improve research facilities and equipment.

Attract, develop, retain excellent faculty and staff
- Bring faculty salaries to competitive levels
- Expand facilities and program supports as required for a major teaching and research university.

Expand opportunities for minorities, females, the disadvantaged, etc.
- Intensify recruitment of women and people of colour to faculty positions in which they are under-represented
- Evaluate classified employment processes to increase personnel from under-represented groups; seek external policy change wherever necessary.

Increase enrolments of outstanding students
- Improve the quality and rigour of academic programs.
- Raise undergraduate admission standards.

Sharpen the university's international focus
- Strengthen the international dimensions of the curriculum.
- Expand the international perspective of faculty.

Improve facilities and equipment
- Give fund-raising priority first to library expansion, second to visual and performing arts instructional facilities, third to computer science facilities.
- Upgrade instructional laboratory facilities and equipment.

Teachers' Performance Appraisal

In the spirit of nurturing autonomy with accountability, all higher education institutions should adopt the practice of performance appraisal of teachers initiated through self appraisal based on objective parameters. Good teaching follows from good research. Therefore, there should be adequate weightage for research work based on quantifiable parameters in performance appraisal of the faculty. Innovations in teaching such as use of new technologies in creating a conducive learning environment should also be factored in. Outcome of performance appraisal should be used by the system for the purpose of merit based promotions and other incentives and awards. Once the institutions adopt objective and transparent procedure for promotions, the current practice of sending observers on behalf of the statutory bodies in the selection committees would be obviated. A system of recognising good teachers in terms of their academic contribution should be introduced at the University, State and National level.

*****

Improving University Teaching

Training of university teachers for faculty development is an institutional responsibility. At present this is done through voluntary exchange of ideas at meetings and conferences than through formal programmes of courses.

Proper Introductory Training

Newly recruited and probationary university teachers need to be trained at least at the introductory level in teaching evaluation techniques, although they have already acquired higher academic qualifications such as M.Phil and Ph.D. This is because there have been sound and valid educational theories and principles that cannot be practiced by a young teacher without proper training in them.

Internal and External Training

The efficiency of a junior teacher in the university can be improved in two ways; first, through the internal training methods organised by the more experienced and efficient teachers of the same faculty to which junior teachers belong. Secondly, through the external training methods organised by the teacher-educators belonging to the faculty of Education in the same university.

Sharing the Classes

The newly-recruited teacher can develop competence in instruction and assessment skills (instructional development) and competence in subject matter (professional development) by sharing the classes with more efficient teachers. The practice of teaching under the guidance of the competent teachers in a real teaching situation will enormously improve the instructional abilities of the junior teacher.

Self-Instructional Modules

It is also possible to train the junior teachers with 'modules'. A module is a self-instructional package designed to achieve a specific objective. It is pre-designed and self-contained and aims at developing professional skills of some immediate need. Each module stresses the link between the training situation and the actual teaching situation. Such packages should be suitably designed by the experienced and efficient teachers in order to improve a specific instructional skill of the junior teachers.

Peer Teaching Method

The new member of the faculty can train himself from "peer teaching" – a teaching method in which colleagues learn lecturing techniques from one another, rather than from 'experts' or 'specialists' in educational methods and practices. This form of training should be held in the normal classroom situation. Peer teaching method gives opportunity for the junior teachers to observe, reflect on, self-review and improve their own methods of teaching.

Teaching and Teaching Techniques

The faculty of Education in a university should take the lead in organising introductory training programmes for newly recruited teachers in other disciplines. The programme may be general in nature and relatively short in duration emphasising on teaching and teaching techniques rather than on the elaborate theories of teaching and learning.

Weekly or Monthly Seminars

The Faculty of Education can also conduct weekly or monthly seminars for groups of junior teachers with a common teaching interest so that they can have orientation to the teaching profession.

In the seminars, the emphasis should be on the improvement of lecturing techniques in the development of skills in organising and conducting classes, the practice of assessment methods and knowledge of effective use of audio-visual aids. The methods used for training must be extended to lecturing and group discussions.

For the teachers who have gained some experience in teaching methods and require training beyond introductory level, advanced and specialised part-time or full-time courses on University pedagogy can be offered.

Effective Teaching

Whether teaching is an art or a science, to be an effective teacher one must develop certain attitudes and qualities which make teaching effective.

The task of a teacher today, is for more difficult than it was a few decades ago. The tremendous explosion of knowledge, development of teaching technology and the availability of different channels of education like TV and Video and Audio lessons have on the one hand provided opportunities which were hitherto not available for effective teaching and on the other hand increased the challenges and responsibilities of the teacher. In the past when the teacher was the main source of knowledge he could afford to be static and lethargic but in the new context such teachers would in no time become targets as dustbins as of the students.

Effective Lectures

A lecture is an exposition of a given subject delivered before an audience for the purpose of instruction. The word lecture comes from the Latin word 'to read'. In medieval universities, the professor lectured to his students from notes. In principle, a lecture is a summary of information organised to give emphasis, in sights, applications and associations that students are unlikely to obtain from text books and also to convey a new or specialised information to supplement what the students can obtain from other sources.

Insights and Interpretations

One of the unique advantages of lecturers is that they can communicate the intrinsic interest of the subject matter. The obvious enthusiasm of lecturers stimulates the students' interest and the interested people stay alert, tend to learn more and understand better. It is therefore in everyone's interest that lecturers have to be extremely enthusiastic in their style. In a lecture it is possible to deal with material that is not available to the audience. Materials needed for a lecturer should be organised in a special way to bring out his or her own insights and interpretations to make conclusions that are interesting. The presentation can be repaid, compared to books and papers and more simplified.

Active Participation

The lecturer must take steps to keep the audience active and participating and keep the students more active. There are many ways in which this can be done, such as asking questions, showing a slide, or an overhead projector. The attention of the students tends to fluctuate gradually and gradually the learning process stops. Finally, the thread of the argument is lost. The time scale of their process is about 10-15 minutes. This needs to be countered by a sort of change.

Key Concepts

Lecturer's function should not only be to transmit factual information but to stimulate and help the students understand the material to be learned by organising, highlighting and explaining its key concepts. Students need to be helped to make a meaning of information, to see how it is obtained and how it may be applied. This requires more thought, preparation and insight on the lecturer's part.

Many students feel comfortable with 'lecturers' as way of learning. Sitting in a lecture room and taking notes would enable one to be more receptive.

Love for Teaching

One of the qualities of effective teachers is that they should have tremendous love for teaching. Only those who have a liking for their profession become good professionals in their fields. Similarly, only those who like teaching can become good teachers. Having become teachers they have to develop commitment and interest in their profession. Teachers without love for teaching can never be effective teachers.

Love for Students

One of the implications of love for teaching is love for students. The teacher who takes keen personal interest in the welfare of the students alone is a real teacher. The teacher should in fact be a friend, guide and philosopher of the students. It is necessary for all teachers to remember that the students and the teachers are not opposite groups but complimentary. Also they are not the two sides of the same coin but are parts of the same system. Some teachers have a habit of making disparaging and discouraging remarks about students. Teachers should learn to encourage and motivate the students instead of blaming them.

Teaching and Learning Go Together

Another important quality of good teachers is that they always try to learn instead of thinking that there is nothing for them to learn once they have become teachers. A teacher who ceases to learn in reality ceases to be a teacher because teaching and learning go together. A teacher becomes outdated unless he keeps himself abreast of the latest developments in his subject. He will also be unpopular and unsuccessful too.

Planning, Preparation and Practice

Planning, preparation and practice make teaching effective. Sometimes for one hour of teaching, more than three to four hours of preparation and planning may be required. With experience, the preparation time may get reduced but even the experienced can do well only with proper preparation. Those who take to the profession of teaching in their early years as teachers in a serious and systematic manner will do well in course of time and with experience they become better teachers. Teaching to a great extent is explaining and those who can explain well i.e. lucidly without being vague are rated as good teachers. It is rightly said that the "heart of the art of teaching consists in explaining."

Humour in Teaching

Humour is another important attribute of a good teacher. Those who teach in a boring, insipid and uninteresting manner are not liked by the students. It is true that humour cannot always form the part of teaching. But without a few doses of humour, reception to teaching may be very low. So every teacher must cultivate the habit of introducing a little humour in the process of teaching.

Inspire the Students

Enthusiastic teachers who can inspire the students are highly rated as good teachers. So one of the essential ingredients of good teaching is the ability to enthuse and inspire the students. The students cannot be enthused unless the teacher has in him a fairly high quantity of enthusiastic spirit. Teaching is not mere passing of information; it is to somehow extend at least a process of inspiring the learners to know more and to learn more.

Humane Attitude

Teachers with a humane attitude are also rated as good teachers by the students. Kindness and spirit of understanding in teachers are valued highly. Rigid, rude and unsympathetic teachers are not only unpopular but ineffective. Kindness does not mean that a teacher should show undue favour to the students. Without compromising on fundamental values, it is possible to be kind and humane. This kindness can be shown in different ways in helping slow learners by not showing impatience and anger and even by financially helping deserving and economically poor students.

Extra-Curricular Activities

Another finding on surveys of the qualities of good teachers is that those who involve themselves in extra-curricular activities are liked more by students than those who confine themselves to classroom teaching. In the present context, a teacher is not a mere instructor, he has to be a promoter, organiser and participant of various activities which makes life in the college dynamic.

*****

New Integrated B.Ed. Course (NIB.Ed.)

First to the Fourth Semester

The total duration of this course, after completing school finals, is twelve semesters (six years). From the first to the fourth semester, a student will study the present TCH syllabus along with other educational subjects like history, health and physical education, natural sciences, school organisation, management and quality control, globalisation and education, women and population, computer education, integrated education for the disabled, general law, commerce and economics, work experience through SUPW (Socially Useful Productive Work), comparative studies of education with respect to inter-state and international levels.

Primary School Teacher Trainee (PSTT)

After completing four semesters, a student must compulsorily serve one academic year in a Government primary school or its recognised schools as Primary School Teacher Trainee (PSTT).

This one year will be treated as the student's fifth and sixth semester. During this period they would be designated as PSTT. The PSTT period is similar to that of the compulsory house surgeon-ship of a medical student before securing the MBBS degree. During the PSTT period the students are exposed to various activities of a primary school like admission, framing the time table, teaching, conducting tests and exams, evaluation, quality control, co-curricular activities etc. After completing the PSTT period, students shall submit a PSTT-report .to the "examination committee" and appear for a personal interview. This committee shall comprise Principal of District Institute of Education & Training (DIET), student's internal guide and an external examiner. PSTT-report shall contain detailed information about the students' responsibilities in school, subjects taught, evaluation of students, school history, statistics of results, reasons for bad quality if any and suggestions to overcome the same, rate of children's dropout if any. If the committee is satisfied about his/her progress after the personal interview they may recommend to the Education Board to award the student a "diploma in education" (D.Ed). It means after getting the D.Ed., degree, one is eligible to teach primary school children.

During the PSTT period the State Government shall pay Rs. 750 per month as stipend to the student. After securing the D.Ed. degree a student will have two options — One can study the further six semesters and get a B.Ed., degree in which case he/she will be eligible to teach at both the primary and the secondary schools or one can discontinue in which case he/she will be eligible to teach only at primary schools.

Entry into the B.Ed course depends on the marks secured both in school finals and D.Ed. Total number of admissions to the B.Ed., course will be decided by the Education Board depending on the requirement of high school teachers. At least half of the students entering B.Ed course shall be from the science stream.

7th, 8th, 9th and 10th Semesters

Out of the remaining six semesters of NIB.Ed, the first four semesters

(7th, 8th, 9th and 10th) shall contain the syllabus of three years B.A. or B.Sc. along with the other subjects like Home Science, Nature Sciences, Astronomy, etc., as compulsory subjects for science students and sociology, history, geography etc. compulsory for Arts students.

The common subjects to be studied by both the Arts and Science students are general law, economics and commerce, history of education, education management and administration, school organisation management and quality control, sex education, women and population, computer education, globalisation, comparative study of education systems in India and in other countries, etc., along with the present B.Ed. course subjects.

Secondary School Teacher Trainee (SSTT)

After completing ten semesters, students shall compulsorily serve for one academic year in a Government high school or its recognised high schools as "secondary school teacher trainee" (SSTT). During this one year (comprising 11th and 12th semesters) a student will be designated as SSTT. The responsibilities, nature of work, submission of SSTT report, etc. will be similar to that of PSTT. After the SSTT period, students will be interviewed by an examination committee comprising District Institute of Education and Training (DIET), Principal, Internal guide and the External examiner. After the committee is satisfied with the performance of the student they may recommend to the Education Board to award a "Bachelor of Education (B.Ed.,)" degree.

During the SSTT period, the State Government shall pay an amount of Rs. 1,000 per month as stipend to the student.

One who secures NIB.Ed. degree is eligible to teach the children of primary, higher primary and secondary schools.

As the NIB.Ed. course reduces the work load of DIET and CTE's, the money spent by these institutions for training of teachers may be diverted to provide permanent infrastructure to the needy schools.

*****

Open Universities and Study Centres

The concept of distance education is an important innovation in this century. It has come to stay and no more a step sister of formal education. It provides open access to higher education to all those disadvantaged groups who could not or did not join the formal stream. It aims to equalise educational opportunities and to train people in various arts and crafts to develop their skills in different jobs. The popularity of the distance education can be gauged from the growth and development of open universities and students enrolment in them.

The first Open University was established in the United Kingdom (UKOU) in 1969. Imbued by its success in helping the distant learners, a number of such institutions have come into existence in several other countries. In Thailand, Sukhothai Thammathirat Open University established in 1975 was the first Open University in South East Asia.

First Open University in India

The credit for establishing the first Open University (1982) in India goes to Andhra Pradesh. The second in the lead is the National Open University (1985) viz. Indira Gandhi National Open University (IGNOU), Kota Open University (Rajasthan). Presently most of the major states in the country are having a number of Open Universities running successfully.

Objectives of Open University

- To provide and promote academic and professional education to enable people to upgrade their educational qualifications in response to individual and social needs.
- To promote research for application in national development.
- To provide educational service to society through the dissemination of knowledge, thereby promoting personal development and professional competence and
- To promote national art and culture and encourage an awareness of ethical principles on the part of the general public to strengthen its sense of national identity.

In Open University system there is no direct interaction between the teacher and the taught. The study centres, to a large extent, overcome the barrier between face-to-face interactions. Hence they are life nerves of an Open University.

Indira Gandhi National Open University (IGNOU)

The Indira Gandhi National Open University has started a few numbers of regional study centres in big cities and many study centres in the length and breadth of the country to cater to the needs of its students. The IGNOU study centres are mainly located in the educational institutions, colleges and conventional universities. The study centres are contact points to the students of the university. The host institutions where the study centres are established provide sufficient accommodation free of cost for the office of the co-ordinator, for the library, audio visual equipments and classrooms for tutorials. IGNOU provides sufficient furniture, library books, office and audio-visual equipments like TVs, VCRs, tape recorder, etc.

Study Centre Co-ordinator

The study centre is headed by a co-ordinator assisted by sufficient ministerial staff. Counselling is done mostly by senior teachers from academic institutions usually on Saturdays and Sundays to suit the convenience of the students who are mostly employed people. From experience it has been found that the students who join the Open University system are a highly motivated lot. They know the value of education which will not only provide them knowledge in their own areas but also open the doors for promotion.

Role of Co-ordinator

The Coordinator is appointed from among the senior academics of the institutions on the recommendation of the Principal or head of the institution. He plays a vital role in the work being the link between students and the headquarters. He is the head of the study centre, is the Public Relations Officer of the University and responsible for the activities of the centre. He renders local help to the students in advising about general and non-academic issues.

The co-ordinator is responsible for drawing up the time table and intimating both counsellors and the students about the counselling classes. He co-ordinates the work of all individual counsellors, maintains proper reports of the students and conducts examinations at the centre. In short, the co-ordinator is responsible for all activities of the study centre and acts as a Liaison Officer between the University, the Regional Centre and the study centre.

Academic Counsellors

Experienced teachers from educational institutions, able administrators from Public and Private enterprises and competent professionals are appointed as Academic Counsellors, depending on the nature of instruction on the recommendations of the co-ordinator. The Academic Counsellor is responsible for overall academic progress of the students and can be compared to a regular teacher in a conventional university. The Counsellor's task is much more difficult as majority of the students are mature and motivated adults and are in a better position to interact with counsellors.

An Academic Counsellor' Responsibility

A counsellor is responsible for the academic counselling, guidance, assignment grading and for the feedback from all the students allotted to him. He should make effective use of universities multimedia systems along with the students.

He has to assist the co-ordinator in intensive coaching programmes, examinations, evaluation of examination scripts, assignments, etc. The success of any programme depends not only on good printed materials, audio-visual cassettes supply, but also on the face-to-face contact sessions at the study centres.

Open University Student Community

Unlike the traditional university students, the Open University students are a cross-section of motivated adult population of the country. Due to various reasons several adults would have missed the opportunity of higher education when they were young. These are adults who want to improve their knowledge while in service, since a university degree will bring them both financial gain and status. Several surveys made on the strength of students of different Open University system have shown that there are several segments of the society who are keen to update their knowledge and seek higher education. Some of them are homemakers, working women, factory workers, office goers, technicians, alternately skilled, dropouts, etc. There are even prisoners who have shown a keen interest in higher studies and achieved.

Advantages

The instructional TV replaces the traditional teacher of conventional education with more elaborate and illustrative material. The student has the advantage of seeing costly and risky experiments, drama, natural phenomenon like volcanoes, earthquakes, etc., which would not be possible in a formal university. In brief just as the nerve centres are to the human body so are study centres to an Open University.

TN Open University

Obviously, the dreams of Tamil Nadu Open University to put Tamil Nadu in a pre eminent position on the educational map of India will come true through establishment of the university. "As we are a UGC-recognised university, the employment opportunities for our students have been stable and good." In all fairness, it has been a dream come true to the university.

While most of the other open universities require a minimum of 10th standard as criteria for enrolment, TN Open University accepts students having studied class VII or VIII. But that does not imply that the competence of students in their respective fields will not be considered. "These students are required to write an additional paper in their first year, to put their basic qualifications to test. While students who have completed 10+2 write 15 papers to obtain the degree, these students will write an additional paper."

The institution offers courses at the undergraduate, postgraduate and doctorate levels. Besides, diploma courses are also available. With so many courses and insititutions committed to the cause of education for all, the message that it is never too late to get back to books comes out, loud and clear.

*****

Continuing Education for Engineers

The growing body of scientific and technical knowledge and its rapid obsolescence call for more frequent occupational refreshing and updating. Several trends also indicate that in future engineers will experience a large number of career changes than hitherto. This means that they will have to acquire new knowledge increasingly and frequently during their working lives. It is necessary to recognise publicly and publicise widely that continuing education programmes are a normal part of engineering profession and that engineering is more a learning profession than a learned profession. Fortunately, technical education institutions and industry have started realising and accepting that the traditional pattern of formal engineering education cannot equip graduates with necessary expertise to harness the fast changing scientific and technological developments. Continuing education gradually evolves from a marginal activity of the universities and technical education institutions to one of their principal activities as is now evident from the varieties of 'correspondence', 'off-campus', 'extra-normal', 'extension' and 'non-formal' programmes they are offering for the professional updating of engineers.

Changing Pace of Science and Technology

A radical change in thinking is needed if technical education is to address itself to the changing pace of science and technology. Scientific and technological changes are so rapid and unpredictable that they preclude anyone from obtaining a knowledge of all that needs to be learnt in a fixed period. Three or four years are far too short to learn all aspects of any discipline. It should always be remembered that engineering is a problem-solving profession. Any valid approach to technical education must encourage development of motivation and skills for continuous and independent learning. Technical education of tomorrow must train professionals who have an interdisciplinary approach to problem solving. Technical education systems have to be redesigned and re-organised to produce a substantial percentage of self-propelled individuals who would be able to grow in any new area and make their contributions.

Professionalism

As part of continuing education programmes, industry-institution interaction needs to be promoted in a big way through apprenticeship opportunities, consultancy, and sponsored research, continuing education of industry personnel, 'adjunct professionalism' in institutional faculty in industry and involvement of industry in the development of curricula and courses. Industrial liaison boards, industry institutional cells and industrial foundations should be set up and operationalised.

Continuing Education in Emerging Technologies

Another important point is that there is serious unemployment among engineers. At the same time there is shortage of suitably trained engineers in several emerging areas such as engineering design, advanced metallurgy, turbo machinery, computer science and micro-electronics. This is an area where the scheme of continuing education could come in. In this century, we will have to keep abreast of developments in several areas such as informatics, telematics, bio-technology, material sciences, oceanography, instrumentation and space technology. A well-conceived and co-ordinated approach to the introduction of emerging technologies in the industry will further increase the need for continuing education programmes. Yet another important issue is that high quality continuing education and retraining programmes should be available through the distance mode.

*****

Quality Enhancement

The academic community should realise that there is an inherent danger in leaving too many problems to the government and non-academic people elsewhere for solution. The teaching community should do some real soul searching and assess in a dispassionate manner, their contribution from the point of view of enhancing the quality of academic life and keeping the universities in good health. Barring a few exceptions, the Indian Universities and their faculty have shown little inclination to bring about the needed transformation/modernisation in the teaching and learning processes in the light of the fast changing needs of the society. At a time when knowledge is increasing at a rapid and accelerating pace, the faculties have got themselves struck with outdated and outworn curricula and course contents. Quality enhancement can be ensured by:

- Continually implementing and evaluating educational innovations
- Redefining their mission and goals
- Using collaborative management strategies
- Generating resources
- Implementing annual themes that chant institutional growth
- Promoting ICT capacity building for students and staff members
- Encouraging student and staff research
- Analysing IQAC enabled student and staff feedback for improvement of its functions and goals
- Providing continued and committed community outreach
- Collaborating with academic institutions, government and non-government organisations
- Close-contact teaching
- Career guidance and personal counseling
- Mentoring and placement services
- Extension work in various areas, sports and cultural programme
- Excellence in Arts/Science Programme

The concerns for ensuring quality in higher education leading to evaluation of performance of universities and colleges:

- Higher education providers are accountable to their stakeholders such as Government, the management, teachers, students, potential employers and the society at large. The ultimate stakeholders as well as direct beneficiaries of higher education are the students.
- At the time of independence, in India there were only 20 universities and 500 colleges. At present, the Indian Higher education system is the second largest in the world with 8 million students, more than 3 lakh teachers, 300 universities, affiliated with more than 12000 colleges and many deemed universities and institutions of national importance.
- By the year 2020, India will be the youngest nation with a higher population in the age group of 30-35. Hence, it becomes imperative to provide enhanced quality based human resources to the rest of the world.
- The Students, the ultimate stakeholders have a unique role to play in ensuring quality in institutions of higher education. Otherwise, these institutions will have very little motivation for quality enhancement.

The involvement of students in the institutional quality enhancement processes is crucial and invaluable, because of the following:

- Students are the largest group within any institution of higher education and, therefore, they are the main stakeholders who have a much stronger voice than any others.
- Students should realise that they have a right to quality education and it is the responsibility of the higher education institutions to provide quality educational experience to learners.
- Students should be equally aware of their responsibilities which in turn will help the institutions to provide quality education.
- The students should demand quality education and demonstrate their commitment to quality education by accepting their responsibilities
- Students must be well informed, committed, participative, motivated and curious and this would provide for valuable contributions.

In higher education, the duty of a teacher is to serve students of different backgrounds and abilities through effective teaching-learning experiences, interactive instructional techniques and engage students in higher order 'thinking' and investigation, group discussions, projects, experiments, internship and application of ICT.

Higher Education plays a major role in the sustainable development of a nation. Therefore, higher education should contribute to the development of human resources, promote social equity, enhance personal development and bring out employable students.

Quality management is the new buzz word in the field of Higher Education. Different stakeholders have different perceptions of quality. Increasing accountability and increase in the size of student population are the reasons for this emphasis on quality.

Stakeholders in Quality Enhancement

Quality enhancement in education has become the mantra of modern times. According to Dr. A.P.J. Abdul Kalam, *"Today quality in higher education has to be provided to the primary stakeholders, i.e. students in an effective manner. It should be aimed through giving students the skill to manage knowledge through research and enquiry, creating an innovative environment through more practical skills, using of high technology, cultivate 'doing-things-right' attitude and have moral leadership for betterment of human resource in the country."*

Every stakeholder of higher education has a role to play in the sustenance and the enhancement of quality. Of all the stakeholders, the students have a unique role to play in ensuing quality in higher education institution. They are:
- Interest of the students in bringing quality enhancement in higher education through innovative thinking and creative power.
- The role of students and their participation in higher education through modern technical skills.
- Suggestion to enhance quality of the primary stakeholders.

Inclusive Economic Growth

One of the major challenges that India faces today is to achieve 'inclusive growth' in a market-oriented economy. Assurance of quality education at affordable price creates a very strong 'safety net' for the underprivileged in our economy. It is to be ascertained through study 'how far has our higher education system helped the lower income groups to improve their ability to earn?'

Internationalisation of Curricula

The steps to develop transnational quality assurance and accreditation system to counter balance the globalisation of higher education could include:
- A common set of definitions and a glossary of concepts regarding international quality assurance and accreditation.
- An agreement on a basic set of principles that define quality assurance and accreditation.
- An initiative to convince the international higher education community, its key actors and its associations that they have to develop transnational forms of self-regulation with respect to quality.
- An initiative to convince national authorities to convince them to seek international cooperation in the field of quality assurance and accreditation.
- An initiative to seek the cooperation of the internationally organised profession in the development of an international regulatory framework with regard to quality assurance and accreditation.
- Initiation of work by experts on the analysis and evolution of standards, criteria and benchmarking procedures used in the existing quality assurance and accreditation systems, in order to investigate the possibility of a definition for internationally agreed minimum standards.

The concept of Quality Management or rather Total Quality Management (TQM) is not new to India. The great Tamil Poetess Avvayyar has given the maxim "*Seivana Thiruntha Sei*"

(Whatever is worth doing, do it perfectly). When a work is executed without any mistake on the first time and all the times, there is total Quality i.e. called "Zero defects."

*****

Total Quality in Higher Education

The world in which institutions of higher learning operate is changing dramatically. Higher education is experiencing substantive shifts in student enrolments. If present trends continue, by the next decade, over 50% of the student body will be over 25 years of age. Meeting the needs of the older, and increasingly part-time, students will require new approaches in the delivery of educational services.

Competition among Educational Institutions

The reason for a focus on quality involves increased market forces and competition in higher education. Students who believe that higher education will provide the key to employment and career growth are increasingly assessing the value of a degree based on their perceptions of quality learning, service, timeliness, and price. Sensitivity to these criteria was not critical in a rapidly expanding economy, in which a premium was placed on a college degree even if the value added by the educational experience was minimal. The expected limited growth of the coming decade will encourage students to assess the value of their educational experiences by something more than a piece of paper. This will encourage greater competition among educational institutions to provide the quality of education desired by today's students.

Geographical Location Not A Barrier

Competition among colleges and universities will be encouraged by technological developments and the reality of long-distance education. Geographical location as a barrier to the size of the area served by an institution will be eliminated. Institutions in Boston will compete with institutions in Florida or California for students and for faculty. Increased competition will also emerge from the private sector. Corporate America already spends billions of dollars on training programs (over $48 billion in 1992) in part in response to their dissatisfaction with the products and services received from colleges and universities.

Positive Future or Defensive Past

In short, the fact is that (1) the environment of higher education is changing and (2) competition for both students and funds will continue to increase, at a time when (3) we are going to accomplish more with less. The result is that colleges and universities in the coming decades/century will not be the same as they are today. Thus, the question that must be addressed is how we as members of the academy will respond to these (and related) trends. Will we respond in a proactive manner and initiate positive, quality-focused, learner-centered programs, or will we respond in a defensive manner, attempting to preserve the past at the expense of the future?

Total Quality Management and Continuous Improvements

Alexander Pope's phrase "Fools rush in where angels fear to tread," has occurred particularly when we seek our colleagues' opinions about the application of total quality management and continuous improvement (TQM/CI) to higher education. Although we, through our collective experience in both teaching and administration (the total years, if combined, would put a person near retirement either as a fulltime university academician or administrator), are convinced of the need to implement TQM-CI within colleges and universities, the core of the academy — the faculty — have and will continue to question and resist its implementation.

Why Total Quality?

Whatever be the reason for reading this book, one of its goals is to help and establish the need that exists to recreate the academy for the twenty-first century. Change may be viewed as an opportunity, not a threat, and the principles and practices of total quality can aid in this transformation.

Growth of Sub-standard Institutions

Due to unprecedented expansion of higher education, there has been deterioration in the standards. The mushrooming proliferation of collegiate education in the far flung areas of the country has resulted in the growth of substandard institutions and has adversely affected the quality of education.

Quality Assurance in Higher Education: Concept of Quality

There are many stakeholders in higher education, including students, employees, teaching and non-teaching employees, government, funding agencies, regulatory bodies, professional bodies and the accreditation agencies. Each of the stakeholders has a different view about quality, influenced by their own interests in higher education. Their views represent their expectations from higher education and its quality.

When higher education is conceived as the production of highly qualified manpower, the graduates are seen as products whose career earnings and employment will relate to the quality of education that they have received. When higher education is linked to training and for a research career, the performance indicators (PIs) then become the research output of staff and students. The third conception in higher education itself is an efficient management of teaching provision. In this view, the PIs are efficiency indicators, such as completion rates, unit costs, student–staff ratio and other financial data. Further, when higher education is conceived as a matter of extending life chances, the focus is on the participation rates or percentage growth of students from less represented backgrounds including adults, part-time students and disabled students. (Barnett 1994)

Definition of Accreditation

Accreditation is an evaluation of whether an institution (or programme) qualifies for a certain status. Accreditation provides the outcome in a binary scale – yes/no or accredited/not accredited.

Internal Quality Assurance Cell

Each higher education institution should set up an Internal Quality Assurance Cell with a view to continuously assess its performance on objective and pre-defined parameters. This exercise should primarily aim at conducting academic audit and to encourage institutions to make continuous improvements to raise their standards. Institutions should make their output performance Public to ensure transparency and accountability.

Definition of Assessment

Assessment gives an idea of the quality of the outputs. Typical outcome of assessment results in a multipoint grade – numeric, literal or descriptive.

Definition of Academic Audit

Academic audit is focused on those processes by which an institution monitors its own academic standards and acts to assure and enhance the quality of its offerings. The objectives of the institution or programmes are taken as the starting point for the audit. The audit is usually done by a small group of generalists and it results in an audit report.

Emergence of Quality Assurance Agencies

In many countries the academic quality and standards are assured by specialised agencies and the process is referred to as quality assurance. The term quality assurance is used in different ways in different countries and contexts. In the United Kingdom, the 'quality assurance' is defined as the totality of systems, resources and information devoted to maintaining and improving the quality and standards of teaching, scholarship and research, and of students' learning experience. Over the past couple of decades, under the pressure of greater demand for accountability, many countries have established quality assurance agencies.

These agencies convince various stakeholders that a higher education institution takes its quality assurance seriously, and that the quality of teaching and quality of graduates leaves no room for concern. With the increased mobility of professionals and skilled workers and the greater need for recognition of qualifications across borders, these bodies are now required to co-ordinate their work and create a mechanism for quality assurance in a transnational context.

Like elsewhere in the world, the rapid expansion of higher education in India has been at the cost of its quality. Quality varies widely across institutions. Though the NPE in 1986 recommended setting up of a quality assurance mechanism, the NAAC could only be established in 1994. It took another four years for the first institute to be accredited in January, 1998.

Transnational Quality Assurance in South Asia

The Association of Management Development Institution in South Asia (AMDISA) has initiated the South Asian Quality Assurance System (SAQS) as a global benchmark approach to quality assurance for business schools. This is a dynamic system which ensures high standards as also responsiveness to changing concerns of the stake-holders. The AMDISA is a SAARC recognised body charted in 1988 as a network of management institutions in South Asia with the generous support from the Commonwealth Secretariat and active involvement of leading management schools in the region.

Ranking and League Tables

Ranking and league tables of higher education institutions are popular abroad. These are beginning to be seen in India. These are lists of groups of institutions that are comparatively ranked according to a common set of indicators in descending order. Different from performance indicators, these are designed specifically as a comparative measure, putting institutions against each other. In most cases, these are produced by commercial publishing enterprises. Most league tables provide a single integrated score that allows an ordinal ranking of entire institutions.

Such rankings provide valuable information to the students, parents, teachers and researchers, policymakers and to institutions themselves as they compare themselves with peer institutions at home or abroad.

IIT – a Global Brand

The smartest, most successful, most influential Indians who have migrated to the US seem to share a common credential. They are graduates of the Indian Institutes of Technology, better known as IITians. Made up of seven campuses throughout India, IIT is one of the most important universities in India. This is IIT Bombay. Put Harvard, MIT and Princeton together, and you begin to get an idea of the status of this school in India. With a population of over a billion people in India, competition to get into an IIT is ferocious. Every year about 3 lakh high school seniors take the entrance exam for just over 3500 seats, which is less than 2%. Compare that with Harvard, say which accepts about 10% of its applicants. Impact of IIT graduates has been on the American technology revolution. There isn't just one area where Indian IIT engineers have not played a leading role. The American companies love the kids from IITs. Nehru, India's first Prime Minister established IIT just after independence to train the scientists and engineers. He knew the nation would need to move from medieval to modern. He could not have imagined that India would be supplying brainpower to the whole world.

Academic Profession in Quality Management

Of all measures, the faculty and its quality has an enduring impact on the quality of higher education. The condition of the academic profession is thus central to many issues in higher education. Traditionally, teachers in India have been accorded the highest esteem. However, over the past few decades, the academic profession is facing a severe crisis. Rapid expansion of higher education has resulted in severe teacher shortages. Teachers' shortages are either due to non-availability of suitably qualified people or arising from the ban on recruitment due to financial distress faced by the governments, particularly in State governments. Most bright people are reluctant to join the profession and those who join, do it as a last resort. They get disillusioned soon after they join when they find that they have no incentives or motivation to perform.

Teacher Quality

Improving the quality of teachers is the key to improve learning outcomes in all educational institutions including higher education institutions. In spite of strong empirical evidence and also the commonly held expectation that teacher quality is most critical in student achievement, there is a crisis of teacher quality all over the world. This is perhaps the weakest link in the education systems worldwide. Hiring good teachers is not easy. Teaching ability is closely related to training or experience. Unfortunately, the prevailing salary structures also do not target particularly high quality teachers. Exchanges between teaching, industrial and applied research professions may provide some incentive relief and relaxation.

Now the trend is such that bright students seek employment in private sector than seek teaching positions. The pay range of a teacher is typically from Rs. 20,000 to Rs. 40,000 per month, which is much less than what private sector can offers. The problem is more acute in professional areas, where students who pass out earn much more from the day they are recruited. In a consumerist society this downgrades the status of a teacher. Students are unwilling to spend many years in getting doctoral degrees, which in many cases is essential for an academic career. There is no monitory growth or gains beyond that point. Promotion schemes are far away. The highest attainable grade is professor in the case of university and reader for colleges. Many teachers achieve this by an average age of 40 years and beyond that there is nothing to look forward.

Attracting and Retaining Good Teachers

The strategy to attract and retain good teachers is not easy. The Career Advancement Scheme has been a boon in attracting and retaining faculty, for it provides opportunities of promotion to faculty members. However, variations in the implementation processes of the scheme require certain improvements. The promotion should be based on a rigorous evaluation of publications in peer reviewed journals. Promotion should be given from the date of selection committee assessment, and not from the back dates. This will require the universities to complete the evaluation process and hold selection committee meetings within a maximum of six months from the date of eligibility of a candidate.

There has been breeding in recruitment and selection process. To curb this, universities and colleges should be given incentives to recruit at least one fourth of their faculty positions from states other than the one in which the institution is located. In order to promote mobility of the faculty, certain proportion of faculty positions should be prescribed to be filled up on contract basis.

Built-In Quality

It should be understood that inspections and examinations do not create quality; quality is built during the curriculum development process. University administrators need to create improvement targets to build quality into the education process. The administrator might set the target at 133% or more of the current process capability, and then work with instructors and employees to create and implement a quality improvement plan on a semester-by-semester basis.

Problems As Opportunities

Administrators should view complaints and quality problems as opportunities to improve the organisation and attitudes within it and to implement reforms. The fundamental principle of quality control is to identify the root cause of a problem so that it will not recur. If the administrator does not search for the root cause and strives to prevent the recurrence of the problem, his or her work becomes haphazard. Search for the root cause thoroughly.

*****

Overview of Total Quality

What is Total Quality?

During the past five years, there has been an explosion of books in the field of Total Quality. Yet in all of the thousands of books and billions of words written on the subject, there is an absence of three essential ingredients: a good working definition, a comprehensive yet concise history, and a clear and simple systems model of total quality. This overview of total quality is intended to fill this void and provide some interesting reading at the same time.

Concept of Total quality

Total quality is total in three senses: it covers every process, every job, and every person. First, it covers every process, rather than just manufacturing or production. Design, construction, R&D, accounting, marketing, repair, and every other function must also be involved in quality improvement. Second, total quality is total in that it covers every job, as opposed to only those involved in making the product. Secretaries are expected not to make typing errors, accountants not to make posting errors, and managers not to make strategic errors. Third, total quality recognises that each person is responsible for the quality of his or her work and for the work of the group.

User Satisfaction

Total quality also goes beyond the traditional idea of quality, which has been expressed as the degree of conformance to a standard or the product of workmanship. Enlightened organisations accept and apply the concept that quality is the degree of user satisfaction or the fitness of the product for use. In other words, the customer determines whether or not quality has been achieved in its totality.

Total Quality Common Language

This same measure—total customer satisfaction—applies throughout the entire operation of an organisation. Only the outer edges of a company actually have contact with customers in the traditional sense, but each department can treat the other departments as its customers. The main judge of the quality of work is the customer, for if the customer is not satisfied, the work does not have quality value. This, coupled with the achievement of corporate objectives, is the bottom line of total quality.

In that regard, it is important, as the Japanese say, to "talk with facts and data." Total quality emphasises the use of fact-oriented discussions and statistical quality control techniques by everyone in the company. Everyone in the company is exposed to basic quality control ideas and techniques and is expected to use them. Thus, total quality becomes a common language and improves "objective" communication.

Mutual Feedback and Closer Interaction

Total quality also radically alters the nature and basic operating philosophy of organisations. The earlier specialised separate system developed early in the twentieth century is replaced by a system of mutual feedback and closer interaction between departments. Engineers, for example, work closely with construction crews and storekeepers to ensure that their knowledge is passed on to workers. Workers, in turn, feed their practical experience directly back to the engineers. This information interchange and shared commitment to product quality is what makes total quality work. Teaching all employees how to apply process control and improvement techniques makes them party to their own destiny and enables them to achieve their fullest potential.

Maximise Value to Stakeholder

However, total quality is more than an attempt to make better products; it is also a search for better ways to make better products. Adopting the total quality philosophy commits the company to the belief that there is always a better way of doing things, a way to make better use of the company's resources, and a way to be more productive. In this sense, total quality relies heavily upon value analysis as a method of developing better products and operations in order to maximise value to the stakeholder, whether customers, employees, or shareholders.

Gaining Experience

Total quality also implies a different type of worker and a different attitude towards the worker from the management. Under total quality, workers are generalists, rather than specialists. Both workers and managers are expected to move from job to job, gaining experience in many areas of the company.

Defining Total Quality

First and foremost, total quality is a set of philosophies by which management systems can direct the efficient achievement of the objectives of the organisation to ensure customer satisfaction and maximise stakeholder value. This is accomplished through the continuous improvement of the quality system, which consists of the social system, the technical system, and the management system. Thus, it becomes a way of life for doing business for the entire organisation.

Central to the concept is the idea that a company should design and build in quality into its products, rather than inspect for it afterwards. Only by a devotion to quality throughout the organisation can the best possible products be made. Or, as stated by Noriaki Kano, "Quality is too important to be left to inspectors."

Probability and Productivity

Total quality is too important to take second a place to any other company goals. Specifically, it should not be subsidiary to profit or productivity. Concentrating on quality will ultimately build and improve both profitability and productivity. Failure to concentrate on quality will quickly erode profits, as customers resent paying for products they perceive as of low quality.

Detecting Defects

The main focus of total quality is on why. It goes beyond the how to include the 'why to'. It is an attempt to identify the causes of defects in order to eliminate them. It is a continuous cycle of detecting defects, identifying their causes, and improving the process so as to totally eliminate the causes of defects.

Self-disclosure of Errors

Accepting the idea that the customer of a process can be defined as the next process is essential to the real practice of total quality. According to total quality, control charts should be developed for each process, and any errors identified within a process should be disclosed to those involved in the next process in order to raise quality. However, it has been said that it seems contrary to human nature to seek out one's own mistakes. People tend to find the errors caused by other and to neglect their own. Unfortunately, exactly that kind of self-disclosure is what is really needed.

Instead, managements too often tend to blame and then take punitive action. This attitude prevails from frontline supervisors all the way up to the top management. In effect, we are encouraged to hide the real problems we cause, and instead of looking for the real causes of problems, as required by total quality, we look the other way.

ISO 9000 and the Quality Movement

At the turn of the last century, England was the most advanced nation in the world. In World War I, England led the charge and during World War II was at least an equal of the United States with one exception. England did not have Shewhart,

Deming, and the other American quality gurus. It was not until the Common Market accepted the firm touch of Prime Minister Margaret Thatcher that the European movement was galvanised in 1979 with the forerunner of ISO 9000. It was Thatcher who orchestrated the transformation of the British ISO 9000 series for the European community. In less than 20 years, it has become the worldwide quality standard.

*****

Prohibition of Unfair Practices in Technical Education, Medical Education and University Bill 2010

A major governance reform is needed. It should have the following features:
- Transparency in governance through mandatory disclosures regarding faculty, fees, admission procedure, infrastructure, etc.
- Punishable under unfair practices include demanding or paying capitation fees, not issuing receipt for fee charged, publishing misleading advertisements, and withholding certificates to compel payment of fees, etc.
- Maintenance of records of admission and publication of prospectus mandatory

The Education Tribunals Bill 2010

Highlights of the bill are as follows:
- The Bill seeks to set up Educational Tribunals at the national and state level to adjudicate disputes involving teachers and other employees of higher educational institutions and other stakeholders such as students, universities and statutory regulatory authorities.
- The state tribunals shall adjudicate cases related to service matters of teachers and other employees of higher educational institution; dispute over affiliation of a higher educational institution with an affiliating university and unfair practices of a higher educational institution prohibited by any law.

- The national tribunal shall adjudicate cases of dispute between higher educational institutions and statutory authorities; higher educational institution and affiliating university (in case of central universities), and any reference made to it by an appropriate statutory authority. It shall have appellate jurisdiction on orders of the state tribunals.
- An order of the tribunal shall be treated as decree of a civil court. If orders of the national or state tribunal are not complied with, the person shall be liable to imprisonment for a maximum of three years or with fine of upto Rs. 10 lakh or with both.

The Foreign Educational Institutions Regulation of Entry and Operation Bill 2010

- Foreign institutions on their own or in partnership with Indian universities can set up operations.
- Twenty years service in home country offering educational facilities necessary to become eligible.
- Programmes offered to confirm to standards prescribed by the authorities and comparable to those offered in home country.
- A corpus fund of Rs. 50 crores to be maintained and 75% of income to be utilised only for educational purpose in India.
- An advisory board to advise the Government on matters connected to foreign educational service providers.

National Commission for Higher Education and Research Bill 2011

- Aims at an over-arching independent authority to determine, co-ordinate and maintain standards in all fields of higher education.
- Promoting autonomy and excellence in a competitive global environment with advice from a collegium of eminent academicians.
- Promoting research and innovation in higher educational institutions.

- States participation in general council of NCHER for policy planning and higher education development.
- National Directory of Academics for leadership positions/ VC selection.
- Independent Board of Research promotion and Innovation.
- Independent Higher Education Financial Services Corporation, for disbursal of funds according to norms set by NCHER.

*****

Revamping of Medical Courses

There is a constant criticism that the standards of medical education in our country is fast deteriorating and is not uniform. It is a known fact that standards vary from university to university, college to college, regular batch to referred batch and even at the same examination from one set of examiners to another. The subjective element takes a greater share in the assessment of merit apart from other considerations. The only method of judging and maintaining the standards of medical education is to hold a nation-wide licensing examination as a pre-requisite for each medical graduate before he is registered to practice.

Regulation in the US

It is worth noting the position in the US which has a reputation of constant endeavour and resilience to adopt changes speedily for betterment. After 12th grade, and further seven to eight years of undergraduate study and Board examinations, Medical Schools in the US awards MD degrees to eligible students. After that another three years of internship in hospitals is compulsory before getting a license to practise medicine. This does not automatically entitle them to practise medicine in all parts of that country. They have to pass licensing examinations held by each state separately for specialised fields. But most States accept the examination conducted by the National Board of Examinations for this purpose. Even after that they have to continuously study and update by qualifying in fellowship tests every year. Hence, it is desirable to introduce a licensing examination mandatory to all for registration before starting practice in the profession. This can also be part of the PG entrance examination or marks at this examination can be given weightage at the PG entrance.

National Board of Medical Examinations

There is already a National Board of Medical Examinations constituted by the Government of India for the specific purpose of granting various postgraduate degrees, including super-specialties. NBME is a better organisation to be entrusted with the responsibility of conducting national examinations including the licensing examination for graduate level as well. The proposal to have a national licensing examination before grant of registration may not be palatable to many medical graduates who will be reluctant to face another examination. But the fact remains that their performance at the final university examinations is not at all acceptable straight away, due to obvious disparities in competence.

Entrance Test

A national level Entrance Test for the UG and PG medical admissions is already recommended by the Supreme Court. The entrance test definitely helps to dispel the notion that merit and scholarship is the prerogative of a few institutions. It is likely that students from newer or even private medical colleges may acquit themselves better. At the same time this examination will be a tool of precision for measuring and maintaining standards of medical education. Institutions would have to strive hard to ensure that its alumni come up to national standards.

Medical Council of India

Medical Council of India publishes, once in a decade, the minimum requirements for 100 admissions to UG and PG courses and the qualifications required for the teaching staff. These are used by the medical colleges when it suits them. The standards in UG and PG subjects are inspected by an Inspectors appointed by the MCI from other institutions once in five or ten years. What they inspect are physical facilities, staff pattern and their experience, but not the standards. In the brief time the inspector spends at an examination, he may see a few sample papers or listen to the answers of a few students. Even if the standards were high at the time of the visit of the Inspector, there is no guarantee that they are maintained on other days. Sometimes, the President or Secretary and permanent Inspectors of MCI inspect institutions to verify physical facilities but not the standards.

The bulky reports submitted by the Inspector and information filled in the printed forms are scrutinised by a sub-committee and their recommendations are finally placed before the General Body which meets once in a year for a day. The main event of the general body meeting of the MCI usually is election of office bearers. The academic items numbering nearly 100 are passed in a few minutes of time. The pace of work and procedures of the MCI are so slow that the comments of the inspectors are available to the institutions a year later. It is indeed a sad state of affair that half of the medical PG degrees in the country are not recognised by the MCI and some medical colleges are started without its approval.

Standards of Medical Education

Standards of Medical Education cannot be determined merely by the buildings, equipment and staff but by testing the graduates produced in these institutions. Every graduate has to be checked before he is permitted to practice. A National level licensing authority must be introduced to register each graduate to replace the random check of the medical colleges by the MCI once in a decade.

MCI is not a suitable organisation to conduct national level examinations which are better entrusted to NBME. The composition of MCI needs to be changed to include more current medical teachers and not ex-teachers or political appointees. There must be flexibility in medical education and no regimentation in the hands of a single organisation with a slow pace of activity and momentum.

Intake Capacity of Medical Colleges

Capacity of medical colleges in Tamil Nadu needs to be immediately doubled to ensure minimum provision of quality healthcare to the population of the state. At present about 3000 doctors graduate from medical colleges in Tamil Nadu whereas the number in Andhra Pradesh, Karnataka and Maharashtra is close to 5000 each. It is projected that the required capacity will be four times the present capacity. Hence, to meet the demand, speedy approval of medical colleges should be facilitated by the state. Both the Central and State Governments are not endowing adequate care or funds to expand and enhance the merit of medical education. For lack of opportunities and high costs for PG courses or specialisation, many are opting to go out to countries like Russia, Germany and Japan, who are now offering courses in English medium at reasonable costs.

*****

6

Higher Education for the Future

Higher Education for the 21St Century

The environment is fast changing. The economy and the psyche of the nation are being tied up with an alarming pace to the outside world. The institutions of higher education may have to learn to live and grow without the budgetary support. Competition is spreading into all areas and corners particularly in higher education. There is no exemption as it can also be a return yielding professional service. This is an endeavour to list the issues that need to be appreciated by the managers of the universities in preparing themselves to meet the challenges of tomorrow and also deliberate on the issue connected with the approaches and attitudes to ensure sustainable self-reliant management of the universities.

Reforming Higher Education

The following reforms are suggested to bring qualitative changes in higher education and to maintain high academic standards.
- The number of working days has to be increased from the present 187 days to 232 days for all degree colleges and also at the university level. Idleness breeds under-care and devilish thinking.
- For all degree colleges first term holidays will be declared as per the university academic calendar and they have to be reduced from 30 days to 15 days.
- Summer vacation for all degree colleges has to be reduced from 90 to 60 days.
- Invigilation work for degree examinations should be made compulsory for all lecturers and readers.

- Academic accountability has to be introduced in colleges by fixing the responsibility on the principals and by delegating some executive powers to punish the guilty and the erring. And at the university level, the same may be fixed on the heads of the departments of the faculty concerned. Quarterly academic inspection has to be done at college level and also at university level.
- Traditional syllabus introduced a few decades ago has to be annually updated, changed immediately and should be made job oriented.
- Traditional mode of setting question papers has to be dispensed with immediately. Stereotyped questions have to be dispensed with forthwith. Objective type of questions should be introduced. Question paper duration has to be reduced from three hours to two and half hours uniformly for all students.
- Boards of studies in various faculties should meet once in three months with experienced lecturers and principals of degree colleges to discuss the day-to-day developments in the curriculum. It has to suggest to the university authorities for the introduction of professional oriented subjects in all disciplines. A change in syllabus is the need of the day.
- Subjects like human rights, human resources management, hotel management, computer management and resource management should be introduced as elective subjects.
- Administrative machinery such as monitoring cell consisting of senior Principals, Professors from the University concerned, Registrar, Coordinator, Members from the Board of Management and also Representatives from Higher Education Department have to be constituted at the university level to regulate and monitor the working of private degree colleges.
- Values of education based on the heritage and national goals, necessary re-adjustments and reforms in the system of education, particularly in colleges and universities, national integration and unity among the student community have to be promoted.
- Teachers have to identify themselves fully in every academic aspect concerning their institutions.

Consultancy Norms and Motivation

The policy on sharing of the staffs' earnings has to be such that the university personnel do their best to do more work. There should be opportunities to pursue the intellectual world itself for motivation up to some extent. Thereafter, it needs to be nourished with incentives.

Proper consultative norms have to be designed. Wherever necessary, orientation programmes have to be reorganised for the benefit of senior officers of the institutions of higher learning to enable them to work in tandem with the changing roles of the institutions of higher learning.

Manpower Planning and Management

The development of technology and use of modern gadgets have reduced workload of staff to a great extent, for example, Word processor, computer-aided teaching/audio visual aids, Photostat machines, printers. Hence, there is need for manpower planning and management. If the latest technology of the system makes the earlier jobs redundant, what are the available strategies to deal with the surplus manpower? Is this surplus limited to only the non-teaching or does it extend to teaching staff also? May be some sort of 'surplus cell for redeployment' has to be commissioned. Job surveys may have to be undertaken to take stock of the available human resources and SWOT (Strength, Weakness, Opportunity and Threats) analysis would help to suggest whether job redesign is possible with the existing people after giving suitable training to them. This has to be tackled in the context of sharing the gains of the efforts of the people putting in additional efforts.

Instruments of Alienation

The Globalisation of commercial outlook may have its pressure on the values. We are becoming increasingly alienated from our people and educational institutions have become instruments of alienation. Education should not be another method of getting alienated from society. The institutions of higher learning should make an introspection and strive with the courage of conviction that they contribute to the social affinity through their programmes and practices.

The exemplary nature of an educational institution — accepted both by the insiders and outsiders of the institution, the efficiency it demonstrates through its staff and students and the utility it conveys to its users would ensure their marketability and hence, their economic standing without foregoing their social responsibilities.

Varsity Management Needs Overhaul

Management of a university has become an extremely complicated task — a task which can be handled only by those trained to manage them. But hardly any attention has been paid to the training of teachers as well as the administrative staff.

While it is believed that no training was required to teach at the university level, such a requirement was considered essential to teach students at the school level. It was unfortunate that it was not being realised that an academic degree did not automatically make a person an effective teacher.

The assumption that the distinction in acquiring new knowledge translates automatically into skills at passing it on, has operated unchallenged in many departments. The main problem facing the universities was the management of change.

If the management of universities were to be effective, they must identify the areas of change and should try to manage, lest there would be a chaotic situation in the system.

Training is needed also for non-teaching staff of a university. They were the most neglected men and women in the campus who were being asked to manage the university without being trained for it. No wonder, the system is cracking at many places.

Economic and Social Progress

The expansion in higher education and the diversification in developing countries ascribe to a combination of several factors. One such factor is the recognition of higher education as a means of economic and social progress. Improvement in general standards of living and rapid urbanisation has also been contributory factors. There is a welcome rise in the number of men and women from different strata of life seeking higher education. There is also a growing number of those already employed who enrolled for higher education to improve their prospects. The cost of higher education with pressure for change in almost all the countries have brought into focus the question of finding adequate resources for financing educational programmes.

Impact

Higher education gains importance as it sets standards. Its impact on the individual who learns and on the society to which the individuals belong, is tremendous because it takes them to a higher level of thinking and understanding of what is going on and how they can contribute to the community.

*****

Educational Priorities in the 21St Century

Educational planning for the 21st century have to examine the links between education and development as it existed in the 20th century. Based on the lessons drawn from such an examination they must determine priorities for the 21st century. The largest majority of our population in South Asia, or Asia minus Japan, Singapore and a couple of other Asian countries, are poor, illiterate and unemployed. They suffer and live in unhealthy surroundings because they cannot afford to live in more healthy surroundings.

Human Rights Oriented Curricula

Development priorities have to be set for the benefit of all and not just for the rich sectors of the world and nation. Development philosophies must be people oriented development projects in a healthy environment, with right to equality before law and equal right to education up to the higher secondary level, right to pursue one's legitimate intellectual and spiritual interest, right to work, right to safety are protected from terrorism.

Aspects of human rights have to become part of the curricula of various school and college level courses. Similarly, environmental issues ought to be included in the curricula, population issues have to be studied at various levels so that a proper historical perspective can be given to the youth of both the rich and poor, highly populated and sparsely populated countries.

A global approach to basic problems has to be inculcated in the students so that they can think globally and act locally. Only such an educational process can empower people at the grass root level and strengthen democracy.

Challenge for Graduates in Professional Courses

There are now hundreds of new professional institutions in every State of our country and there ought to be some special tasks associated with nation-building for the graduates who come out of these centres of medical, engineering, business management and other newly designed streams of study.

Nation-Building

"A nation is built in its educational institutions." College essentially a corporate body of teachers, students and administrative service staff working together for the promotion of knowledge, the imparting of skills to the young and progress of the community and the nation.

Success of the Educational Institutions

The relationships among these various groups and those between different groups and the public including parents and others who come in contact with the colleges will have to be of a high quality. It is such sincere and dedicated relationships which will ultimately lead to the success of the educational institutions.

Quality Leadership

Education, etymologically, signifies the attempt to draw out the best among the taught and helps them give quality leadership to the nation. Along with magnificent buildings and excellent equipment, there is a need for dedicated teachers and efficient management for an educational institution to flourish. Above all, there is a need for the support of the community in which the institution functions.

One In One Hundred

If India has been able to make a mark in the world today, it is because of its readiness to change with the times. The new professional colleges are providing better facilities and equipment of global significance. At the same time, students have to remember how privileged they are in our global village where hardly one person in one hundred gets the opportunity of higher education. We are living in a fast changing world, but we are also placed in a world where almost half the people are still eking out a mere existence on less than a dollar a day despite some marvellous achievements in science and technology.

Hallmarks of Democracy

True education needs an atmosphere for free exchange of ideas, opinions and thoughts. There should also be facilities and avenues for discussions and debates among students and teachers besides games and sports facilities. The skills necessary for facing life do not all come from books and lectures, but through corporate living and concerted action, doing things together in a spirit of camaraderie. The democratic spirit is imbibed in no small measures by young people during their school and college days, in the classrooms, libraries, hostels and sports and games fields. Cooperation, not confrontation or unfair competition, is the hallmark of democracy. The spirit of give and take that is the base of a democratic society is learnt in the educational institutions.

Socio-economic Realities

More than the intellectual ability or the technical skill, what makes us valuable to society is devotion to a good cause. We as a nation having great resources, technical and human, and have proved our merit not only nationally but also globally. But we cannot jettison some 400 million fellow Indians who are absolutely poor. This thought is important because our higher education should not make us ignore the socio-economic realities. An educated person must take interest in what is happening around him or her. If the educated do not take interest in the higher goals of life and fundamental aspects of science and philosophy, they are not truly educated.

Knowledge of the Society

The destiny of India depends on her spiritual strength rather than on material prosperity of half of her children. The spirit of India is broken when the other half is suffering from various disabilities. One cannot wash away this reality in India today. Along with material sciences, social science and management sciences, we have to devote some attention to the sociology of knowledge and the dangers of over-specialisation. Just as every educated citizen ought to have knowledge of the material world and its sciences, it is important that he should have knowledge of the society in which he lives and how his knowledge is going to benefit unto the last in society.

New Avenues for Employment to Empower

The new millennium must be both a challenge and a message of hope to the millions whose lives are not touched by the great achievements of science and technology in the past three centuries but overshadowed by the threat of poverty and misery. At least some of us must start new industries which will open up new avenues of employment for those who are unemployed today. All our future actions as engineers, managers, computer experts, information technologists and specialists of various kinds must be geared to pull up the huge segment of fellow citizens from the abyss of ignorance and inequalities, social injustice and economic deprivation and empower them to stand on their own feet.

Modern Means to Improve Human Condition

The modern means of communication, the latest devices for exchange of information, the fastest means of production and labour-saving, and the latest inventions and discoveries in engineering, medicine, management and information and communication technology (ICT) will create plenty of comforts and leisure for the educated. All this will have to be used to promote human rights and improve the human conditions in general. It should not suppress the natural rights of the many for establishing the special privileges of the few.

Balancing Regional Expectations and Global Objectives

In the colleges and universities, the curriculum and educational process are to be dynamically and integrally linked to issues of regional development. The objective is to strive for a balance between the regional expectations from these publically financed institutions and their global objectives in education and research. This would require a complete reorganisation of academic life in colleges and university campuses with a fresh direction to the students and faculty. In the long run, this involvement in development would endow the colleges and universities with the capability to guide and assist people's initiatives, thereby infusing life in the campuses with a sense of societal relevance.

*****

Humanistic Education

The term 'education' connotes rearing. Rearing implies a number of things including guiding, trimming, disciplining and grooming for the harmonious development of total personality. Its meaning encompasses the mental, moral and physical dimensions and endows education with the responsibility for gearing optimum growth in all respects.

Those of us who shoulder or share even a part of these obligations are therefore called upon to provide necessary inputs for realising the goals set. Educational planners and administrators should in this context, not even for a moment forget that education and life are co-terminous. As one lives, he/she continuously undergoes education. *"Education must be conceived as an interdisciplinary concept as a factor of multi-dimensional development of which, man is both the end and the instrument." Life itself is an education.*

The ancient Indian concept takes "education" as an instrument of emancipation which dismantles all restraints to diverse experiences. This implies the opening up of intakes and sharpening of the senses for the same.

A Humanistic approach to education presupposes among various other things, a reverence of the kaleidoscopic mystery of human life and experience. It challenges the assumptions of our educational methodology and it seeks to liberate us from the bondage and tyranny of customs and untested orthodoxies. Humanism implies that education affords young men and women an opportunity to become human, by discovering new meanings and fresh facets of human existence. Humanistic education is open to more extensive interpretations of life than it is possible in our educational environment today.

Human Values in Education

Human beings require human excellence in addition to their physical needs, helping which are common to all living beings. The best medium for helping man to develop his supra animal qualities is education with human values to develop not only the intuitions, and psycho-spiritual development but also help in overcoming the limiting forces that divide human beings on various grounds, like differences in colour, religion, nationality, caste and community and teach the essences of all great religions, sciences and philosophies. "The main thrust should be to deal with the main aims of human life. It should be an approach to human life and a prescription for happy living" and to human understanding and well-being in all aspects.

Five Levels of Humans

"Education in Human values should be developed in every human being as it helps other levels like the physical, the intellectual and the mental. It is useful for human beings at all ages but is all the more useful and has a lasting effect on younger people. We have to consider the main characteristics of a human being and the relevance of human values in the all-round development of one's personality. A man has five levels of being, i.e. the physical, the intellectual, the emotional, the psychic and the spiritual.

Five Basic Human Values

The five basic human values are truth, righteousness and good conduct, peace, love and non-violence. These values correspond to the five basic characteristics of human nature: physical — good conduct and righteousness; intellectual — truth; emotional — peace; psychic — love and spiritual — non-violence.

Technical Education

There is need to generate updated and appropriate technology. Scientists, engineers, managers and workers have to be organised so that they can translate science and technology to produce useful goods and services that are beneficial to society. Inadequacy on this front is causing a setback in the technological environment.

The major objectives of education, whether technology or humanities, are to socialise the individual by making him develop roots in the tradition and attitudes of his/her society to equip him with basic information and intellectual tools that would help him find his way through life and train him to earn his livelihood in conformity with norms of economic conduct accepted by the society.

*****

Physical Education

Sports and Physical Education is an integral part of the learning process and will be included in the evaluation of performance. Physical education is closely correlated with mental and social development of the individual. Physical education should aim at making a person physically, mentally and emotionally fit and develop his personal and social qualities which will help him to live in harmony with others and become a good citizen. The outcomes of wholesome and methodological programmes of physical education are:

Sound Mind and Body

This is a vast subject; it includes the acquisition of good habits in food, sleep, hygiene and the use of physical exercises to regulate the various functions of the body and mind.

Fitness

Not only muscular strength and physical stamina should be developed but the skill, dexterity and endurance which sports and games develop and, which are an excellent preparation for many occupations should also be encouraged.

Training of the Senses

It should be the aim to develop a quick perception of the eye and ear and a quick response of all the parts of the body to any call made upon them and a coordination and mastery over reflexes, as for instance in gymnastics and balancing.

Principles for Developing Programmes

- The physical education programme should be planned for desirable outcomes keeping in mind the interest and capacity of the participants.
- The traditional forms of play and physical activities that have developed in our country should receive due emphasis in the programme.

Higher Education for the Future

- The activities provided should develop in each student a sense of personal worth and pride.
- A sense of sharing responsibility in a spirit of democratic cooperation should grow from experiences in playground and also in the gymnasium.
- The programmes offered should supplement other programmes of education and not duplicate them
- The programme should reach all rather than a select few.
- Special instruction and coaching should be provided for students with talent and special attitude.

Change in Attitude

Physical education should include developmental exercises, rhythmic activities sports and games, outing activities and group works. Development infrastructure, integration and evaluation of physical education at all levels of education would generate adequate awareness, great interest and awakening in the programmes of physical education.

There should be a change in attitude and approach of teachers towards physical education. The traditional practice of preparing selected students for sports and games competitions should be replaced by mass participation of students in physical education activities. All teachers should also take pride in participation in these programmes.

*****

Women's Education

Women's Education

Women's studies should prepare them for playing an equal role, not necessarily identical, with men in society. Research studies should consider the areas of disability, the handicaps the impediments and the prejudices that women face and devise ways of educating and enabling men and women to remove them.

A change is needed in the outlook and approach of both men and women. It needs the preparation of women to be able to claim and maintain an equal status. It will not come to them as a gift. Education truly holds the key for such a change and preparation. Science and technology offer the real chance for a life of freedom, dignity and equality for women consistent in conformity with their biological differences and disposition.

The new challenges that education and research in general and women's education in particular will have to face are immense. Another area where the women's universities could play a significant role is in deciding the direction of the women's education by themselves.

Women's Education and Varsities

The history of women's education in India can be traced to the Vedic Age, when women had the same status in society as men with equal rights to education. Women were given good religious education. They were also taught fine arts like music and dancing. References to these can be found in the Vedic hymns, Taittriya Samhitas.

With the advent of the Muslim rule in India there was a decline in the status and education of women. It was at the efforts of Christian Missionaries, although their aim was to spread their religion, girls schools were opened and continued with sustained vigour. The cause of women's education was also strengthened by the efforts of the social reformers.

Women's Education in Independent India

With independence in 1947, came more opportunities for women's education. The National Committee on Women's education under the chairmanship of the late Durgabai Deshmukh was set up in 1958 to suggest measures for the improvement of women's education in the country. Emphasising the need for bridging the gulf between men's and women's education, the committee called for the cooperation of semi-officials, local bodies and voluntary organisations in promotion of women's education. It is now realised that equality of educational opportunity is not synonymous with the identity of opportunity. The crux of the matter about women's education lies not so much in the assumption that women were inferior, superior or equal to men, but in fact they were different—a girl's physical, intellectual, emotional, social, moral and spiritual needs and changing social roles that she has to play postulates a special type of education for her.

Women's University

Women's universities need to avoid merely duplicating the work of the existing universities. They should give new direction to the courses. This will help in proving the girls with an education in conformity with their attitudes and aptitudes and one that would be a proper preparation for their future vocation, not only as wives and mothers but also as individuals and professionals.

Vocational Training for Women

A majority of women in India today go out to work, almost certainly before marriage and after their children have grown up they can fend for themselves. Further, economic exigencies also compel many married women to work, in order to supplement their husband's income. Hence, it is important to give them a vocational training that will serve as an "insurance policy". Education of women should also aim at equipping them to make creative use of their leisure, both for their personal development and for the improvement of the society at large.

True Architects of Future

Education of women seems to be in fact more important than that of men, for "If you educate a man, you educate an individual: if you educate a woman, you educate a family" for "Women create men and women—they do so mentally, physically and spiritually as mothers, wives and teachers. They are the true architects of the future. Women civilize men and thus preserve civilisation.

Factors Responsible for Poor Progress in Women's Education

Domestic duty

One of the main causes for poor progress in women's education particularly in the rural areas is that they are required to work at a very young age in various domestic chores. Some are required to work as paid and unpaid workers.

Social Factors

Marriage of girls is a determining factor in their education.

Inadequate Infrastructural facilities

There are poor physical facilities which act as a deterrent factor for women education.

Defective Curricula and Policies

Although equality of men and women has been enshrined in the Constitution and guaranteed in the laws of the land, there has been gender bias in the curricular provisions. The topics have been given in the textbooks depicting women as home makers, wives and mothers. Women are shown as non-achievers, passive, timid and dependent whereas men are shown as high achievers, courageous, daring and active participants.

All these above factors coupled with ignorance, poverty and mass illiteracy have contributed to the poor progress in women's education.

Solutions for Progress of Women's Education

- The media should be utilised for promoting awareness among masses on the importance of women's education.
- Local leaders, voluntary agencies and political people should also be involved in the promotion of women's education.
- The economic conditions of the parents should be improved and some compensatory assistance be given for spacing their daughters for education.

- Employment opportunities should be made available to educate women in various sectors of the society.
- Curricula as well as textbooks should be oriented accordingly and sex bias should be abolished as fast as possible.
- Early childhood education should be expanded.
- Philanthropic and social service agencies may be requested to extend assistance to the girls of poor families.
- Early (Childhood) marriage of females must be prevented by law enforcing authorities.
- Female literacy rate of 24.83% which is almost half of that for males with 46.89% needs to be raised at least to the national average rate of 36.23%.

Dress Code

The girls will become confident and will not feel shy of working along with men later in their career. At the same time we should not sacrifice discipline in colleges and severe punishment should be given to those indulging in ragging within the campus or outside. The states should be armed with statutes to deal with mischief mongers.

The college authorities may impose some sort of dress codes. Students may also realise the importance of dress codes. The visual media and blind imitation of what is showy in western culture by youth of both sexes are major culprits in prompting pseudo, ultra-modern fashions causing violence. Parents and teachers should approach their adolescent stage problems with caution and responsible care.

Education as an Agent of Change for Women Empowerment

The National policy on Education 1986, viewed education as a premier instrument for promoting equality of status and opportunities between men and women and between groups divided by class, caste and other forms of historical oppression. It regards education as an agent of basic change in the status of women. It states that the national education system would play a positive interventionist role in the empowerment of women. It would also foster the development of new values, through redesigned curricula, textbooks, decision makers and administrators and active involvement of educational institutions. It also states that women's studies would be permitted as a part of various courses, and educational institutions would be encouraged to take up active programmes to further women's development.

Women's Study Centres in Universities

Universities can do a lot for promoting educational empowerment of women. Women's study centres can play a major role in changing the attitudes of conventional academics and educational administrators towards the societal role of women. By the end of 10th plan there were about 66 centres for women's studies in universities and colleges. Within the university structure, centres/cells of women's studies are set up to conduct research on women's issues, to promote extension services to develop gender free curriculum for different subjects, to document and disseminate women related information.

Women's Representation

The reservation for women teachers/students has been granted in a few university Acts only. Karnataka State University Act, Kurukshetra University Act and Maharishi Dayanand University Act are some of those providing for at least one woman principal to be represented in their Syndicate. The Karnataka State University Act also provides for two women students and one women graduate to be represented in the university Senate.

Facilitating Women's Educational Empowerment

The following are some of the measures that can facilitate women's educational empowerment:
- More colleges and Universities should be opened for women's higher education.
- Incentives like scholarships, free books, etc., should be provided to enable girls from rural areas to pursue higher education.

- Girls should be encouraged to enter more professional courses.
- Departments of Adult Education, continuing education and extension centres should undertake large scale extension programmes in order to activate girls and women in the surrounding areas to take advantage of educational facilities of various types.
- To increase the proportion of rural girls in higher education certain percentage of seats may be reserved for girls.
- All agencies involved with preparations of curriculum, prescription of textbooks and organisation of educational processes will have to increase awareness towards women's issues.
- Appropriate voluntary agencies, women's groups, etc., should be involved in giving new perspectives for the issues of content and process of education.

Role of Distance Education in Women Empowerment

To overcome the rigidities, compulsions and limitations of formal system of education and make new efforts to develop non-formal education begun four decades ago in the Indian University system. Women who mostly remained outside the formal system for a variety of reasons are expected to be beneficiaries of distance education. Distance education is a home-based and learner-centered education, which is free from the constraints of time and place. India has 14 distance teaching universities, which are popularly called as 'Open Universities' offering a number of academic programmes. Besides, over 100 conventional universities also offer a variety of distance education programmes. Distance teaching methodologies can be used for educational advancement of women.

Suggestions for Women Empowerment in Higher Education

- Awareness programmes regarding the distance education courses for women in urban, rural and tribal areas will provide opportunities for them to gain knowledge about existing educational facilities.

- The courses for women in distance education should be application-oriented so that it will help them in their economic and social empowerment.
- The course materials should be simple, preferably in regional languages to make women more comfortable to use.
- The gender component should be incorporated in the syllabus of all disciplines.
- The fee should be affordable for weaker sections of the society especially women.
- Gender sensitisation programmes should be organised to benefit teachers and learners.
- Confidence building and personality building programmes are essential to help women to overcome resistance to distance education.
- Women should be motivated and trained to use technology for faster and easier learning.
- Separate channels for local T.V. and radio must be introduced to promote distance education for women.
- Study centres with libraries, should be opened in each village to facilitate women's education.
- A good response is required from the distance education providers to enquiries of the learners from various places.
- Recognition is also required for distance education degrees among the educational institutions, employers and the society.
- The quality of the study materials should be enhanced and availability should be made in time for the learners.
- The contact programmes in Distance Education should be flexible to so that the timing is suitable for the working women in urban and rural areas.

Women's Educational Equality is Equality of Mental Faculties

In the human domain, excellence is the excellence of the mind and excellence in performance, whatever be the task equality is equality of mental faculties. Freedom is a concept; dignity is a concept and self-esteem is a concept. These are matters of the mind rather than that of the body. One must therefore look for equality in the world of knowledge, not in dress, not in habits, not in any external manifestations. Women must choose to maintain whatever feminine characteristics and equalities that nature has endowed them to adore and remain equal with men. They need neither to imitate nor copy men. Women's studies should therefore concentrate on the nature of opportunities that now emerge for women to prepare themselves for playing an equal role—not necessarily identical role—with men in the affairs of the society. The research studies should consider the areas of disability, the handicaps, the impediments and the prejudices that women face and devise ways of educating and enabling men and women to remove them.

*****

Architecture and Education

Monuments

Architecture is the matrix of civilisation. Historically architecture has showcased man's intellectual capacity and skills right through the ages. Indian monuments bear testimony for its rich architectural heritage. Ancient Indian's rich outstanding quality of architecture is evident from its monumental temple structures, sculptures, etc.

World Class

The Moguls had an aesthetic sense and a remarkable skill in construction. Be it a palace or a tomb, everything showcased the architectural skill and knowledge present at that period. The Taj Mahal is one of the world's most outstanding monuments. The entire complex was proportionally designed accordingly to a series of geometrically related grids, explaining not only the tomb's perfect balance but also that of the entire complex. The magnificent design, the exquisite garden, proper layouts are world class even now. We may boast of advancement in every sphere, but today we can't bring out such masterpieces in architecture.

Landscape and Greenery As Catalyst of Changes

Architects play a pivotal role to give an aesthetic value to the building and give a facelift to the structure. Eco factors should also be taken into consideration. The rich heritage, culture and architecture of our country should be replicated in the construction. Whether it is a complex or a residential apartments or an industry, landscape and greenery should be made mandatory. The architects are the catalyst of change who bring about novel designs and novel techniques in the construction industry.

Visiting Faculty in Architecture Department

It is no secret that there is a severe dearth of full time faculty in most architectural institutions in the country. Many schools of architecture depend on visiting faculty members who are practicing architects. However, if visiting members of the Staff outnumber their full-time counterparts by a big margin, as is the case of many schools, fixing the accountability for teachers' actions and general control of the instruction schedule becomes very difficult. This may lead to dilution of academic standards.

An important pre-requisite for the success of any educational institution is the harmony of relationship between its students and the faculty. This is all the more vital in the case of architecture studies which demands a close academic interaction between the former and the latter. Further internal assessment marks in this course being very high, combined with considerable subjective element in evaluation, many departments have found this to be the bone of contention between students and teachers.

Teachers have to maintain a high level of integrity and any extraneous consideration is never allowed to interfere in the assessment of students' works. Regular meetings are held between the representatives of students and the faculty members to thrash out any problems which they may face. It is ingrained in both the students and teachers that they should always safeguard the interests of the department as a whole, rather than think of any issue as the one of staff verses students. This philosophy has paid rich dividends and as testimony to its success.

*****

Technical Education in the 21st Century

Competitiveness is going to demand higher standards of ability and understanding and expertise that will be acquired only through quality academic inputs of international standards. In this 21st century, greater economic interdependence among nations and advances in communication technology are bringing into reality, the concept of the world becoming a global village. Many are being confronted by common economic, social multicultural and educational problems.

Engineering Education Today and Tomorrow

Engineering education is one of the principal instruments of change for achieving human resources development. There has been a significant qualitative change in the job requirements of engineers. Quality, productivity, excellence and values are some of the concepts and indices for assessing the performance. There is considerable scope for improvement in many spheres, including industry–university interaction, contributions of professional societies, etc. Some of the critical issues requiring attention are the current trends toward introduction of narrow specialisations, accreditations, etc. Strong and urgent corrective actions are necessary to respond optimally to the emerging challenges such as globalisation of markets, enhanced quality requirements, liberalisation of economy, etc.

Socio-economic Development

Science, Technology and education and in particular, technical and management education, are the principal instruments of change for achieving socio-economic development and a decent standard of living. Human resources development with acquisition of the relevant technological knowledge and skills is recognised to be capable of making up for the lack of material resources.

Compulsions of a Changing World

Resource allocation and enforcement of standard quality, challenges of globalisation of markets, competition from other countries, international markets (e.g. ISO 9000) and the dire necessity to earn 'forex' have all necessitated a reconsideration of the traditional attitudes and the strategies.

The compulsions of a changing world have to be accepted and managed. Pragmatism should guide the policies and actions.

Forward Look in Education

Education has been recognised as the most crucial and significant factor in activating and optimising the welfare of the society through its ramifications in almost all spheres of life. Economic development, social welfare and cultural progress are the ultimate goal of any nation. There are many internal and external challenges in attaining these goals in an ever changing world of science and technology.

Education is the most effective instrument to meet these challenges. Only education can imbue people with knowledge, a sense of purpose and the confidence essential for building a dynamic, vibrant and cohesive nation, capable of providing its people with the wherewithal for creating better fuller and more purposeful lives.

Updating Education

Updated education is the core and crux of all development activities at all levels starting from the workers to the top level managers and administrators. Stagnated water becomes polluted; so also knowledge. One should continuously update his knowledge and skills in the fast changing world of science and technology otherwise he will be rejected by society. Curriculum revision and renewal is the only means through which the education system can become a real instrument of social change and development. In the face of all this, our efforts sometimes dissipate because of lack of such updated education among the masses and expected results cannot be achieved as there is lack of community involvement. The curriculum is to be updated to match the challenges and required curriculum materials are to be designed including applications of the mass media and educational technology. There is awakening to modernise the whole of the education system in order that it may cope with the increasing challenges and demands.

Key to Real Progress

We have to plan for real progress from now on, as the demands of the 21st century may not be easier ones. If we want to have a breakthrough it should only be through education. The new inputs are:
- Instructional processes should be based on the needs, abilities and interests of learners.
- Better organisation of space for group learning and independent learning will have to be applied.
- A teacher should be a facilitator in helping the student to learn rather than a transmitter of knowledge.
- Methods should be adopted to monitor the progress of student's learning at every stage and to provide guidelines.
- Information technology should find an extensive role in all teaching and learning methods.
- Conventional face-to-face teaching will be slowly reduced and self-study through various resource materials will be encouraged.
- Open education channels should be developed fast.
- Multimedia libraries should be established and promoted in place of libraries with mere printed material.
- More credit-based modular education programmes will be developed and implemented.
- There should be greater emphasis on the faculty and staff development through regular in-service education and training programmes at all levels.
- Apart from in-service education, continuing education programmes with credit approach will be promoted.

- Curriculum will be designed scientifically and linked with career development.
- The education system should re-link learning with life and this is very essential to achieve our aims.

Future Education

Education for future must be a global one and a multipurpose social service which must reward human resourcefulness and commitment. Nowadays it is widely understood that knowledge must be continuously acquired, put to use and supplemented by a lifelong retaining system.

National Qualifications Framework

A qualification is an award which recognises that learning has taken place and a standard has been achieved. In a competitive world of today every individual is striving hard to achieve a standard in a particular skill. The attainment of particular standard of knowledge is now tested in terms of its employability, irrespective of its expertise and innovative ideas that have more opportunities and better prospects, both within the country and at global level. Increasingly, firms are looking to higher levels of knowledge and skills among their employees in order to gain an advantage over their competitors. In a globally competitive world, the balance between two firms goes in favour of those who have an edge in knowledge and technology. Qualifications provide this recognition of a person's skills and knowledge. Keeping the changing needs of the industry and the diversity of manpower requirements, the countries like New Zealand, Australia and England have introduced an innovative structure called National Qualification Framework (NQF) in their educational systems.

Emergence of New Structure of Knowledge and Education

The emergence of new structures like the National Qualification for Framework (NQF), which is designed to develop knowledge, skills and understanding in broad areas of study and vocations created a new phenomenon in education. The NQF provides opportunities to people to receive national recognition for their skills and qualifications. The NQFs introduced in the advanced countries offers greater flexibility for the learner and removes many traditional barriers of learning such as attending to a formal training course in an institution. The NQF is designed to cover general, vocational and industry based education and training and each is registered at an appropriate level on the framework.

Influence of NQF Levels on NVQs

In the UK, the National Vocational Qualifications (NVQs) are designed at 5 levels. The levels reflect increasing levels of complexity and responsibility in a job role. Roughly speaking level 1 applies to jobs which are mostly routine and predictable whereas level 5 applies to jobs which are very complex and involve significant responsibility for the work of others (senior managers). Therefore, not all occupations have NVQs at all levels but eventually all occupations will be represented within the NVQ framework (From Abattoir workers to Zoo keepers). In New Zealand the framework has eight levels, ranging from achievement comparable to school certificate at level 1 to postgraduate qualifications at level 8. The emergence of NQFs and the organisations involved in setting standards, awarding qualifications and accrediting providers helped to popularise the framework among the job seekers and employers.

Half-Life of Knowledge and NQF

There is a relationship between NQF and the Half-Life of Knowledge (HLK). The half-life of knowledge is a concept popularised by World Bank experts. It constitutes the speed of acquisition and deterioration of knowledge. The table below shows that half-life of knowledge can be divided into Long Half-life of knowledge (LHK) and Short Half-Life of Knowledge(SHK) depending upon the knowledge type, acquisition time, finance and the positive externalities.

Half-Life of Knowledge

S.No.	Subjects	Long Half-life of Knowledge	Short Half-life of Knowledge
1.	Knowledge Type	Academic, basic, Theoretical	Vocational, Practical
2.	Acquisition Time	Long years, months	Short-days, weeks, months
3.	Quick Econ Return	No	Yes
4.	Social Externalities	High	Low
5.	Finance	Families, State	Workers, businesses
6.	Examples	Basic socialisation, Citizenship, language, mathematics, logic, reasoning, theoretical parts of professional training	Industrial processes software use, specific technical and professional skills.

It is a known fact that knowledge can be embodied in persons through the development of skills or disembodied through the advancement of technology. Now the skilled manpower of the third world countries is migrating to the West (due to lucrative pay and life styles) making the scarce native experts of the advanced countries to concentrate on highly paid sophisticated jobs. The half-life of knowledge in the table is of short-term duration and is offered NVQs. The NVQs can be obtained by anyone including those who are in formal educational institutions undergoing training in a comprehensive curriculum. NVQs provide opportunities of employment to those who are in the formal institutions.

"Brain Squeeze" in the Third World

The excess reliance on skills that are in demand in the global labour market imposes a "brain squeeze" in the developing countries where the cream of young minds opt for such skills, leaving the basic sciences, mathematics and social sciences deserted. In fact most of the universities in the developing countries were developed during the colonial period and modelled on the development of liberal arts and science courses. They need to be re-organised now to suit the emerging conditions of knowledge based on economy and social conditions. The universities are now facing a challenge as major innovations are taking place in independent specialised institutes and the entry of lumpen elements in research projects are hijacking project money. The traditional universities are concentrating on fundamental research and in the creation of knowledge, which has a long half-life of knowledge that takes care of the long run interest of the society and economy. But the policy makers in the developing countries are not in a position to see the relevance of these institutes to protect interests of the nation rather than helping the industrialised economies with reverse subsidy. It is likely that in the near future these societies face excessive supply of certain skills and a shortage of people with basic sciences.

Learning Method in Western Countries and the US

In Western countries particularly in the US, there is a lot of emphasis on learning by doing—by questioning and challenging assumptions. You are not expected to be an obedient and double listener accepting what the professor tells you. You have to explore experiment and question everything including what is being taught to you. In this way what you learn is not based on belief but in actually seeing it and analysing it yourself. Such knowledge stays with you forever, because it enters into your bloodstream and does not merely remain in some unknown recesses of your brain. It becomes a part of you. And when you need it, it comes to you as a natural, intuitive insight. It also helps you to develop your own independent thinking, such a system combined with a cross-disciplinary approach nurtures creativity. No wonder so many innovations and inventions happen in the West.

Continuous Change of Curriculum

The change in curriculum should be a continuous and ongoing process; each university should undertake innovations for periodic revision of the curriculum every two to three years and an intensive revision every four to five years depending on the developments in the subject area. In the exercise of autonomy in this regard, the process for revision of curriculum should be reviewed, simplified and made less cumbersome and time consuming. Apex bodies like UGC and AICTE may evolve appropriate mechanism of overseeing the quality of curricular changes envisaged by the institutions and provide feedback for improvement wherever required.

Research Fund for Faculty Members

No faculty member should suffer in his/her research endeavours for want of funds. In order to facilitate this, certain funds should be made available to faculty members against duly worked out and approved research proposal. In return, the faculty member should be accountable to maintain progress of research of acceptable standards as should be evidenced by publications in reputed journals.

Self-Financing Courses

All universities and colleges should be given the autonomy to start self-financing courses, particularly in new and emerging areas where job opportunities exist subject to the overall framework provided by the funding and regulatory bodies. Rules and regulations on this may be reviewed with a view to dispensing with avoidable hassles.

Admission Policy

Any uniform prescription for admissions applied to all higher education institutions in such a vast country as India is going to put several institutions with very special character in difficulty. Though the Centre may evolve a national system of entrance examination for various programmes, the institutions may be given a free hand to join it or conduct their own entrance examinations. The Government of India may consider establishing a National Testing Service on the lines of Educational Testing Service of the USA as envisaged in the NPE 1986. Higher educational institutions may use a suitable combination of the scores obtained both in the entrance test and in the qualifying examination for admissions. A composite index may be evolved by way of giving proper weightage to other vital parameters such as percentile scores in classes X and XII, extra-curricular activities, interviews, etc. There should be absolute autonomy for this purpose up to the level of university. However, the mechanism adopted by universities and other higher education institutions should be fair, transparent and well publicised in advance to ensure that there are no malpractices.

Non-Academic Support Staff Outsourcing

To the extent possible, appropriate non-academic activities could be outsourced to achieve better efficiency and greater effectiveness, thus reducing the overall burden of administering a higher education institution. The universities and colleges should have only a small component of non-academic support staff but adequate technical and academic support staff. The institutions should strive to achieve a ratio 1:1.5 to 2.0 between the teaching and non-teaching staff including both technical and academic support staff.

Tribunal Set-up

A Central Higher Education Tribunal should be set up for expeditious disposal of litigations on service matters relating to both academic and non-academic staff in the higher education system. There is also a need to encourage the state to set up similar state Higher Education Tribunal for the same purpose.

Upgrading of Infrastructure

In respect of self-financing institutions/courses in government and government- aided institutions, it is desirable that fees are kept at levels which meet the actual cost of imparting education and create some reasonable surplus which should be utilised for upgradation of infrastructure and facilities without allowing commercialisation, with a mission of service and not exploitation. All institutions should be required to adopt certain disclosure standards with a view to containing malpractice in relation to fee. All institutions should provide free scholarships to meritorious and deserving students from lower socio-economic strata of the society. Institutions should also encourage and facilitate availability of education loans for higher education.

Financial Auditing

The system of audit, including internal audit in respect of both government and private institutions, should be strengthened with a view to ensure proper expenditure management and compliance with financial rules and regulations. The outcome of the audit reports should be discussed and acted upon for improving the overall financial management in the higher education system. Audited statements of every year should be made public.

Potential on par with the Best

We have become leaders in IT and are surging ahead in biotechnology. India can become a developed nation if there is fast development of knowledge. We have the potential to be on par with the best. We have to make the fullest use of the educational opportunities in the university. What you learn in the colleges and universities is not an end in itself. You should not feel that when you leave the university your studies are over. Learning is a continuous process.

Higher Education for the Future

Knowledge Power

Our Nation's future is inextricably linked to developments in Science, Technology and Managerial skill and capabilities. Changes in our economy and the need to effectively meet the challenges of Globalisation compel us to have a workforce educated in Science, Technology and Management. In today's world knowledge is power. Mere abundance of natural resources will not do. Several countries like Singapore, Taiwan, South Korea, China, Malaysia and Israel proved themselves to be extremely innovative in order to move economically ahead of us.

Clear Vision and Goal

The engineers of tomorrow must be analytical and have the capacity to arrive at solutions based on global information and must have the ability to work in a competitive environment. Universities should have a clear vision and goal-oriented missions to produce professionals with these capabilities.

*****

Education Technology

Education Technology has rich potentialities and possibilities for accelerating the pace of human progress in general and for bringing about development in various aspects of education in particular. It would help in surpassing the limits of time and distance. It has capabilities of bypassing several stages and sequences that are normal in the process of development.

Status and Promises

Educational Technology consists of all modern media, methods and materials and needs to be used in a very well-integrated manner for maximising the learning experiences of students at various levels. It implies a behavioural science approach in teaching and learning and makes use of relevant scientific and technological methods and principles developed in psychology, sociology, linguistics, communications and other related areas.

It also seeks to incorporate the management concepts of cost effectiveness, systems approach and the efficient deployment and utilisation of human as well as material resources. It helps in optimisation of educational outcomes through the development, application and evaluation systems, methods and techniques in the field of teaching and learning.

Media in Education

We are in a world of Electronic Media involving Radio, Television, Films, Tape Recorders, VCR, VCP, Computers, etc. These methods and materials must be deployed and displayed in the field of education with the help of these media for providing efficient and effective learning experiences. Education can reach a take-off stage with the help of modern technologies and can be made available to masses in remote areas of the society. This would remove disparity in the educational facilities available to the disadvantaged and provide individualised instruction to learners conveniently suited to their needs and pace of learning.

Planning and Production

Educational Technology should therefore be viewed not as a panacea for all the ills in the educational system. Nor it should be deployed in a piece-meal and haphazard manner. It should be utilised in a well-integrated and well-planned manner, without lopsided and single medium approach. Selection of media is, of course, important from the nature and objectives of learning, but planning and production with cooperation and participation of students as well as teachers would ensure more effectiveness and credibility.

*****

Public Relations

Public Relationship, as a profession, is probably the youngest in our country. In our changing social and economic environment, it has proved its importance as an effective management tool. Public Relations are basically a philosophy of the management, an attitude of an organisation, a business or a public institution. Though important as a catalyst of social change, Public

Relations field is yet to develop as a scientific discipline like other management disciplines. There is a great need of training for its development. Public Relations is highly specialised and developed in Western countries because they give due importance to training.

Objectives of PR Education

- To make the students aware of the significance of the philosophy of communications in their personal social and professional life.
- To make students aware of the job directions of this discipline.
- To calculate in the mind of students a sense of responsibility and accountability in the use of the mode of communications.
- To develop the skills required in the area of communication for public relations and advertising.
- To provide a base in PR and advertising courses for interdisciplinary tie-ups.
- To provide a university with a global and national view of the growth and development and needs of advertising of PR.
- To provide university youth with the socio-economic and political demographic environment as they relate to the jobs of PR and advertising. The detailed syllabi for such courses have also been prepared.
- The PR Education should consist of not just public relations courses but of study in all disciplines linked through a communication core. Since communication is a sheet anchor of public relations, a study in communications process with reference to communication revolution in the country is essential.

PR Responsibility

Public Relations is a profession with great responsibilities — varied and sometimes vexing. A PRO's job is tight-rope walking between two poles — one end is the management and at the other the Public. Only education and training can make him a miracle man; education is his magic wand.

*****

Information and Communication Technology (ICT) In Education

Relevance of ICT in Education

The long-term relevance of information and communication Technology (ICT) in education is characterised by the following possibilities:
- Global access to knowledge.
- Sharing of experiences and best practices.
- Consistent higher quality education.
- Self-paced and self-based learning.
- Effective learning for solid fundamentals early in learning lifestyle.
- Experimental learning.
- Creative computer-based content can facilitate more effective delivery of curricular content and can also be an effective supplement for teachers to improve learning levels.
- Computers also have a potential to deliver standardised training to teachers including distance learning.

Student Enrolment in Higher Education

The age group of 17-26 years is suited to be enrolled in higher education. From the existing data it is a matter of great concern that approximately 80% are out of the higher education system. Mere 20.4% of the said age group is enrolled for higher education. In countries like Canada, USA and Australia the students' enrolment of the same age group is between 80% and 88%. Since the progress of higher education in India is very slow and inadequate to cater the need, it could empower very limited people ignoring the interest of the rest. It is relevant to note that in all the said countries higher education is available in their mother tongue; Malaysia and Indonesia, besides German and Spanish countries, have adopted English (Roman) script for their national languages and Russian script is also nearest to English, to facilitate easy interaction with English language. When we emphasise globalisation and international standards, we conveniently overlook thinking of advantages in adopting a uniform languages script, relative to the script of knowledge sciences.

Higher Education to build Nations

Higher education is not just an extension of school education. It is an important and major activity in the life span of an individual that will help to mould the destiny of a nation. You may lose your economy, you may also perish as an individual, but if your education is in your hands, you can rebuild all that is lost. This is proved beyond doubt after the World Wars. Japan, Germany and even Soviet Union could rebuild their economies and societies because they have their 'Own' education system.

Teacher Calibre – The King Pin

The King Pins of an institution are its teachers. In an institution if good teachers have joined the teaching profession, it is because they value academic freedom, enjoy teaching, learning and have made pursuit of excellence in their mission. Then quality automatically follows. It is generally believed that a just and fair system in rewarding good performance is crucial for teacher motivation. But, if one were to ask teachers of institutions that are highly rated, it would be found that they set their own goals and drive them with self-discipline for performing at the peak of their capability. The source of their motivation may be self-determined goals, peer appreciation, publishing articles in journals of repute, invitations for sharing their research work in conferences and seminars, etc., and not the desire for obtaining material gains such as rapid promotion in service or position of authority. Rewards and recognition follow them because of their hard work.

Quality performance – Infrastructure

Recruitment of high caliber teachers is necessary but may not be sufficient for ensuring quality in their performance. They would require support of infrastructure such as a good libraries, laboratories equipped with modern facilities essential for carrying out teaching and research at international standards and more than these a sympathetic understanding of their academic needs by the administration. Only then they may be able to work at the frontiers of knowledge by keeping themselves updated with the latest developments in their field.

Knowledge Generation – External Provider

The character of higher education, which is directed towards long-term goals of a knowledge-based society, needs autonomy not only from governmental bureaucratic institutions but also from market pressures. Higher education is the site for innovative foundational research and generation of knowledge. If it is reduced to mere transmission of operational technologies, a national society will remain at the mercy of external providers. A growing, autonomous higher education is a reflection of a mature society. At present, India has among the lowest percentage, even among the developing countries, of the relevant age group studying in its higher educational institutions. State funding is essential to ensure wider access to higher educational opportunities.

Private Higher Education – Policies to be Adopted

Private presence in higher education has become inevitable.
- Private players must be given the right to establish and administer higher education institutions.
- This would imply even a higher-fees paying system for it to be viable.
- Appropriation of seats by the state goes against that right and amounts to nationalisation, where they do not depend on any state aid and abide by the laws of the land.

- The regulation is warranted because the right to administer does not mean the right to mal-administer and that recognition by the state must imply minimum accountability.
- The right to regulate must be exercised in a manner that implies reasonable restriction which does not question the concept of private provision of educational services.
- Every private institution is free to devise its own reasonable fee structure, but profiteering and capitation fees be prohibited.

*****

M-learning (Mobile learning) and E-learning

The field of education through technology is a vast one with subtle distinctions among its various branches. Distance learning incorporates all forms of instructions in which the instructors and the students are physically removed from one another by time or space from traditional correspondence courses to web-based instruction. Electronic Learning or E-learning incorporates all forms of online instruction using personal computers (www3.telus.net). M-learning is the follow-up of E-learning which for its part originates from D-learning (Distance learning).

The term 'M-learning' has lately emerged to be associated with the use of mobile technology in education. Mobile learning simply means 'learning on the move', like on I-pads, laptops, mobiles and other handheld devices. In other words, the new term simply attempts to differentiate between learning that takes place in formal context, such as a classroom. In this the learning process takes place anytime, anywhere while we are moving in our environment. According to Clark Quim (2003), "it is E-learning through mobile computational devices. Traxler (2005) defined it as 'any educational provision where the sole or dominant technologies are handheld on Palmtop devices (Mostakhet al 2005). Another popular definition of M-learning is the delivery of training by means of mobile devices such as pocket PCs, mobile phones and palmtop computing devices, PDAs, tablets, e-book readers and similar handheld devices. While defining mobile-learning one confronts tension between functionality and mobility. There is a continuum from the point of view of functionality in the devices used for E-learning and M-learning. This continuum goes from desktop computers to laptop computers to PDAs or handhelds or palmtops to smartphones to mobile phones.

Mainly, two kinds of words are associated with mobile technology 'Portable', which means that we can carry those devices that we call mobile. Secondly, 'wireless', i.e. there are no wires connecting the devices. From the educational point of view, it is the mobility of devices that is interesting, i.e. we are moving when using the technology. A person just happens to be moving while conducting educational activities. It deals with 'convenience', i.e. rational time management and other such things. However, it gains some pedagogical relevance as well when we say that a person, a student or a teacher is moving because it is possible for him or her to be moving and simultaneously conducting educational activities like studying or teaching. We can consider this perspective from the point of view of higher learning concerning relationships between higher educational institutions such as universities and the surrounding society. The walls of educational institutions become permeable, while in work and leisure; university and home; the public and the private, blend amicably. We may call this relationship as a convenient relationship between university and its surroundings where people carry out their activities.

Differences between E-learning and M-learning

Many authors view M-learning simply as the natural evolution of E-learning which completes a missing component of the solution, i.e. adding the wireless feature or a new stage of distance and e-learning. However, there are quite a few differences between E-learning and M-learning on various points.

Comparison between E and M- learning

Sl.No.	E-learning	M-learning
1.	Computer	Mobile
2	Bandwidth	GPRS, G3, Bluetooth
3	Multimedia	Objects
4	Interactive	Spontaneous
5	Hyperlink	Connected
6	Collaborative	Networked
7	Distance & Learning	Situated learning
8	More formal	Informal
9	Simulated situation	Realistic situation
10	Hyper learning	Constructivism, Situationalism, Collaborative

Pedagogical differences between E-learning and M-learning Environment

Sl.No.	E-learning	M-learning
1.	More text and graphics based instruction	More voice, graphics and animation based instructions
2	Lecture in Classroom or in Internet labs	Learning occurs in the field or while mobile

Differences between E-learning and M-learning Environments with respect to the mode of communication between Instructor and student

Sl. No.	E-learning	M-learning
1.	Time delayed (Students need to check e-mail or website)	Instant delivery of e-mail or SMS; matter from stored e-books and cloud computing
2.	Passive Communication	Instant Communication
3.	Asynchronous	Synchronous
4.	Scheduled	Spontaneous

Student-to-Student Communication

Sl. No.	E-learning	M-learning
1.	Face-to-Face	Flexible
2.	Audio-teleconference Common	Audio and video tele-conference possible
3.	E-mail to E-mail, or messengers	24/7 instantaneous
4.	Private location	No geographical boundaries
5.	Travel time to reach the Internet site	No travel time since wireless connectivity
6.	Dedicated time for group meeting	Flexible timing on 24/7 basis
7.	Poor Communication due to group consciousness	Rich communication due to one-to-one communication, reduced inhibitions

Feedback to Students

Sl. No.	E-learning	M-learning
1.	Asynchronous and time delayed	Both asynchronous and synchronous
2.	One-to-one basis possible	One-to-one basis possible
3.	Mass/standardised instruction	Customised instruction
4.	Benchmark based grading	Performance and improvement based grading
5.	Simulations and lab-based experiments	Real life cases and on site experiments
6.	Paper based	Less paper, less printing labour cost

(**Note:** With the introduction of pen-drive 3G-5G, GPS, Wi-Fi, mobile Internet connectivity to laptops, I-pads, tablets, mobile phones and smart phones, the differences between E-learning and M-learning have been virtually narrowed down)

Advantages of M-learning

Mobile technology extends learning beyond the walls of classroom. It offers greater flexibility in where and when learning happens. Following are the advantages of M-learning.

Portability

These mobile devices, due to their portability, can be carried from class to class or wherever one goes and information can be acquired while interacting with one's peers. Portability can make a difference in a wide variety of settings, namely the classroom, a field trip or outside the school environment (June 2003).

Collaboration

Handheld devices allow the learner groups to distribute, aggregate and share information with ease, resulting in more successful collaboration. According to Perry, wireless technologies, notably PDAs are affording benefit for 'family learning' as learners are able to use them for various literacy tasks, noting reading e-books and taking them home to continue working on them along with their parents (Perry 2003).

Motivation

Teachers report that learners using handheld wireless technologies demonstrate an increased autonomy in learning, as the learners show increased self-directedness in learning and take the initiative in finding ways to use the handheld devices for learning. Perry says that giving learners wireless technologies 'lights up' their enthusiasm.

Disabled Learners

To a disabled learner, the added value of M-learning is three fold:
- Any assistive technology benefit afforded by M-learning is more portable so the support available to the learner is available at more places and more times.
- Mobile technologies are generally cheaper than PCs and laptops, so are more likely to be affordable.
- Mobile technologies are private and personal in use and have none of the students self image problems that may be associated with traditional assistive technologies.

Use of SMS in M-learning

One of the most straightforward applications of the usage of mobile devices as educational supporting tool is messaging. An SMS system (despite its debilitating language spelling, needing a mental dictionary on abbreviations) is considered to be a useful to spread information about lectures and classes, corrections in the schedules, etc. In certain cases, students find it more convenient than e-mail or Internet as information always comes on time through SMS.

Conclusion

Ubiquity of mobile devices in the classroom has allowed for M-learning to take place within the classroom environment. These devices are now encouraging students to participate in face-to-face lessons with their mobile devices. Like the fields of distance education and e-learning before it, mobile learning needs to achieve acceptance and then status and then certification, eventually at university degree level. Universities and colleges need to be convinced to accept M-learning as their normal means of communication with all their students on changes of timetable, submission of deadlines, enrolment procedures and other administrative necessities. The course modules for PDAs, handheld devices, palmtops, tablets, smartphones and eventually for mobile phones should be developed. Furthermore, books on mobile learning need to be written. On technology side, wireless Internet is a must for M-learning to take off. To cater to huge chunks of data that is common on most educational websites, there is a need for high-speed wireless data transfer. But, this should be at affordable costs to the general public.

*****

Life-Long Education

Every individual must be in a position to keep learning throughout their life. The idea of life-long education is the keystone of a learning society. The concept of life-long education covers all aspects of education, embracing everything in it and extending through our entire life. All tangible and permanent aspects of education must be life long. That is why life-long education is not an educational system, but the principle on which the overall organisation of a system is founded, and which should accordingly underlie the development of each of its components.

The concept of life-long education, however, acquired a new significance, a new meaning and mass application and has generated a new awakening, an awareness and interest throughout the world. This is in reaction to or in response to the prevailing situations and existing systems of education which are far from the concept of life-long education.

Way of Life

Life-long education questions the basic premises of traditional education systems, reverses established procedures and destroys some myths and dogmas deeply rooted in our systems. It is far more dynamic, more flexible, more open and a more humanistic education. It is co-terminus with life affecting all aspects of life and vice-versa. It is not only a philosophy of education, but also a philosophy of life. It is not merely a way of education, it is a way of life.

Books to Reach the People

One of the major, revolutionary developments in the world has been the advent of printing of books, thus opening out the avenues of knowledge and communication to vast numbers of people.

Without books one has to rely on human memory and on tradition. These have their value but obviously a limited value. The books bring us the experience of our forebears. But if the books do not circulate, only the elite will have them. Printing brings an expansion of the opportunities of gaining knowledge and therefore of making progress of various kinds. Take the sciences; scientific knowledge today is not the result of the effort of anyone but is made up of knowledge accumulated by tens of thousands of scientists. Books play an enormous role in distributing this knowledge.

If books are essential, the contents of the books are important. The outward appearance of the book is important, as everything good and beautiful is important. It encourages a good taste.

It is for the consideration of the writers essentially and also of others like the publishing trade, that if books are to go far, they have to be cheap. Books can be cheap only if they have large circulations. Books will have large circulations only if they are written in crisp and absorbing style which can be understood by large numbers of people. One step should lead to the other. Otherwise limitations come in and as a consequence the reading public does not expand.

Teacher Competence and Quality of Learning (Pursuit of Excellence)

It is an acknowledged fact that higher education's mandate would effectively be carried out not through the drawing on "a Frigidaire of facts" or a compendium of routine information but through the basis of instruction on imaginative curricula which take the latest advances of knowledge in their sweep. Further, it necessitates the giving up of a 'cosmetic commitment' in favour of a true one to the pursuit of excellence, apart from upgrading teacher's orientation capacity to evolve "new understandings, new insights, new relatedness, new wealth, new joys" realisable through academic pursuits.

Quality of Education

The nexus between teachers' competence or capability and the quality of higher education though long recognised and emphasised, have been non-issues in most of the states. A compulsory training for university teachers is a must. The unwarranted assumption that teacher's high academic attainments in the discipline would ipso facto make for a high pedagogical capacity, forgetting that the best curriculum would become ineffective, if handled by indifferent or incompetent teachers.

The Educator

The initiatives taken so far to provide pedagogical staff development have been "sporadic, piece-meal and tentative" as exemplified by the setting up of a variety of centres or units and allowing them to languish for want of adequate financial support subsequently. UGC rating exercises and public accountability as also the mooting of the idea for staff colleges are needed. It helps to promote awareness among university teachers and planners of higher education of the need to shed their primary identity as academic political scientists, chemists, linguists or physicists and regard themselves as educators. Such an awareness has had the effect of defining staff development in relation to not only academic knowledge and research capability but also administrative and community service which can be undertaken only by academic staff colleges.

As suggested by the UGC, the academic staff college has developed an eight-week orientation course divided into two or three modules and a three weak Refresher Course. The curriculum for the staff orientation comprises four components (a) Awareness of linkage between education, society and economy (b) Philosophy of education (c) Subject up-gradation and (d) Management and Personality Development, which can be broadly classified as general and subject components; the weightage to be given to them respectively is decided by the Advisory Committee of the ASC concerned. But efforts have to be made to disabuse the minds of some of the trainees having such mistaken notions, as they need only an exposure to new developments concerned, which is actually taken care of in the refresher courses.

Managerial Life-Long Learning

It is a known fact that learning does not stop after graduation or post-graduaton. It is continuous and lifelong. Surveys have already indicated that there is a need to have constant industry-academic networking. The challenges for both industry and academics are:
- Concept of application and application to concept.
- Executive education to necessarily act as an instrument of change.
- Appropriate mix of faculty which acts as a facilitator in the executive education.
- Response of B-schools to specific corporate needs.
- Increased competition ensures that the best B-schools stand out.

A Triangle of Corporate, Accreditation and B-schools

This triangle is very essential for the development of the corporate world, society and the students. What has been outlined above is a broad framework and the B-schools are required to develop their own models to meet the aspirations of the stakeholders more so the students. With the changing lifestyles of the students, it is essential for the B-schools to understand the underlying issues and develop the programmes and the courses that address the marketplace.

MBA

There are around 1.5 lakhs of seats for MBA in the country out of which only 10,000 to 20,000 are in Quality institutions. The need for MBAs will never cease in a country such as India. At least 30% of the recruits in the Indian Institutes of Management are opting for jobs abroad.

In order to take advantage of the favourable economic climate of the country, we need to have not just those who will work in the higher echelons of the corporate world, but also those who will fill up the middle level vacancies.

The availability of qualified faculty for MBA is a challenge that the institutions face. This is because education is not as well paid a profession as it should be. Management education in India is largely exclusivist.

To excel in business, one need not necessarily have a solid academic background. All it needs is a right combination of various skills, which include communication and interpersonal skills.

Business schools should be producing leaders who are able to think in terms of sustainable environmental and social framework. They should be able to maintain this balance.

The Business schools have to produce good technical analysts along with leadership skills. Leadership skills will mean focusing on big issues like sustainable growth.

Models of Management Education

1. The Pragmatist's Model
2. The Professional's Model
3. The Humanist Model

1. The Pragmatist's Model

Pragmatist's model is based on pure utilitarianism. In human history, its roots go back to the concept of literacy both in terms of alphabets and numbers, abilities to use language, and make calculations. It is in a developed form that now includes interpersonal communication and communication skills, working on computers and playing smart in business deals. Recently, the model has been branching into developing aggression and killer instinct in young managers. It has become part of formal education. The road leads from English medium schools to prestigious colleges and then to management institutes. But largely, it is a process of acceleration, learning without teaching, picking up on and off from others, which are certain benefits and attitudes currently in fashion. It is not entirely a new process without history and roots. It has always been popular and hence okayed. We can only criticise it, but we cannot reject it because it is based on realities of life of the growingly materialistic world. Apparently, it treats education as merely a means to serve and an end, not an end in itself.

2. The Professional's Model

The professional's model is an alternative to pragmatist's model, viewing managers as professionals and not as businessmen or bureaucrats. The process started with the setting up of Harvard Business School in 1906. In the beginning and for long, teaching courses were descriptive and fitted well with the pragmatist's model. Then came the big revolution in the late fifties with the publication of Ford and Carnegie Foundations' reports in the United States. Their implementation led to making all management courses contain only scientific inputs; a new type of the subsequent years witnessed massive build up of scientific research and Proliferation of Management education all over the world. But now almost everywhere, there is a progress reassessment of current research focus and curricula of business schools. Their relevance and quality of the performance thus far is being seriously questioned.

Professional's model is also vulnerable to criticism. The sociologist would not grant the professional status to the organisation man. The systematic body of knowledge supporting managerial practices is not yet sufficiently large. Mandatory certification of qualification to practice management is still a distant dream. And, evolving a code of ethics for the practicing manager has yet to be conceived.

3. The Humanist's Model

In order to meet criticism of exclusion, the third humanist's model, has in recent years come back into vogue. Its basic promise is that all organisations function as human systems and therefore, elements such as emotions, values and institutions need inclusion. The Harvard Business School in 1995 has revamped its MBA Programme and to label it more meaningfully for leadership and learning to achieve. This revamped programme is focused on three areas for learning values and qualities, skills and knowledge in that order. The inclusive element is reflected in the following items of coverage under values and qualities.

- Ethical Commitment
- A Commitment to continuous personal Improvement
- Self-esteem
- An Orientation of action
- Synthesis
- Entrepreneurship
- Leadership

All these changes will mean a major reinvention in the field of management education. For continuous education in future, we have to use all the three models of management education.

*****

Higher Education in National Development

Changes

Far-reaching changes are taking place in several walks of life—economy, polity and science and technology all over the world. The Indian polity, economy and science and technology are bound to be influenced by these changes. In fact the Liberalisation measures initiated in recent years are going to touch other sectors of the society.

Series of Reforms

Higher education cannot remain aloof and be a silent spectator of these dramatic forces. In other countries educational planners and academics have taken cognizance of interaction between higher education and the dynamic changes. As a result of this, a series of reforms have either been introduced or are being contemplated in developing countries. International bodies like UNESCO are also realising the importance and need for higher education.

Radically Different

The nexus between development and education was not clearly discernible or vividly demonstrated in the past centuries since education was accessible only to the elite. But the situation now is radically different with the welfare measures introduced by the public organisations, particularly by the Government, as the people are educated.

Level of Prosperity

The Education Commission rightly observed that "in a world based on science and technology, it is education that determines the level of prosperity, welfare and security of the people."

Development

Higher education, unlike other levels of education promotes development by

- Providing skilled manpower.
- Helping to spread science and technology.
- Generating new knowledge through research.

Higher education is thus crucially linked with national development in terms of its role in ensuring self-reliance in science and technology knowhow, in producing leadership in every department of societal functioning, in generating skills crucially needed in sectors of development and in generating social criticism so vital for the life of democracy.

Functions of the University

The three major traditional functions of a university are
- Development of the individual.
- The preservation and development of culture.
- Maintenance and further development of technology.

The central purpose of institutions of higher education is to educate (adults as well as young people); and the aim of education is to develop each individual as fully as possible to make him/her more human.

Requirements of the Future World

Requirements of future Higher education is vulnerable because it has been vested with too many hopes, saddled with too many responsibilities and held accountable for too many solutions. When we are dealing with the requirements of the future world, there are bound to be risks.

Supplier of Advanced Skills

Certainly higher education will be more needed in the future than in the past as a supplier of even more advanced skills, as an entry to even more desirable and better quality of life for individuals, as a supplier of even more needed social commentary, as a basis for social reform, and as a preserver and enhancer of ever-expanding cultural heritage.

Higher educational institutions in India will be tested on these anvils.

Updating Knowledge

In view of the rapid developments taking place, it is possible that what was learnt ten years ago or yesterday may have become obsolete today, for new discoveries are overtaking the existing knowledge. Therefore, there is a need to update knowledge of the people in all fields. One way of doing this is to read the latest literature, books and journals in one's own field and there is no substitute for this. There is a need to arrange for continuing education so that every practitioner in a profession is given access to the new developments in the field.

The University — Dynamic Agent of Change

In a developing society aspiring for structural changes through democratic means, the university has a crucial role to play as an agent of change. It has to prepare a cadre of leaders equipped in terms of both attitude and professional competence to initiate the process of change. It has also to serve as an effective agent of social criticism and prevent society from committing actions counter to progressive transformations. For a university to perform those tasks effectively, it has to have, essentially, the sensitivity to comprehend and even anticipate the changing social realities and cultivate dynamism within its organic whole which can make its responses quick and effective. Thus to be a dynamic agent of change, the university itself has to be opened to changes in its internal structure.

Access to Higher Education

Growth of the Indian university system during the colonial period was symbolic of the growing influence of the anglicised middle class. The post-independence period saw several deliberations in order to identify an exhaustive agenda for national development. The enrolment figures in Indian Universities have increased impressively over the years. In spite of this, access to higher education is very low. University education still remains the exclusive privilege of a few. Though there is generous provision for scholarships/interest free loans, access to higher education is still limited.

Supply and Demand

The courses and curricula offered by the university have to respond favourably to the needs of the society. There is a need for short-term middle-technology courses. Most universities are offering long-term high-technology courses. As a consequence, there is a gross mismatch between supply and demand; whereas we have a surplus of engineers, there is an acute dearth of technicians.

Finance

The Finance has been a chronic problem in many state universities. It is with great difficulty that many universities manage to disburse salaries of the employees in time each month. There is hardly any money left for improvements and developments. The funds earmarked in most state government budgets for education and their resources are not "elastic". As such, the allocations made by the Central government should be stepped up and expedited. Further, block grants should be earmarked for higher and technical education. It is most essential to create a body which will look into the financial requirements of the universities from time to time. There is an urgent need for establishing a University Finance Commission once every five years to go into this problem and make recommendations to the State and Central government. So long as universities have financial worries they will not be able to pay attention to other aspects of their work. They need to be put on a sound footing if they are to perform their role effectively.

Administration

The Indian Universities suffer from a high degree of centralisation. The trend of most of the institutions is that the various tiers in the system — Deans, Principals and Heads of Departments have not been delegated with authority to commensurate with their responsibilities. The style of functioning of any university which was evolved when it was small continues even today when it has to deal with thousands of students and teachers instead of a few hundreds. Lack of decentralisation/delegation is a single major factor which adversely affects the management of the universities.

The management of a college is forced to depend on the University for every minor decision. There is a strong case, for reversing the centralisation trend and for strengthening the different units of the university organisation. They should be enabled to operate as semi-autonomous units within the system.

Purpose of Higher Education

In the absence of clarity about the purpose of higher education, the task of effective university administration becomes very difficult. In spite of education commissions and committees, there still exists much confusion about the purpose of education. There is hardly any manpower planning. There is no relation between the demands of the society and what the universities produce.

Mismatch

This mismatch of a demand and supply is a serious problem which universities alone cannot tackle. "In the past, societies evolved slowly and absorbed the products of education easily and willingly, or at least managed to adapt to them, the same is not always true today." Some societies are beginning to reject many of the products of institutionalised education.

Manpower Planning

It is a common phenomenon in India today to find hundreds and thousands of graduates without employment, where as people are not available for the kinds of skills that the society needs. The demographic pressure being what it is, will further accentuate the irrelevance of the present day liberal education. It is true, in a democratic society like ours there cannot be a perfect manpower planning, but some plan of education is better than none.

Size of the University

Enormous expansion has taken place within each university. Where there were only four or five hundred students, today there are forty or fifty thousand of them in a medium-sized university. "Human beings have the painful awareness of the consequences of putting on too much of weight which is dysfunctional to the body. It is time that educational planners had some idea about the size of the university in terms of number of students, staff and institutions within it."

Universities - Part of a Larger System

The expectations of the society from the universities are very high, for they are temples of learning and scholarship. But when these institutions are faced with crisis, there is a sense of disappointment. Universities are parts of a larger system; what happens to the system as a whole has its effects on the sub-system too. The performance of the university administration is therefore, much influenced by the conditions in society. The management of academic institutions is more vulnerable and challenging.

Autonomy and Accountability

Universities are the large public institution in charge of the education of the youth. The Governments spend considerable amount of money on these institutions. Therefore, the management of universities is of great importance to the nation. Since independence, several committees and commissions have examined the structure and working of the universities and have made recommendations. The most important of them all is the autonomy and accountability.

Autonomy is the freedom given to an institution to do its work or perform its assigned tasks without hindrance from others, particularly outsiders.

Encyclopedia of Higher Education

It says that institutional autonomy refers to the belief that institutions of higher education should be left alone to determine their own goals and priorities, and to put these into practice, if they are to best serve society as a whole.

Components of University Autonomy

The components of university autonomy as per Robbins Committee of British Government higher education are:
- Freedom of appointment
- Freedom to determine curricula and standards
- Freedom of admission
- Freedom to determine the balance between teaching and research
- Freedom to determine the shape of development

For the sake of convenience the above five could be listed under three categories:
1. Academic Autonomy
2. Administrative Autonomy
3. Financial Autonomy

Academic Autonomy

Academic functions of the university are to design the academic programme at various levels, admit students and appoint teachers to teach them. It has also the task of evaluating the performance of the students and certifying them. To ensure there is hardly any outside interference in the discharge of academic functions. It must, however, be pointed out that there could be outside interference in matters of students' admissions and examinations. But much depends on the systems and procedures developed by a university and the integrity of those managing the university at various levels.

Administrative Autonomy

Administrative autonomy implies the freedom to hire and fire the teaching and non-teaching staff and make arrangements for teaching and research. However, in prescribing their qualifications emoluments and other service conditions, universities are required to follow either the state or central Government norms. Otherwise, the universities are autonomous.

Financial Autonomy

Financial autonomy refers to the freedom to raise resources and freedom to spend these as the university authorities desire. State universities are dependent on state governments and central universities are dependent on the UGC. In this area universities do not have the same type of freedom which they have in academic and administrative matters. Central universities enjoy a greater degree of autonomy than their state counterparts.

Public Interest

One among the reasons for the curtailment of the university autonomy is the conduct of universities themselves. There are cases where autonomy is misused by the chief executives and that gets a bad name for all the universities. Simply "The higher education community earns independence by what it does in the public interest, not by what it does for itself alone or by what it demands for itself alone. It has no inherent right, regardless of its conduct, for support and independence."

Part of the Society

Autonomy is an opportunity to play an important role — that is of educating the youth. The government should recognise the key role of a university. It is to be stressed that while exercising their autonomy, universities should remember that they are social institutions and they are part of the society in which they exist.

Accountability

The autonomy and accountability are two sides of the same coin. Public institutions are accountable to the nation; their performance should be accounted for and assessed from time to time. Accountability has been defined as: The duty of those responsible for the development and implementation of policy and /or managing affairs, and resources and to demonstrate not only prosperity but also how economic, efficient and effective their polices and/or management have been over a period of time.

Countries all over the world are facing financial stringencies and have therefore started looking at the performance of universities. Are the universities discharging their functions economically and efficiently? They are being asked to justify their activities and their actions for their use of resources and their performance, not only to external financial bodies but also to other influential groups in society.

Accountability of the institutions is judged by their use of resources and performance in terms of:
- economy in acquisition and in use of resources;
- efficiency in the use of resources;
- effectiveness in achievement of institutional, departmental and
- individual objectives, through the successful implementation of strategies, action plan; and
- teaching quality.

Research in Universities

"The ideal aim of a university is to make the life of learning and science possible, in an institution whose greatest function is the advancement of learning and whose rank in the academic hierarchy ultimately depends upon the contributions made by its members, to the sum of human knowledge and enlargement of the range of human thought."

Production of Results

In the changed context, the objective of research is no longer the expansion of knowledge, but production of results useful for new products and processes. Therefore, resources assigned to research depend more and more and stem from consciousness that they are essential components of investment in the development of a production system; consequently, the percentage of gross domestic product assigned to research has become an important index for its qualification.

The university system should move to the centrestage. It should utilise its autonomy for innovations in teaching and pursuing high quality research. The universities should make use of the three programmes that are UGC initiated.

1. Special assistance programme
2. Assistance for major and minor research projects
3. Setting up of Inter university centres for providing common facilities for research in Nuclear Science, Astronomy and Astrophysics, Atomic Energy, etc.

National Laboratories

With a view to promoting research in the country, the government has set up a large number of national laboratories dealing with a variety of areas in Science and Technology (S & T). Similar institutions have been set up in Social Sciences and Management studies. When we look at the developments in Science and Technology in the advanced countries, we find that the support for it in India is very weak. There is a need to further strengthen R&D in the country. The gap in the infrastructural facilities and capabilities between specialised agencies, national laboratories, in the industrial undertakings and the university system needs to be taken care of. If research in the universities is weakened, the whole falsie of development in the country would suffer. After all, the university supplies the manpower need by the industry and the laboratories.

If India is to compete favourably with other countries in this era of market-oriented economy, the industry and the government need to pay more attention to research. What is being done at the moment to support research in the universities is woefully inadequate and if sufficient attention is not paid in time, the nation will have to pay a heavy price and we will be forced to depend on others.

University-Industry Interaction

All these years, the Indian manufacturers and producers enjoyed a certain amount of protection and concentrated on the domestic markets. With the liberalisation of the economy, the Indian industry will have to become strong enough to withstand the competition from outside. The industrial sector consists of large, medium and small industries. Both public and private industries have played a significant role in the development of the country. In spite of these developments there has been no substantial interaction between the higher education sector and industrial sector. They worked in isolation from each other. In the university teaching and research there is not much input from outside. Similarly, industries are shy of making use of expertise available in the university system. Such isolation has to end and the two sectors need to come together in their own interest and in the interest of the nation. This is of great urgency today.

The main complaint of the industries was that what was being done in the university system, whether teaching or research was not of much relevance to them. When they employ products of the university they have to spend another year or so in training the students so that they could meet their requirements. Industries consider this a waste. Similarly, they find that the research concerns of the university system are not in congruence with their needs. They were also not confident whether they could use the university scientists in consultancy work, for they feel that the orientation of the university academics does not suit them.

However, things are changing. Some interaction between university and industry is taking place today. This interaction could broadly be divided into four categories general research support, cooperative research, knowledge transfer and technology transfer.

Intelligent Use of Technology

One must keep in mind that a productive and profitable industry–university relationship rests on continuous supply of new knowledge and well-educated engineers and scientists with an entrepreneurial spirit together with "grassroots" contact between industry and university "researchers". A technologically literate public together with technologically literate politicians is essential for the intelligent use of technology in society.

Expanding the idea of Return from Education

The better educated tend to live longer and healthier lives. In addition, better educated women tend to have a smaller number of better quality children and are less likely to experience maternal mortality. These are private benefits having a public character as well.

Human Capital

Societies that choose smaller number of higher quality children will, in 20 years time or so, have a much higher endowment of human capital upon which they can rely for development, as well as reduced exposure to the pressures and strains that accompany larger populations.

*****

Revamping the Colleges and Universities

Rich Undergraduate Programme

It should be mandatory for all universities to have a rich undergraduate programme and undergraduate students must get opportunities to interact with the best of faculty. In all the famous universities, great teachers, even Noble Laureates, prefer to teach undergraduate students.

Interact with Undergraduate Students

The university faculty, especially the senior faculty must be provided an opportunity to interact with the undergraduate students. It is the younger student studying in UG classes who is in the best position to raise basic questions on a host of issues while participating in the entrenched discourses of various disciplines.

In many universities, the faculty serving undergraduate colleges is given some opportunities to participate in postgraduate teaching at the university. Similarly, provision for the university faculty should be made to serve in undergraduate classes to enrich their intellect with the rejuvenating pedagogic experience.

New Universities with Undergraduate Courses

When the state intends to create new universities, it should begin with undergraduate education and build on this base their postgraduate programmes, thus becoming not only role models for the colleges in their states but also a resource for them.

Private University Corrective Mechanism

In the field of higher education, private initiative requires a credible corrective mechanism to do away with the ills associated with it currently. It would be necessary that the present practice of family members who sometimes don't have the experience or the competence relating to education, occupying the controlling position of the governing systems of the private educational institutions be prevented. Similarly, the practice of conferring academic designations such as Chancellor, Vice-Chancellor and Pro-Vice Chancellor on members of the family has to stop.

All private institutions which seek the status of a university will have to submit to a national accreditation system. The Private universities should not be allowed to confine themselves only to "Commercially Viable" sectors of education, such as management accountancy and medicine etc, but should also encompass areas of social and natural sciences by establishing comprehensive universities.

Foreign Scholars

Nation's higher education can be enriched with the learning experiences by opening our doors to foreign scholars and making our rules more flexible. Interaction with the best minds of the world would enhance the quality of our universities.

The best of foreign universities, amongst the top 200 in the world want to come to India and work. They should be welcomed.

Competitive Remuneration

Measures are needed to bring people who enjoy teaching and research back to the university. Resources in terms of laboratories, libraries, research assistance, etc. as well as competitive remuneration would be needed to attract and also to retain good people to our universities.

Retired Re-hired

Higher education has lost a generation of academics due to the inability of universities to find place for their scholarship. Positions of retaining academics are lost. Retired academics are re-hired to teach and are paid meagerly for each session. This is indeed a national shame and not a strategy of developing higher education in world's most promising country.

Key Determinant

Quality of teaching is the best indicator and a key determinant of the overall quality of institutional life. Higher education must give the highest priority for attracting good teachers and giving them a positive and motivating environment.

Student Feedback

Research and publications can serve as important criteria for assessing the scholarly dimensions of a teacher's personality. Students are in a unique position to provide an experiential assessment of the quality of teaching. Student feed back at the end of each semester should become a routine.

Statutory Agencies

The higher education institutions in India are regulated by many statutory agencies such as AICTE, BCI, COA, INC, MCI, MCTE, PCI, DEC, UGC and so on. In addition, there are regulations on the institutions by Central and State universities, as well as Directorates of College and Technical Education in each state leading to undesirable cubicalisation of knowledge, unwarranted fragmentation of disciplines and separation of knowledge from application and skills.

Single Higher Education Authority

All higher education, including engineering, medicine, agriculture, law and distance education is to be brought within the purview of a single, all encompassing higher education authority.

Healthy Competitive Setting

Universities need the autonomy to operate in a healthy competitive setting. The leadership of the university must be driven by the objectives of the institution. They need to set their own policies and thereby experiment with strategies on university governance.

Leadership of the University

The role of VCs is to attract the best of students, faculty and staff to the institution by making their institution very attractive to these talents. The role of a VC is to provide academic leadership to the university, develop and execute the vision of the university including its growth and to ensure that the university is academically healthy and financially sound.

Professional Fund Raisers

The universities should employ professional fund raisers who have the skills to identify the unique selling points of the university and persuade potential donors and investors to invest in the university.

Academic Content

Universities are to be made responsible for academic content of all courses and programmes of study including professional courses.

Undergraduate programme should be made mandatory for all universities and the students of undergraduate programme must get the opportunities to interact with the best faculty.

Higher Education for the Future

Undergraduate programme has to be restructured to enable the students to have opportunities to access all curricular areas with fair degree of mobility.

The vocational education provided by the polytechnics, industrial training institutions should be under the purview of universities by providing necessary accreditation.

The barriers to entry into universities for students going through vocational training should be lowered to enable them to upgrade their knowledge at any stage of their careers.

New governing structures are to be evolved to enable the universities to preserve their autonomy in a transparent and accountable manner.

Inter-University Centers

Modern higher education system requires extension facilities, sophisticated equipments and highly specialised knowledge and competent teachers. It would not be possible for every university to possess the best of these infrastructures. Therefore, it is important to create a number of inter-university centers (IUCs) in diverse fields to provide the best of these possibilities and to attract the participation of several institutions of higher learning to avail them.

IITs and IIMs

Institutions of excellence like IITs and IIMs are to be encouraged to diversify and expand their scope to work as full-fledged universities, which shall act as pace setting and model governance systems for all universities.

Upgrade as Universities

Best colleges across the country may be identified and upgraded as universities and cluster of other potentially good colleges may be encouraged to form universities. All levels of teacher education should be brought under the purview of higher education. A National testing scheme for admission should be evolved.

Incentive Pattern

Quantum of Central financial support to state-funded universities be enhanced substantially on an incentive pattern, keeping in view of the needs for their growth.

Expansion of the higher education system be evaluated and assessed continuously.

Higher Education for All

Privatisation of higher education is not a new phenomenon in the world economy. In many countries of the world, the private sector has come to play either a limited or predominant role in higher education. Privatisation is due to stagnating and declining public budgets for education, on the one hand, and on the other increasing social demand for higher education, manifested in slogans like, *"Higher education for all."*

Better use of Resources

The problem of non-viable institutions with low enrolments, poor facilities, and offering the usual traditional courses, would have to be squarely tackled with determination, to make better use of available resources for accelerated higher educational development.

Revamping Course Structure

The structure of course in higher education needs to be revamped so that the nexus between degree and strength of the fresh graduates are so trained as to suit the employment market. The higher education council would do well to make an in-depth study of courses and come up with its recommendations to make the Higher education system more meaningful and relevant to societal needs and the current aspirations of the people.

Postgraduate Education

For maintaining high standards and for giving the needed thrust to programmes of development, the postgraduate system calls for a transformation of its character through the introduction of a modern scientific outlook and other essential measures to suit our national needs and an extension of its coverage so that the education of the people becomes not a peripheral pursuit but a central objective. About 50% of postgraduate students are in colleges, it is necessary that the UGC should review the position in terms of the norms of postgraduate education. Those colleges which have potential to fulfil the criteria of postgraduate education should be adequately aided and encouraged and others should be made to continue Postgraduate education to maintain the standards.

Interdisciplinary Courses

University departments should be so strengthened as to function as viable units of teaching and research. Interdisciplinary courses should be introduced at the undergraduate level. Special efforts should be made in this regard at the postgraduate and research levels. Individuals, groups and departments in universities and colleges should be given every support in their pursuit of high quality research.

Advanced Research and Fund Allocation

Advanced research calls for the development of indigenous instrumentation capability and culture. Efforts in this regard should be encouraged through the setting up of universities in Instrumentation Service and Regional Instrumentation centres. While Universities will continue to be involved in fundamental research, it is essential that they should collaborate with national laboratories and industries in application oriented research. Both fundamental and applied researches demand the highest intellectual qualities. It is to be viewed with concern that three-fourth of the Government of India's fund allocation for research goes to the national laboratories, only 2.5% to 3% of the research allocation goes to the Universities. It is high time that the question of funding research needs to be re-examined imaginatively, with a view to apportioning a bigger slice of the cake to the universities engaged in both fundamental and applied research of high quality. Otherwise, it is justly feared that the caliber of teachers and students working within the university system to produce and reproduce both knowledge and scholarly work is bound to deteriorate.

Teacher-cum-Discoverer

"Engagement in research, meant for research work is a major pre-condition for creative teaching and stimulation of creativity." Research refines the teaching competence of a teacher. Research gives the teacher a more personalised experience of knowledge generation in his discipline and provides him newer insights into the structure of knowledge. Even if this influence be intangible and imperceptible, it is considered extremely valuable and tellingly operative in effective teaching. The very gamut of any research activity demands that the teacher remains a teacher-cum discoverer and consequently may be mentally better attuned to view knowledge as a growing entity. The fact that matters is, if universities are unique institutions where research, scholarship and teaching are integrated into a matrix of academic activities, they be interdependent. Their boundaries are to diffuse. Teaching without scholarship becomes dull and repetitious. Research without teaching is irrelevant. Practice without research becomes voodoo and scholarship without instruction becomes sterile.

Discovering New Knowledge

It should be the responsibility of the university academics to stimulate independent and critical thinking in their students and introduce them to an experience of generating knowledge as well as its methodology. All this is to be attained through teaching, it is essential that the students need to have opportunities of being taught by those who involve themselves in research too. This contact takes the students nearer to research and prepares them for the thrilling task of discovering new knowledge. Even so, the researcher in the teacher may stand out as a model for the students who are researchers in the making.

Complementarities of Teaching and Research

It would be clear, then those complementarities of teaching and research is inherent in both the processes when they are perused continuously for improvement. Whenever a conscientious teacher sincerely undertakes research, the outcome is bound to impinge upon the different aspects of his teaching functions in terms of clarity of knowledge, designing of newer strategies, and more intimate contact and interactions with students (the young minds he is to teach).

University Autonomy

The Government's intervention in the direction of securing a kind of physical control over the university, the appointment of Vice-Chancellor, the functioning of the Senate and Syndicate, and affiliation of colleges tantamount to seizing the basic authority of a university as an autonomous body, etc. If anything goes wrong due to this interference, the blame is squarely laid at the door of the university.

Government's Consultation

The Government's Consultation/interference with the university in the matters such as the kind of plan that a university should opt for, what Postgraduate or research departments it should or should not establish, what provision it should make to generate the man-power necessary for the growth of local industries or how it could meet the menace of unemployment are all reasonable, healthy and welcome in the larger interest of the nation.

Distance Education Tools

Teachers have to equip themselves with new tools of their trade in order to utilise interactive methods of instruction such as projects, seminars, stimulatory exercises, problem-solving sessions, tutorials, video-cassettes and video-discs, and sophisticated computers, they will be required to use their creative talents in the interests of distance education which would greatly enhance the reach as well as the scope of a higher education.

Character Building

The teacher plays a crucial role in the building of a student's character, temperament and of high quality research. Teacher is an instrument of educational change as much as education is an instrument of social change and national development. If the teacher is not motivated or inspired but is discontented and frustrated, if he is not pepped up with adequate supply of the basic necessities, then we cannot expect from him a genuinely professional role which is appropriate to current needs.

Commercial Commodity

Higher education has become commercial commodity available for those who have fat purses to buy. Truly speaking education is becoming increasingly expensive. To make matters worse a deep crisis of values has overtaken our country. The basic drawback is that higher education is confined to career-oriented instruction with no emphasis on cardinal moral and culture values. The result is that it has been turning out militant, brash and self-centered youth with no concern or vision for the nation. Most of the universities and colleges, regrettably enough, have become academic wastelands and have turned out to be places where pebbles are polished and diamonds are dimmed. Holistic education having been neglected and has gone with the wind.

Shelters of Mediocrity

The creeping inertia and decadence have overtaken our higher education institutions (universities) because of petty intrigues, power politics, extraneous interferences, vested interests, academic quackery, stultifying obscurantism and growing cynicism. Conspicuous lack of adequate participation and involvement on the part of educationists, teachers, students and the administration has led to our centres of higher education degenerating into shelters of mediocrity and emptiness. With their idealism waning and vision fading our universities by and large are just sustaining themselves still as mere centres of examination, operating creaky and leaky machines for churning out diplomas and degrees of no value in the employment market. With the mushrooming of colleges and universities and the rapid rise of enrolments there is hardly any scope for experimentation, innovation and quest for excellence. Quality has been grievously defaced and mediocrity has gained upper hand.

Sow Seeds of Human Creativity

If mediocrity is to be replaced by excellence, individuals should be developed to the limit of their potentialities by recognising their individual differences and providing relevant education to them in harmony with their immanent talents, traits and aptitudes. In this way the higher education institutions sow seeds of human creativity, nurture their growth for fruit and harvest and promote values of culture and humanism.

Strategies to Revamp

Consolidation and expansion of institutions of tertiary education, development of autonomous colleges and autonomous departments revamping and redesigning of curricula, innovations in teaching methodologies and evaluative techniques, strengthening of research and reorientation of the faculty, creation of an intellectual climate conducive to the pursuit of scholarship, efficiency and excellence providing for mobility of teachers—all these are strategies to revamp the universities to perform in high order.

Improving Facilities – Fund Allocation

Developmental programmes as well as schemes for improving the existing facilities in colleges and universities need adequate financial resources. High level of funding should be ensued for tertiary education by raising the allocation from the prevailing 3.7% to 7% of the GNP in the central Government budget. Further 25% of the education budget must be set apart for higher education.

Funding – Roadblocks

Funding procedures need to be redefined and simplified. The existing system of university finances has to be suitably reorganised on the basis of certain criteria. Universities should be treated with understanding and imagination. There should be some inevitable safeguards in financial matters and reasonable economy in expenditure. Sufficient grants should be extended for enabling the recipient institutions to discharge their administrative and academic obligations with speed and efficiency. The grant-in-aid authority should refrain from exercising too much control and adopting a rigidity of approach in the name of checks and balances. Such an attitude would act as a road block impeding the smooth administration of university finance.

Free From Regimentation of Ideas

The autonomous status of the universities is a basic need to discharge effectively their principal functions of teaching, research and service to the community. Only an autonomous institution free from regimentation of ideas and pressure of party or power politics can pursue the truth fearlessly and build independent thinking and a spirit of enquiry in its teachers and students.

Government Interference

The crisis and chaos arising out of maladministration of a university and abuse of power indulging in corrupt practices in matters of student admissions, staff appointments, college affiliations, building contracts, equipment purchase, etc., are ostensible reasons for the government to interfere into the functioning of the universities. To deal with the drawbacks and deficiencies promptly and sternly there needs to be in-built machinery within the university structure. But when the government assumes such powers as dismissing or suspending a Vice-Chancellor, affiliating or disaffiliating colleges or granting permission for setting up of educational institutions by over-riding the decisions of the university in an arbitrary manner, one cannot help observing that university autonomy is well on the road to an unceremonious burial.

Streamline Higher Education

One of the serious dilemmas tormenting higher education is deterioration in standards arising out of mechanisation and scrutinising of teaching and evaluation consequent upon admission of an increasing number of students to colleges and universities. There is no interpersonal contact between teachers and students – which was possible when classes were compact and manageable. With more and more centralisation of curriculum designing prescription of books and modalities for examination, teachers of affiliated colleges, who have very little or no say in the evaluation of their wards have become examination oriented. The students are led to attach disproportionate importance to external examinations, which put a premium on their memory rather than testing their all-round capabilities and talents. A concerted attempt must be made by the entire fraternity of universities to thoroughly streamline the higher education systems, ensuring greater reliability, objectivity and validity.

Essential Reforms

Developing question banks to assist paper setters, ensuring objectivity in evaluating answer scripts, declaring results in terms of marks/grades experimenting with open book examination, diagnostic evaluation introducing flexibility in curriculum development and combination of courses, integrating evaluation with the process of teaching and learning – these are some of the essential reforms that our universities would do well to attempt with a view to making the evaluation process genuinely effective.

Ideas and Ideals, Skills and Techniques

The University is for the transmission of ideas and ideals, of skills and techniques. These have to be transmitted from one generation to another and the ideals and the ideas may be the same but the skills and techniques have been changing from age to age, and unless we are able to reckon with the modern challengers, we will be left behind.

Basic Wisdom

Universities have to teach some basic wisdom to understand and solve the problems of today. If the universities are producing people with degrees who seek certain jobs, then the universities may have solved the unemployment problem to some extent.; But they will not have produced men who can understand or solve the problems of today.

Produce More Than Mediocre cadres

The future of this country ultimately depends on her young men and women, most of who are in colleges and universities today. We are anxious to find out what stuff they are made of. They are large in number but what really counts, if our country is to progress, is the quality of our human materials. The future of India does not depend on her numbers or even on her past, except in so far as the future grows out of the present and the present grows out of the past. It is possible for a country to make progress to some extent even with people of mediocre quality. India has large numbers of them. Obviously, that is not enough. If a great country like India is to be greater, it is essential for her to have men and women who must be more than mediocre. Universities should produce such kind of people.

Uniform Standards – Serious Challenge

Our Universities have provided first generation learners, especially from remote and rural areas, under-privileged sections of the society and women with opportunities for their development. Hence, the maintenance of uniform standards poses a serious challenge. A pragmatic approach to provide adequate attention to both the objectives may prove to be the only solution to the problem.

University Work

A university's work, however, does not consist simply setting up of buildings. What goes on within those buildings – its programmes and performances – are what determines the stature and the future of the university.

Status of Recognition

Students need to have access to information on the status of recognition and accreditation so that they can make informed choices. It is also necessary to inform students on the possible existence of fraudulent providers. It is important to regulate the way advertisements are made to make sure that no wrong information is imposed.

*****

Higher Education in Tamil Nadu

A college exists for the formation of character, intellectual and moral, for the cultivation of the mind, for the improvement of the individual, for the study of literature and the classics and those rudimental sciences which strengthen and sharpen the intellect. The primary aim of a college is to give to its students a sound education in preparation for the responsibilities of mature citizenship through the disciplines of a broad, rich and extensive curriculum. The essential components of a college are as follows:
- Students
- Teachers
- Curriculum
- Management

Students

The modern objective of sending a student to college is highly materialistic. The main aim of a student in pursuing his higher studies in a college is to secure a degree with good a percentage of marks in the examination to take up a lucrative job and also to go abroad for further studies. It is an irony that "learning stops, once a person secures a good job with a five figure salary with perks"; so laments R.S. Suguha. A survey was made to know the views of the students on *"Education for life or for livelihood "*. Surprisingly 20% of the students who were contacted for this purpose laid emphasis on "education for life", whereas the rest forcefully argued that education for livelihood. It is evident that only a minority was for value based education. This trend is universal and not peculiar to our country alone.

"Man making education" is nothing but perfect teamwork between the teacher and the students. It is true that the success of the present system of higher education largely depends on the quality of the teamwork.

Teachers

Alexander, the famous Macedonian conqueror, once said, candidly indebtedness to his teacher, Aristotle, "I am indebted to my father for living, but to my teacher for living well." Thus a teacher is an inspiring guide to students to shape their lives in such a way as to enable them to live a life of happiness coupled with contentment. A.M. Sinha considers teachers a blind role-model for his students. The aim of the teachers is to train their students to question papers that are also set by outsiders. "Teachers are the immortal souls of this sacred soil. They never die. They merely fade away."

"Teaching... is the noblest of the professions not because of any pecuniary considerations but because it gives the greatest satisfaction, when the work is well done that the teacher has kindled one more spirit, and lighted one more lamp so that in its ever-increasing luster, darkness and ignorance may ultimately fade away."

Teachers like, Harold J. Laski and A. L. Mudaliar were creative geniuses. They were able to inspire their wards with their dynamism and by their scholarly works. For them teaching and research must go together. Once Dr. A. L. Mudaliar remarked that "no college could be said to have worked successfully which does not, besides teaching that is imparted to the students, contributes to an increase in knowledge through research and other activities of the teachers in that college." This kind of endeavour will enable both the teachers and the taught to participate actively in the process of learning.

Curriculum

It has been often stressed by educationists that education should be turned into "a proper vehicle for imparting and cultivating the right social values among students." A curriculum is to be prepared satisfying the need for cultural, mental and physical development of students. It "should promote the spiritual, moral, cultural, mental and physical development of students." It should prepare them for the opportunities, responsibilities and experiences of adult life.

Issues in Higher Education

The institutions of higher education in Tamil Nadu are suffering from malfunctioning. A college can boast itself as rather fortunate if it is able to work for eighty to ninety days in an academic year in comparative tranquility. During this short span of time what is happening in the campus of a college is quite known to everyone. The academic year starts usually in the third week of June. The first task that captures the attention of every teacher is the admission work, which continues upto the middle of September every year. The Principal and the senior members of the staff are not free to divert their attention to class work till then. Not even 50% of the classes would be held during this period. Students would be loitering in the verandahs making filthy comments and nobody bothers about them. If it is a postgraduate college, a few teachers would come forward to engage the second year postgraduate classes at least for half a day. Parents would be waiting for interview indefinitely at the doorsteps of the Principal's room. In the meantime, the prospective candidates of the College Union Election will organise a strike on flimsy grounds demanding either protected water supply or better lavatory facilities. As soon as, the college admissions are over, the next item of the agenda of the Principal is the Students' Union Election. When it is announced, the campus will witness hectic activities pushing aside the academic work. The elections for Students' Union are bitterly fought among rival groups aided openly by different political parties as if it were the public General Elections.

As a consequence, the mood of friendship disappears from students. The academic atmosphere in the campus will be vitiated due to campus politics. The impact of the election will be felt in every activity of the college whether it is the inauguration of the College Union which is usually conducted in many colleges several months after the election or the celebration of the College Day which is another headache for the Principal.

It is a fact that the Government Colleges struggle to function even for 100 days in an academic year amidst indiscipline of all sorts that involves the people engaged in the process of learning. Nonetheless, there is a genuine effort on the part of a few students at the far end of the year to get through the University examinations. If luck favours, 10 to 20% of the students will be successful in obtaining a degree, either B.A. or B.Sc. or B.Com. "The degrees or diplomas which the students obtain are considered symbols of achievement and status." In reality, to quote S.C. Dube, "Higher education has become a ritual without meaning or purpose."

Growing Pressure on Higher Education

One of the biggest challenges that the State of Tamil Nadu faces today is the growing pressure on higher education. Better economic opportunities and upward social mobility are the two reasons which make more number of youngsters in India attempt to enter the institutions of higher education but in Tamil Nadu the principle of reservation, observed by the Government, provides ample chance for the students, particularly from the lower strata of the society, to swarm the portals of the colleges in large number.

Educational Atmosphere

The educational atmosphere in Government Arts Colleges is terrible. A kind of academic anarchy reigns supreme on the campuses of these institutions where the objectives of higher education are thrown to wind. It appears that there is no system of discipline, enforced by the authorities. "Let things go" is the attitude of every member of staff, both, teaching and non-teaching. No one, starting from the Principal and ending with the last grade servant of the college, is serious about his or her work. A total non-committal tendency prevails in the campus. A few are sincere and dedicated to their work, but they too remain unmindful of what is going on in the surroundings.

Left in Wilderness

A timetable is given to every department and to every individual. It is adhered to more in its breach than in its observance. Classes are cancelled without any rhyme or reason. No possible alternative arrangement is made whenever a staff member goes on leave. Most of the time, the students are outside their classrooms. They are literally left in the wilderness. They are like sheep without a shepherd. No guidance is available to them. Even poor students are victims of social vices such as smoking and drinking. In such an atmosphere roughly about 15% of students dare engage themselves in the learning process and yet another 10% of students are forced to attend classes due to external compulsions. The rest consider the college campus a place for past-time. They need a pretext for leaving the classrooms. It is a pity that no systematic and organised efforts are being made by the authorities to keep them engaged at least for two hours a day.

Specialised Short-term Courses to Foreign Students

The newly initiated international centre of Madras University offers specialised short-term and degree courses to foreign students. The centre is a single window for admitting students, counselling, helping them find residential accommodation and solving visa and other documentation problems. It offers learning programmes in Indian music and dance, Ayurveda, Siddha, performing arts, archaeology, tourism, Indian heritage and culture, and traditional medicine systems. The Madras University has been identified as a university with potential for excellence by UGC.

Education and Training for Tamil Nadu to Prosper

Tamil Nadu is a state, short in natural resources. It has a population pressure above the national average. We need to adopt a development policy that is appropriate for a state with scarce natural resources. Fortunately, we have come to a stage of development in human history where knowledge has become a resource. Tamil Nadu is endowed with a population that has a great potential for advancement through education and training. The future of Tamil Nadu has to be designed and built on the foundations of education training and innovation. The reforms and restructuring needed are fairly well known. They are within the competence of Tamil Nadu to accomplish and to sustain. These are imperative not for prosperity, but even for its survival. What is needed is the will, not only on the part of the government but on the part of all individuals including all political parties.

Physical Education Department – A Foremost Neglected Department

The Physical Education Department is yet another area of human resources which is far-neglected. The Physical Director occupies a place of importance in the hierarchy of the college which is analogous to that of a Minister without portfolio. He is one of the members of the staff who is at the beck and call of the Principal. It is not false if he is described as a shadow of the Principal. Since he is totally free during the working hours of the college, the Principal prefers to keep him as his constant companion to face the wrath and fury of the agitating students. The hidden talents of students in the field of sports remain unutilised.

Unquiet College Campus

"Students politics in pre-Independence days had some ideological thrust, but present day campus politics reflects only group rivalries and factional fighting often instigated by political personality clashes. Ideology is missing and goals are in distract and student activism is no longer part of ideological movements but outbursts of sporadic violence provoked by political and other rivalries." As education begins at home, the parents have the paramount duty of shaping the formative years of the child. Students are now drifting like rudderless vessels in a turbulent sea. In other words, they lack both guidance and direction. The electronic media, like the T.V., mobile phones and cinema have misguided the youth inducing them to commit crimes like theft, violence, addiction and eve-teasing.

Concept of Accountability and then Profession of Teaching

An institution of higher education is not a commercial enterprise. It is not in the business of manufacturing, processing or selling commodities. An institution of higher education is not a political party. It is not an ethical society.

Autonomous Colleges – An Overview

Some areas of academic programmes have remained unchanged in spite of the availability of freedom to change them. The examination system has remained unchanged. The autonomy granted by the UGC is often misused by some institutions.

Francis Soundararaj has made an in-depth study of the functioning of autonomous colleges and found out the areas of their constraints which are as follows:
- The inability to offer new courses and degrees without the concurrence of the parent university
- Lack of financial autonomy to diversify courses or to offer optionals.
- Dependence on UGC or state funding for the execution of academic programmes.
- Non-recognition of internal assessment by parent universities.
- Non-recognition of achievements of outstanding students of autonomous colleges by universities for awards.

Dr. M. Abel rightly remarks: "Autonomy and accountability are two sides of the same coin. Autonomy without accountability will be directionless, while accountability without autonomy will be stagnation."

Right Person for the Right Job

It is our tradition to choose a right person for the right job. Even Thiruvalluvar confirms it. In the 517th couplet of his celebrated work *Thirukkural*, he says:

> *This deed, by these means, if he can perform*
> *Test him; if convinced, assign it to him.*

Only after evaluating the task, the means and the person to do it, the task should be assigned to him.

But this cherished tradition of our society has been totally ignored. In the present-day, teaching has become the last resort for job seekers. In other words, it is the last choice in the job market. As a result, incompetent and undeserving people are appointed as teachers in colleges. Therefore the department of education has a large number of indifferent teachers on their roles: Developed countries, like Japan, are "gifted with committed teachers who work with a true spirit of dedication and unflinching loyalty." That is the reason why they make phenomenal progress in the sphere of Science and Technology and live in prosperity. Poverty is ashamed to appear on their soil.

In Japan, all the fresh appointees are required without any exception to undergo a period of induction training for one year. It is gratifying to note that the Japanese Ministry of Education, Science and Culture sends nearly 5000 teachers to foreign countries every year to broaden their international perspective and to update their knowledge in the chosen field. "To attract excellent quality people to the realm of education and to improve the standard of education, teachers' salaries are fixed at three times compared with other public employees.

Average Enrolment of Students – Colleges and Universities

Average enrolment per institution in India is about 550, though this has little meaning since there are a few institutions with more than 10,000 students, while some have less than a hundred. It is not necessarily true that the universities are big while the colleges are small. There are some colleges that have large number of students, while there are also a few universities that have less than a few hundred students enrolled. There are a couple of hundred universities and colleges, mainly in the metropolitan cities, that have more than 5000 students enrolled. There are another 1000 institutions with enrolment ranging from 1500 to 2500. The remaining colleges have a few hundred students only; such small colleges are usually in small towns and rural areas. A large majority of them are non-viable, understaffed and ill-equipped; two-thirds do not even satisfy the minimum norms of the University Grants Commission, the apex body for regulation of higher education in the country. Thus the sizes of institutions are highly variable and the system is extremely fragmented.

Enrolment Structures in India and Developed Countries

The structure of enrolment in India differs from that in advanced nations with mature systems of higher education in several ways. One, enrolment of women in India at about 40%, is still less than that of men, while generally, more women than men are enrolled in higher education in advanced countries. Two, enrolment of part-time students or mature students is still low even at the postgraduate level in India. Part-time students form a significant proportion of the enrolment in developed countries. In the UK, more than 40% students are enrolled as part-time students; at the Postgraduate level, their numbers are almost twice that of full-time students. Three, in India, most students who enroll complete their degrees. Large dropout rate is a major concern in advanced countries. Four, India has ever-increasing application-to-acceptance ratios, particularly for more reputed institutions. In most developed countries, due to reducing number of young people, application-to-acceptance ratio remained stagnant or decreased due to declining number of young people seeking higher education. And, finally as seen from diversity of students at the institutional level, most students are from the same level. Due to cultural differences students travel large distances for higher education in many advanced countries where the parents' involvement in the lives of adolescent children is minimal. In India, enrolment of women is growing fast, and part-time studies and enrolment of mature students are appearing on the scene.

Promoting Equity

Equity, the quality of being fair and impartial in higher education is viewed as the ability of the brightest students to study in the best universities, regardless of their socio-economic backgrounds. However, family backgrounds and places of residence do have influence over access of higher education opportunities. There is a large variation in the availability of universities and colleges across states in rural and urban areas. Disparities in enrolment amongst various socio-economic and ethnic groups exist. Despite significant improvements, enrolment of women continues to be less.

The strategies to improve the inclusiveness in higher education would be as follows:

- Rural and urban disparities – enhance access to rural population.
- Interstate variation – focus on states that have lower GER than the national average.
- Gender disparities – special attention to higher education of women.
- Inter-religious group disparities – special focus on promoting higher education amongst most backwards, tribals and scheduled communities.
- Social groups within religion – special focus on farmers, agricultural labourers, manual workers and lower castes within religions.
- Disparities across income groups – support to poor and marginalised to access higher education.
- Disparities across occupation group – special attention to agricultural labourers, other labourers and the self-employed in rural areas, and casual labourers in the urban areas
- Inter-caste disparities in GER – special attention for promotion of higher education among the SCs, ST and OBC.

Study Abroad Scheme

As a first-of-its-kind in the country, the Tamil Nadu Government has initiated to upgrade skills of students and professors attached to State Government colleges on a study tour to leading universities in the UK and to undertake joint research programmes.

Tamil Nadu Government has signed a Memorandum of Understanding (MoU) with the South India British Council for Higher Education in a bid to expose students to international standards of education as part of their curriculum on 14th December, 2013. Students under this programme will experience international exposure with greater understanding of the multiple perspectives of international issues.

The students and faculty chosen for this programme will be nominated to study at various universities in United Kingdom and in the universities in Asian and Far East countries. The Study Abroad Programme provides opportunity to the meritorious under-privileged, postgraduate students in Government Arts and Science Colleges.

A total of three professors and 14 students were finalised after applying rigorous selection modules to enable them to accommodate themselves to the new culture and language. All the selected students from state-run colleges would fly abroad for one semester at a foreign institute in 2013. It is to be noted, among the 14 students selected 13 are women.

*****

8

Conclusions, Recommendations and Suggestions

Solutions for Effective Functioning

Share faculty

Institutions and Universities could share faculty and facilities among themselves for cost reduction, to reduce wasteful expenditure.

Credit System

As for curriculum reform each university has to concentrate on its core strengths rather than the present system in which all universities routinely ran all types of programmes and departments. The credit system should be introduced in all colleges to enable the individual to earn credits in subjects of their choice and develop specialised skill in chosen fields.

Periodic Training to Non-teaching Staff

In administration, the academic heads have to evolve common service and leave rules for non-teaching staff in all universities. Outside experts could be brought into conduct periodic training to non-teaching staff in files handling.

Mix Freely

There is no need to look down upon women as the weaker sex needing protection. If the students mix freely with each other in their teens, they understand the problems of the opposite sex and react responsibly in the society.

College Credibility and Accountability

Colleges need to accept both credibility and accountability of their own students. A group is looking in to the statute changes that are required to allow the colleges to provide degrees. An autonomous institution could provide degrees, while the university under which the institution comes, could separately or at the back of the same degree give the college's rating by the National Assessment and Accreditation Council (NAAC). In the case of non-autonomous colleges that have undergone the accreditation process, the degree would have the name of the college and its NAAC rating. In the case of colleges which are not autonomous and have not undergone NAAC accreditation process, the degree would be given with the detail that the institution has not undergone the process. This would make the degree credible and accountable.

"Every individual is a resource – of time, skill, and goodwill. So if we all do something together then there is no problem that we cannot solve."

Quality Time

Teachers should be facilitators, when teachers have too much evaluation they have no quality time for students. Now teachers do only manual correction of multiple-choice questions. There is only one correct answer and computers themselves can do the evaluation. It will be quicker and more accurate.

Enrolment Ratio

The gross enrolment ratio in higher education is 12.4% in the country at present, much less than the global average of 25% to 27%. Developed countries have a registered GER 50% to 70%

Fixing Mandatory Working Hours for Professors and Teachers

If UGC has its way, then it might become mandatory for University professors and teachers to clock a minimum of 40 hours a week at work. They will have to be physically present for at least five hours a day on campus and earmark six hours a week for research. This move to fix work load for academics in terms of hours spent on site is misplaced. It reflects the bureaucratic mindset of administrators in India. While less bureaucracy is desirable in all spheres of public life, education is one area that desperately needs to be unshackled.

Effective Educator

Universities and Colleges are not factory floors. The output of teachers cannot be measured merely by number of hours they are physically present on campus. A lot more goes into the making of an effective educator. A teacher can be present eight hours a day but that does not necessarily make her/him competent or effective. In assessing the productivity and efficacy of teachers, the crucial factors are their research and student's feedback. Neither of these can be gauged from mere attendance.

Teaching and Research

Top quality universities and colleges in countries where education is of much higher quality than in India do not lay down such absurd rules. Teachers and Professors are expected to take a certain number of classes a week, be available between two to four hours in office per week to interact with students and produce original research in their areas of specialisation. Much emphasis is placed on how up-to-date they are with latest developments in their teaching and research as assessed by the students and peers respectively.

Flexible Working Hours

Flexible working hours give teachers the freedom to spend constructive time in libraries, seminars, refresher workshops, etc. — all of which are vital inputs to their knowledge base. It is virtually impossible to enforce and monitor the proposal that the UGC has come up with. Instead of trying to fix input, a regulatory system can be evolved to measure the output.

Counterview for mandatory working hours

The UGC proposal to mandate Professors and all teachers in full employment at universities to work 40 hours a week should be welcomed. Higher education in India, much like primary and secondary school education, suffers largely from teacher absenteeism. Requiring Professors and teachers to come to class and holding them accountable if they don't – would be a big step forward in providing quality education to Indian youth.

Forty Hours a Week

There is a section that believes that requiring a workload of 40 hours a week from teachers is to overkill them. But 40 hours is really not very much. All that UGC requires is that professors be physically present on campus for five hours every day. This doesn't mean that they have to take five hours of classes – direct teaching hours are limited to 16 a week for assistant Professors and 14 hours for more senior teachers. Professors will be free to spend rest of their time in libraries, conducting research or meeting with the students who wish to discuss problems or ideas with them. With class size in India being big, it makes sense to have teachers available for longer periods than in American or British universities.

Primary Responsibility

It is all very well to suggest that the level of a Professor's commitment to teaching be judged through student evaluations and papers published in reputed journals. But we all know how little credence is given to students' feedback, particularly when big names of Professors prove to be unpopular. Incentivising teachers to publish more is a good idea. But this should not come at the cost of teaching which after all, is the primary responsibility of those in the educational profession. Universities in Britain and the US are facing criticism, for just this; the emphasis placed on research is so high that teaching, particularly undergraduate teaching, suffers as a result. And in India, where there is no practice of Professors hiring teaching assistance to share their work load, encouraging teachers to put in paper publishing above classroom hours would be a big mistake.

Using a degree of flexibility in how teachers spend their time is a small price to pay to improve the standards of teaching in our universities.

'Students develop an interest in a subject only if they like the teacher'.

Motivate

A good teacher is a person who can motivate his or her students. The tips for the same are:
- Before you motivate others you should motivate yourself. You should be enthusiastic. Exhibit your passion for training your students.
- Be a role model to your students and inspire them.
- Establish a rapport with your students. You should attract your students towards you. The more the students like you, the better they learn and participate in activities.
- Be a friend, but not a philosopher. Give concrete examples with which the students are familiar.
- Always give a pat on the back. Use phrases such as "Well done. It is a good attempt." or "I liked your argument very much", "It is a good point" or "you have been very creative."
- Always sound positive. Instil confidence in your students. Tell them that it is easy to develop their speaking skills and make them believe your words. Make them believe that they have the potential to express themselves clearly.
- Use strategies that do not threaten them. It is very important to learn and practise in a non-threatening environment.
- Participate: It means to take part in an event or activity. It implies that the teacher should come down to the level of students. It is possible only if he undergoes a paradigm shift and has a positive attitude towards his students and adopts a result-oriented approach.

Mingle with Students

Mingle with your students and participate in activities such as group discussions and role play. Empathise with learners who need your special attention. Know your students' strengths and weaknesses.

Future Challenges in Management Education

Higher education in general and management education in particular has undergone a radical transformation in India, more so, in recent years. Globalisation and borderless economies have become the driving forces in B-schools. The importance of professional management is being recognised not only in private but also in other sectors like government, social services, VSOs, financial institutions, etc., necessitating academic institutions to deliver quality management education. The international markets are changing and the B-schools are developing curriculum, which have to be of international standards.

Key Factors Relevant For Management Education

Understanding the Market Place

The management education needs to understand the key stake-holders-faculty, students and the corporate world. The phenomenal growth of business schools, in the last thirty years has led to the expansion without adequate understanding of the market, industry–institute linkages and the widening gap between the skills required and acquired.

Growing Needs

In addition to the above the conventional management education with specialisation in marketing, finance, Human Resource, etc., has undergone a change. With the growth of new sectors like hospitality, health services, insurance, investment banking, pharmacy, retail, the need for sectored specialisation have increased. The sectored specialisations are also leading to functional specialisations. This necessitates the academic institutes to prepare themselves for growing needs of the sector and functional specialisations.

Future Needs of the Industry

The conventional technology programmes are giving way to technology management programmes, combination of engineering and management, pharmacy and management, law and management. This is typically called combo-programmes. These programmes will address the future needs of the industry.

Healthy Sign

Profiles of the students are undergoing phenomenal changes. Students are no longer interested in accepting a job as is offered by the corporate. They are now prepared to wait, to have a job of their choice. This has resulted in minimisation of losses. It is a healthy sign. The students are well read and informed, thanks to the information explosion. This would mean that faculty must be well prepared to understand the students learning processes and are required to be a step ahead of the students.

Need for Strategic Planning

- The B-schools must develop a strategy planning document and address some of the fundamental issues like:
- Greater accountability
- Higher cost of education
- Increasingly important role of universities in regional, national and international economic development.
- International relationships and Globalisation of management education.
- Changing pedagogical methods through developments in communication technology.
- Greater emphasis on social responsibility in academics.

(The above is only an indicative lists and not an exhaustive list)

Plan for Future

The B-schools must chart their plan for future, taking into account a 'trilogy' of changing factors like supply-demand patterns, societal expectations of institutions, employer expectations, business schools missions and niches.

Curriculum

There are a number of areas or issues that need attention. There are several set of possibilities but the major ones are:
- Breadth of curriculum
- External and transitional environment
- International dimension
- Information service society
- Cross-functional integration and
- Soft skills

Faculty Preparation and Development

Faculty is a major stakeholder in the institutional development. Research, training and continuous learning are essential. Upgradation is an ongoing process. Faculty needs to develop themselves with a strong research base. Doctoral programmes provide the opportunity.

As in the corporate world, the development of the faculty members also does not stop after joining a B-school paradoxically. B-schools offer many development programmes to the corporate sector but little emphasis is given on self-development. For B-schools the major agenda should be lifelong learning perspectives. Specific faculty development programmes should be evolved and offered.

Accreditation

Accreditation is a primary requirement for a B-school to compete and progress. It provides a threshold level with standards significantly above the entry level and also acts as a mechanism to induce quality in learning.

*****

Role of NCHER

Objectives of the Commission for Higher Education and Research (NCHER) should be as follows:
- Be responsible for comprehensive, holistic evaluation of higher education sector.
- Strategise and steer the expansion of higher education.
- Ensure autonomy of the universities and shield them from interference by external agencies.
- Act as a catalyst and also as a conduit to encourage joint/ cross disciplinary programmes between and amongst universities and institutions.
- Spearhead continuous reforms and renovation in the area of higher education.
- Establish robust global connectivity and make it globally competitive while creating our own class standards.
- Promote greater engagement and enhance resources to state universities with an aim to bridge the divide between the State and Central universities.
- Ensure good governance, transparency and quality in higher education.

Connect with industry and other economic sectors to promote innovations.

Devise mechanisms for social audit processes and public feedback on its performance and its achievement.

*****

Community College

Introduction

The Community College is an alternative system of education, which is aimed at the empowerment of the disadvantaged and the underprivileged (Urban poor, Rural poor, Tribal poor and Women) through appropriate skills development leading to gainful employment in collaboration with the local industry and the community and achieve skills for employment and self-employability of the above sections of people in the society. The Community College is an innovative educational alternative that is rooted in the community providing holistic education and eligibility for employment to the disadvantaged.

Origin

In Tamil Nadu, the Community College movement started with the inauguration of the Madras Community College by Arch Dioceses of Madras, Mylapore and by Manonmaniam Sundaranar University, Tirunelveli in 1998. Tamil Nadu Open University started approving Community Colleges in India for offering Tamil Nadu Open University Vocational Education Programmes in 2004 and recognised so far 205 Community Colleges in Tamil Nadu and 2 Community Colleges in other States as Vocational Programme Centres. The success of TNOU-Model motivated Government of Tamil Nadu to issue G.O.163 for the recognition of Community Colleges and the TNOU has established 205 Community Colleges all over India run by Christian Dioceses, Religious Congregation, NGOs, Philanthropic Trusts and Civic Bodies like the Chennai

Corporation. The Movement is spreading to different parts of the Country and IGNOU also started Community Colleges.

This community college system started in 1995-96 and during the year 2006-7 it was on its peak. The number of community colleges, the students' strength and the beneficiaries were richly improved during this period.

Vision

The vision of the Community College is to be: *of the Community, for the Community and by the Community* and to produce responsible citizens. The Community College promotes job-oriented, work-related, skill-based and life coping education.

The Community College initiative is in conformity with the Indian political will that has priorities in education, primary education, information technology education and vocational education.

Concept

A community college is an alternative educational system with a difference. It aims at the empowerment of the poor, marginalised and disadvantaged sections of the society. A community college promotes skills development, Knowledge dissemination and positive change in the attitude. The concept of community college matches education with employment and self-employment opportunities and it is an effort by the local community. It collaborates with industry, employers and community leaders. Further it responds to industrial, employment and social needs. It teaches — Life skills, Communication skills, English as a tool for better and effective communication, Computing skills, Work-skills, Hands-on-Experience and Preparation for Employment.

The Motto of Community Colleges is "including the Excluded and Giving the Best to the Least." A community college helps the individual to discover his own talents and capacity through a formal education which is either unaffordable or inaccessible otherwise.

The key words of the Community College system are access, flexibility in curriculum and teaching methodology, cost effectiveness and equal opportunity in collaboration with industrial, commercial and service sectors of the local area and responding to the social needs and issues of the local community internship and job placement within the local area, promotion of self-employment and small business development, declaration of competence and eligibility for employment.

Present Scenario

The Community College Movement has become a National Phenomenon spreading in many States of India. We have 322 Community Colleges in 20 States in India. The table below indicates the growth of the Community College movement in India.

Table -1

Sl. No.	Name of the State	No. of Community Colleges
1.	Tamil Nadu	215
2.	Puducherry	05
3.	Andhra Pradesh	11
4.	Karnataka	25
5.	Kerala	13
6.	Maharashtra	08
7.	Madhya Pradesh	06
8.	Gujarat	02
9.	Goa	01
10.	Jharkand	13
11.	Chattisgarh	01
12.	Odissa	07
13.	Himachal Pradesh	01
14.	Haryana	02

15.	West Bengal	04
16.	Uttar Pradesh	04
17.	Punjab	01
18.	Assam	01
19.	Jammu Kashmir	01
20.	Bihar	01
	Total	**322**

Aim

The purpose of a Community College is to provide skill based, livelihood - enhancing education and eligibility for employment to the disadvantaged and under privileged like the urban poor, rural poor, tribal poor and women. Providing appropriate skills development in collaboration with local industries thus leading to gainful employment is the major target of Community Colleges. According to the latest report available, Community Colleges are present in 20 states of India. There are around 322 Community Colleges and they have served more than 65,000 people in these years, out of which 75% have got employment, 15% of them have been motivated to opt for higher education.

Tamil Nadu Vision 2025

Tamil Nadu's vision to raise the Gross Enrolment Ratio to 25% by 2025 sets the road map for all-round development in the higher education sector. The 12th Five Year Plan also envisages a observable target of additional enrolment capacity of 1 crore students including 10 lakhs in ODL and 33 lakh students in skill granting diploma programmes and remaining 57 lakh students in further expansion of degree programmes with accelerated expansion of postgraduate and doctoral programmes. To implement Tamil Nadu's vision, the TNOU has started strengthening the Community Colleges System in Tamil Nadu.

*****

Bibliography

G. Ram Reddy, *Higher Education in India – Conformity, Crisis and Innovation*, Sterling Publishers Private Limited, New Delhi, 1995.

J.V. Vilanilam, *The Challenges before Higher Education in the 21st Century*, B.R. Publishing Corporation, New Delhi, 2007.

J. Mohanty, *Current Issues in Education*, Cosmo Publications, New Delhi, 1992.

S.K. Chakraborty, *Ethics in Management*, Oxford University Press, New Delhi, 1995.

S.K. Panneer Selvam, *Prospectives on Higher Education*, A.P.H. Publishing Corporation, New Delhi, 2010.

Dr.S.K. Panner Selvam, *Higher Education*, A.P.H. Publishing Corporation, New Delhi, 2009.

V.C. Kulandai Swamy, *Higher Education in India – Crisis in Management*, Viva Books Private Limited, New Delhi, 2003.

Sudhanshu Bhushan, *Restructuring Higher Education in India*, Rawat Publications, Jaipur, 2009.

Dr.Rabindra Sen, *Higher Education and Administration*, Crescent Publishing Corporation, New Delhi, 2009.

Dr.P.K. Manoharan, *Higher Education*, A.P.H. Publishing Corporation, New Delhi, 2009.

Pawan Agarwal, *Indian Higher Education – Envisioning the Future*, SAGE Publications, New Delhi, 2009.

D. Swamiraj, *Higher Education in India*, ESSES Publishers, 1997.

R.P. Singh, *Private Initiative and Public Policy in Education*, Federation of Managements of Educational Institutions, New Delhi, 1993.

Dr. P. Rajaraman, Ph.D, *Higher Education in Tamil Nadu – Maladies and Remedies*, Vizhigal Pathippagam, 2007.

Amrik Singh, *Fifty Years of Higher Education in India*, Sage Publications, New Delhi, 2004.